Resist the

Resist the Punitive State

Grassroots Struggles Across Welfare,
Housing, Education and Prisons

Edited by Emily Luise Hart,
Joe Greener and Rich Moth

First published 2020 by Pluto Press
345 Archway Road, London N6 5AA

www.plutobooks.com

British Library Cataloguing in Publication Data
A catalogue record for this book is available from the British Library

ISBN   978 0 7453 3952 8   Hardback
ISBN   978 0 7453 3951 1   Paperback
ISBN   978 1 7868 0529 4   PDF eBook
ISBN   978 1 7868 0531 7   Kindle eBook
ISBN   978 1 7868 0530 0   EPUB eBook

This book is printed on paper suitable for recycling and made from fully managed and sustained forest sources. Logging, pulping and manufacturing processes are expected to conform to the environmental standards of the country of origin.

Typeset by Stanford DTP Services, Northampton, England

Simultaneously printed in the United Kingdom and United States of America

For
Lucas, Eleanor, Iris and Finlay

Contents

PART III: SUBVERSIVE KNOWLEDGE AND RESISTANCE: RECONCEPTUALISING CRIMINALISATION, PENALITY AND VIOLENCE

Acknowledgements

We would like to thank colleagues in the School of Social Sciences at Liverpool Hope University, University of Liverpool in Singapore and the Department of Sociology, Social Policy and Criminology at the University of Liverpool for their support and collegiality. Thanks also to The School of Law and Social Justice Research Development Fund for providing the finances to host the conference that laid the foundations for this collection. Thanks to Joe Sim, Steve Corbett and Chris Grover for reading drafts of the proposal and offering advice. Thanks also to the European Group for the Study of Deviance and Social Control for providing the platform and critical space that led to the development of the ideas behind this book. Thanks to the team at Pluto Press and in particular David Castle for all the help and enthusiasm for the project. Finally, enormous gratitude for the hard work of all the contributors to this collection, for their diligence, patience and enthusiasm for the project and for responding to what were at times pretty tight deadlines. Massive thanks and we hope you are happy with the final book.

Emily would like to thank fellow UCU activists on the University of Liverpool UCU committee and all those who joined us on the picket lines. Many thanks also to Dave Whyte for his support as her research mentor and friend. I have been lucky enough to spend time with some pretty amazing critical women in Liverpool over the last few years and they have provided support, friendship, wine and inspiration, special mention to Ala Sirriyeh, Kay Inckle, Kirsteen Paton, Zoe Alker, Daniela Tepe-Belfrage, Samantha Fletcher, Kellie Rudge-Thompson, Tracy Ramsey, Laura Penketh, Rose Devereux, Nicki Blundell, Philomena Harrison, Jo McNeil and Lucy Hanson. Thanks to fellow Community Action on Prison Expansion activists, in particular those involved in our fight in Wigan: Nicole, Heledd, Marion, Solvi, Tony, David, Paul, Jan and others. To my students past and present, who got behind the USS strikes and who have embraced the abolitionist arguments. Thanks also to Anna Marshall, Liz Stack, Fiona Pender and David Evans, you have listened gracefully to all my moans. To Mum, Dad and Lucy for always cheering me on. To Andrew for the last 20. To Finlay and Iris, keep on resisting … .

Joe would like to thank all those people who have been a source of academic support and political inspiration over recent years and especially Laura Naegler, Christian Perrin, Eve Yeo, Pablo Ciocchini, Laura Vitis, Will McGowan, Anna Anderson, Guy Jamieson, Rose Devereux, SUGAH, Michael Lavalette, Laura Penketh and Julia O'Connell Davidson. The deepest gratitude to my mum and dad (Jenny and Joe) and my two sisters (Helen and Megan). And, finally, not forgetting Laura Meehan and Eleanor for bringing joy and happiness into my life every day.

Rich would like to thank activist colleagues past and present in the Social Work Action Network (SWAN) for commitment and comradeship in the project to rebuild radical social work: Michael, Iain, Vasilios, Laura, Alissa, Dan, Linda, Mark, Malcolm, Jeremy, Sue, Bea, Peter, Bob, Rea, Carol, Simon, Nicki, Nick and Terry. Also big thanks to colleagues in the worlds of the survivor, mental health, disabled people's and psychocompulsion movements for all the energy and inspiration: Guy, Carys, Trish, Noreen, Liz, Denise, Paula, Helen, Mick, Ann, Alex, Jay, Rick, Anne, Joanna, Richard, Debbie, Paul, Roger, Roy, Lynne, Linda, and Phil. To colleagues at Liverpool Hope for support and friendship over the years: Rose, Nicki, Kel, Scott, Philomena, Tracy, Hakan, Steven, Lucy, Dave and Steve, as well as colleagues from SUGAH and students. Not forgetting Mum, Kirstin, Andy and the rest of the Williams Clan, and never forgetting Nan and Grandad. To Lucas, my little ray of light. And, above all, to Nicola for everything, always.

Introduction

Rich Moth, Emily Luise Hart
and Joe Greener

In recent years, a diverse range of groups including some of the most marginalised of our fellow citizens have been subjected to a range of deeply harmful policies and practices by state institutions and their corporate proxies. Recent scholarly activity has drawn necessary attention to these draconian developments and gone some way to describing and explaining the violence inherent in recent political developments (Cooper and Whyte, 2017). Our primary objective in this book is to highlight emerging examples of resistance to these various forms of state–corporate social harm and violence with reference to specific arenas of welfare and criminal justice policy and practice.

This collection contains contributions written by engaged scholars and activists, who are at the forefront of campaigning and resistance in a number of substantive policy arenas including mental health, disability, welfare, education, social housing, prison expansion and migration and illustrate the contribution of these emerging movements for social justice in response to increasingly punitive state actions.

In doing this, however, we are trying to attempt to break down the divide between activism and academic scholarship by elevating activist practice and knowledge in these various fields of social science.

One of the major areas of debate is around issues concerning *strategies of resistance* deployed by campaigners. On display across the following chapters is a series of examples of political organising which demonstrate different 'forces and relations of movement production', to use Barker and Cox's terminology (n.d.). The forces of movement production might be described as the current institutional factors, technological tools available, wider state of politics and political alliances – the possibilities available from the repertoire of collective action (Davenport, 2009). The relations of social movement production are the social labour that goes into creating a political movement and in particular the tensions and unities within the organisation and with others outside. This would include issues around how to relate and interact with each other in the course of protest. In examining the forces and relations of social movements, every chapter examines some of the multiplicity of practices, pressures, contradictions and opportunities that lead to (or inhibit) successful oppositional political organisation.

Each chapter examines strategies that have been utilised and developed by various grassroots networks, movements, activists and engaged scholars. We explore how these strategic approaches and differing modes of struggle combine, overlap or exist in tension with each other within the lived realities of activist campaigns and networks. We demonstrate through the contributions in this collection that social movement activist practices rarely fit neatly into discrete scholarly categorisations such as the tripartite *real utopias* framework of reformist (symbiotic), prefigurative (interstitial) and revolutionary (ruptural) orientations as suggested by Wright (Wright, 2010).

In summary, the book examines the relationship between activist interventions and contemporary theorisations of state crime and social harm. In particular, the chapters: consider the role of activism in redefining punitive welfare and criminal justice reforms as forms of social harm; present case studies of campaigning interventions by various social movement networks to explore contemporary strategies of resistance to such policies; and, within this, examine the contribution of activist scholarship to political challenges to oppressive state and corporate practices.

While there has been considerable analysis of the social, cultural and political 'damage' caused by austerity, less attention has been directed to contestation of and resistance to these punitive policy interventions. Cooper and Whyte (2017), for example, did an excellent job at highlighting the violence and brutality of austerity and the far-reaching and multiplicity of effects it was having on people's lives. We, however, examine what forms of resistance were arising to fight the onslaught of punitive policies and practices. In recognition of the importance yet complexity of these grassroots movements, we also wished to examine how various crises of social reproduction have become increasingly important as sites of and backdrops to resistance and the implications of these processes for wider aims of societal transformation. Moreover, those texts that have addressed recent protests and resistance have tended to do so either from a perspective outside of direct engagement with, or participation in such social movements (Winlow, Hall, Treadwell and Briggs, 2015) or have been concerned with a more general examination of the role of intellectuals in social movements rather than engaging with particular campaigns or substantive areas of knowledge production (Haiven and Khasnabish, 2014). Consequently, the collection seeks to fill this gap by identifying real-world instances of resistance to punitive policy agendas, assessing the challenges and opportunities that these represent, and examining the role of activists and engaged scholars in the formation of subversive knowledge and development of grassroots movements.

STRUCTURE OF THE BOOK

Echoing the above core aims of this collection, the book is divided into the following three parts:

I   Challenging state–corporate power: theories and strategies of resistance
II Resisting the punitive welfare state: housing, mental health, disability and immigration
III Subversive knowledge and resistance: reconceptualising criminalisation, penality and violence

The chapters in the first part theorise various strategies of resistance that challenge state–corporate power and consider the core features, interactions and tensions between them. The opening chapter is written by the three editors and proposes an 'integrative transitional approach' for resisting punitive state–corporate policy agendas. The chapter brings together, on the one hand, analyses of economic and social crisis tendencies under contemporary capitalism and, on the other, an overview of demographic shifts and their implications for contesting draconian policies and state–corporate violence. Based on these insights, and drawing on Gramscian and social reproduction theory, we argue for a transitional political strategy that integrates demands spanning both productive and reproductive spheres. This approach, we contend, enhances the potential for workers and social movements to build and strengthen the kind of diverse and broad-based alliances of resistance necessary to challenge not only punitive state–corporate policy interventions but also the capitalist social relations which underpin them.

Chapter 2 explores activists' endeavours to build upon the prefigurative politics of Occupy Wall Street and to use prefigurative resistance to fight the housing crisis in New York. Drawing on ethnographic research with the post-Occupy movement, this chapter focuses on anti-gentrification resistance and the Anti-Eviction Networks emerging in late 2013. Laura Naegler focuses on prefigurative politics as a form of creative resistance that aims to build the 'new society in the shell of the old', while taking away power from authority by rejecting its legitimacy.

Chapter 3 addresses the role of the 'academic' and the struggle for the contemporary university. It considers universities as state-ideological apparatuses, sketching the key role of university education and research in reproducing class power before asking how academics can challenge this role and can support counter-hegemonic struggles. Tombs and Whyte develop this discussion within the context of the 2018 UCU dispute over attacks on members' USS pensions and argue that the resulting demand to 'reclaim' the university remains based upon a mystification of what the university is, as a site of a 'pure' forms of knowledge production, insulated from economic or political demands. The need, therefore, is not to seek to 'save' the university, or even maintain professional autonomy, but is to find ways that deepen our organic connections to social struggles.

Part II starts from the premise that there are key areas of resistance and emerging and renascent forms of activism around the increasingly punitive nature of the welfare state.

Chapter 4 focuses upon recent grassroots housing campaigns in London, predominantly led by working-class women, who took on the daunting position of resisting government and for-profit organisations, global and local institutional power. Lisa Mckenzie argues that citizenship is not simply the struggle for rights and legal norms, but also involves more lived and affective dimensions such as values, feelings and the need for social solidarity. With specific reference to questions of inequality, social class and locality, Mckenzie states that the power maintained within an institutional political sphere too often puts out the precarious flames rising from small grassroots movements of this kind. The chapter contributes to the wider discussion on class and its relationship to the development of neoliberalism, linking how institutional 'official' politics deal with local movements who have a deeper ethno-graphic understanding by contextualising small protest groups within the wider issues of class inequality and especially within a housing crisis. In Chapter 5, Peter Beresford provides a critique of the alliance that has developed between neoliberal politics and psychiatric ideology, which has coupled individualisation and medicalisation; welfare benefit cuts and hostility with psychiatric stigma. This is done from the Mad Studies perspective and explores psychiatric system survivor organisa-tions challenging the punitive neoliberal state.

Chapter 6 provides an analysis of the Grenfell crisis and the future for housing after this appalling event. In particular, Robbins examines the potential for change and what grassroots movements have emerged from the ashes of the tower. He suggests that housing campaigns are essen-tially local but that the housing crisis has become a global pandemic and that finding a cure requires collective action that is not restricted to national borders.

In Chapter 7, Williams-Findlay provides an account of the last four decades of activism by the disabled people's movement and argues that the recent erosion of the rights of disabled people under austerity has deeper roots than recent austerity-related policy shifts. Roots that can be traced back to a legalistic conception of enhanced individual rights, which culminated in the Disability Discrimination Act 1995. The resulting formation of the grassroots network Disabled People Against Cuts (DPAC) went beyond an exclusive orientation to individual legal rights and advocated campaigning on wider material issues, placing disabled activists at the heart of the anti-austerity movement. However, Williams-Findlay argues for continued work to reclaim a radical histor-ical materialist social model of disability to inform more fundamentally transformative political interventions.

In Chapter 8, Ken Olende examines the emergence of the 'hostile environment' policy and the Windrush scandal that arose from it. It provides an overview of resistance to this agenda, and looks at how cam-paigning interventions have led to a government retreat on Windrush and indicates the possibilities for such challenges to derail the wider 'hostile environment' project. The chapter also provides observations on the potential for greater trade union involvement in challenging this agenda to strengthen and deepen resistance.

The final part of the book examines forms of activist knowledge production that reconceptualise state–corporate practices as forms of social harm around criminalisation, penality and violence.

Chapter 9 examines the relationships between social movements, academic research and the surveillance state. Using the example of undercover policing, Schlembach argues that despite carefully managed moves towards opening up the culture of secrecy, this has happened not so much through increased transparency but rather accelerated co-optation. This is due to criminological knowledge being tied up in uncomfortable ways with the institutions that control access to the desired data and information. This raises methodological, theoretical and political issues and consequently the hidden practices of undercover policing will need to be exposed through alternative means.

Chapter 10 draws upon the issues emphasised by abolitionist activist scholars in their struggles to challenge government plans to build six new mega prisons in England and Wales by 2020. Scott argues that local communities can be unaware of the toxicity caused by the building of prisons: for the communities, for the surrounding environment and for the prisoners. The chapter therefore highlights how sociologically and criminologically informed arguments can play an important part in garnering support from local communities in resisting prison expansion. The chapter highlights the role and contribution of critical scholars and activists in generating emancipatory knowledges and building resistance and how we are all 'ordinary rebels'.

In Chapter 11, Julia Downes explores both the potential and challenges faced in doing accountability work on gendered violence within the 'British Left'. Drawing on empirical research with women and non-binary survivors who have experienced violence from fellow activists within grassroots social movements, she examines how traces of a 'criminal legal imagination' can recirculate within British Left grassroots social movements faced with gendered violence within their groups. This chapter argues how learning from the perspectives of survivors and experienced transformative justice practitioners can help to map out a framework for transformative justice within the British Left and open up pathways towards cultivating accountability as a crucial practice in dismantling the punitive state. This includes the development of an anti-carceral feminist imagination to contest the reliance on punitive state responses, such as the law, police, courts and prison, to resolve gendered violence.

Chapter 12 examines the Prevent agenda and states that while there is a wide body of writing and commentary that systematically critiques Prevent and its impact, there has been little study of the *movement* against it. Rob Ferguson explores the successes, limits and challenges that this movement has faced with a primary focus on education. He examines how education as one of the state's central terrains for combating 'extremist' ideas and promoting 'British values' has also been the foremost site of resistance to Prevent.

REFERENCES

Barker, C. and Cox, L. (n.d.) 'What have the Romans Ever Done for Us?' Academic and Activist Forms of Movement Theorizing. http://mural.maynooth university.ie/428/1/AFPPVIII.pdf (accessed 21 May 2019).

Cooper, V. and Whyte, D. (2017) Introduction: The Violence of Austerity. In V. Cooper and D. Whyte (eds). *The Violence of Austerity*. London: Pluto Press, 1–34.

Davenport, C. (2009) Regimes, Repertoires and State Repression. *Swiss Political Science Review*, 15(2): 377–85.

Haiven, M. and Khasnabish, A. (2014) *The Radical Imagination: Social Movement Research in the Age of Austerity*. London: Zed Books.

Winlow, S., Hall, S., Treadwell, J. and Briggs, D. (2015) *Riots and Political Protest: Notes From the Post-Political Present*. London: Routledge.

Wright, E.O. (2010) *Envisioning Real Utopias*. London: Verso.

PART I

CHALLENGING STATE–CORPORATE POWER
THEORIES AND STRATEGIES OF RESISTANCE

1

Resisting the Punitive
State–Corporate Nexus

Activist Strategy and the
Integrative Transitional Approach

Joe Greener, Emily Luise Hart and Rich Moth

INTRODUCTION

The case studies that will be presented in this book illustrate the extent to which a 'punitive turn' across a number of policy domains is a prominent and pervasive feature of neoliberalism in the UK. However, before the book turns to these examples of policy implementation, this first chapter will outline a broader understanding of this phenomenon and its implications for activist strategy. Consequently, the chapter has two main aims. The first is to locate these punitive tendencies as a feature of the 'integral' state under contemporary neoliberalism, which utilises increasingly draconian and divisive means to maintain a degree of legitimacy for this system. These threats to consent-making processes are an effect of neoliberal reconfigurations of the interrelated spheres of production and social reproduction that underpin harmful and detrimental processes, such as work intensification in the former and crises of care provision in the latter. However, neoliberal reforms have also resulted in demographic shifts both within labour markets and across society more widely that are engendering new patterns of contestation and resistance. Our second major aim in the chapter is, therefore, to explore the strategic implications of these shifting contexts and demographics for strategies of resistance and the development of oppositional currents and coalitions. In particular, and building on our analysis of these shifts, we propose a framework for activist strategy which we call the 'integrative transitional' approach (ITA). ITA takes account of these wider changes in social conditions by incorporating political demands that span productive and reproductive concerns and in so doing, we argue, has the potential to enhance activist efforts to build and strengthen diverse and broad-based alliances of resistance to punitive state–corporate policy agendas.

CONTEMPORARY CAPITALISM AND THE 'INTEGRAL' POWER OF THE PUNITIVE STATE

The enactment by the state of an increasingly punitive approach to welfare and criminal justice policy is a core feature across the contributions in this book. In this chapter, we examine the strategic and practical implications of that policy shift for building oppositional currents and political resistance. However, before doing so, it is necessary to delineate the nature of the state and its relationship to the economy. We consider the state and economy (including its constituent capitals) to be structurally interdependent elements within the wider capitalist system (Jessop, 2008; Ashman and Callinicos, 2006). For us then, the state should be regarded as the *capitalist* state. Moreover, the latter institution, as Gramsci argued, is best understood as the 'integral state'. This is because power and control in capitalist society is enacted and maintained through two integrated modalities: on the one hand, the deployment of *force* by institutions such as the police and army ('political society'); and on the other, securing *consent* via complex mediating systems including those of education, the media, charities, NGOs and trade unions ('civil society'). These civil society organisations play a significant formal and informal role through the creation and maintenance of a pervasive 'common sense' favourable to ruling social groups (Davies, 2014; Thomas, 2009). However, it is important that consent and coercion are not counterposed or understood in a dualistic way. Rather, these two elements are dialectically related and complementary, and it is by counterbalancing them that the state secures order and maintains the relative legitimacy (or *hegemony* in Gramscian terms) of the dominant class within capitalist democracies (Thomas, 2009:164).

The Transition from Keynesianism to Neoliberalism

The exact 'mix' of consent and force deployed by the integral capitalist state at any particular historical moment is contingent on situational factors. Consequently, in order to understand the current 'punitive turn', it is necessary to map the political and economic context that has shaped these policy shifts. In this section, we will therefore provide a brief account of the transition from Keynesian interventionism to neoliberalism, consider its implications for economic and social policy reform, and outline how this provided a basis for the emergence of a more punitive and coercive approach to public policy.

In the post-war period from 1945, the dominant political-economic theory was a Keynesian approach characterised by a mixed economy, nationalisation and state provision of welfare (Ferguson, Lavalette and Mooney, 2002). These policy agendas represented an attempt by the Keynesian state to secure hegemonic power by abrogating class conflict and generating popular consent through welfarism (Esping-Andersen, 1990). Social policies in areas such as education, housing and health care were oriented towards universalism and reduced dependency on markets, while criminal justice policy was characterised by comparatively lower levels of incarceration (Wacquant, 2009). However, this model was destabilised by the economic crises of the 1970s. At this juncture, a shifting balance of forces led to reorganisation of the state along neoliberal lines in an attempt to bolster the structural power of capital while reducing the state's social protection functions.

The emergence of neoliberalism was marked by significant developments in relation to both the economy and social provision. In relation to the former, neoliberalism instigated the subordination of economic and social policy to markets (Fine, 2012) and capital's shift away from more productive areas of the economy towards financialisation (Harman, 2009). Recent broader changes in the structure of the economy have also intensified the sense of precarity for workers, with an increased prevalence of mechanisms such as zero-hour contracts and the growth of the 'gig' economy reinforcing material and employment insecurity (Doogan, 2009). In terms of social policy, neoliberalism has accelerated retrenchment and market reconfigurations of formal welfare institutions such as the NHS, social care and benefits systems, thereby further privatising 'care' tasks either to the private sector or individual households (we will characterise this in terms of social reproduction later in the chapter).[1] Furthermore, social and economic policies have been developed in ways that support the interests of financialised capital, for instance, the reconfiguration of social housing as primarily a market for investors rather than provision to meet social needs and the involvement of large corporations in many aspects of government service delivery from social care to prison expansion.

From Social Protection to Disciplinary Proletarianisation

The process of transition from Keynesian to neoliberal political economy and its consolidation represented an attempt to transform the background conditions of capitalism (Fraser and Jaeggi, 2018) by increasing the structural power of capital at the expense of labour. A central feature of this transition is a shift from *social protection* to *disciplinary proletarianisation* within the arenas of welfare and criminal justice policy. This change is, we contend, central to an analysis of the punitive tendencies foregrounded by the contemporary capitalist state. The neoliberal era has seen an increasing integration (and subsumption) of welfarist agendas for the management of poverty and inequality within the structures of criminal justice policy. This is driven by a significant re-orientation of these policy agendas towards an overarching aim of managing economic insecurity by enforcing participation in deregulated labour markets. This punitive dynamic of coerced labour market engagement spanning welfare and criminal justice policy constitutes what we call disciplinary proletarianisation. This describes a shift in emphasis from consent-based forms of domination to more directly violent and coercive practices in order to manage various crisis tendencies within contemporary capitalism, with the aim of driving down wages, weakening the political position of the working class more generally and creating favourable conditions for financialised accumulation. In order to realize this outcome, both policy domains are increasingly oriented to a 'behaviourist philosophy relying on deterrence, surveillance, stigma, and graduated sanctions to modify conduct' (Wacquant, 2009: 288). Accordingly, the rehabilitative goals of welfare and penal policy have been eroded and more punitive orientations have taken centre stage. While the exercise of coercive measures by the state to engender labour market participation is nothing new, the austerity phase of neoliberalism has heralded a concerted effort to enforce such compliance across much wider populations, simultaneously rolling back levels of welfare support to those groups previously regarded as exempt from the labour market (Roulstone, 2015).

Processes of disciplinary proletarianisation are buttressed by the deployment of stigmatisation. Mainstream political narratives under neoliberalism are grounded in a position that emphasises citizens' obligation to be economically productive and reframes profoundly socially structured experiences, such as poverty and unemployment, as personal and moral failures. This ideology then legitimises the utilisation by politicians and the mainstream media of denigrating frames of reference (for instance, 'strivers and skivers' rhetoric) to stigmatise and demonise particular marginalised groups including migrants, benefit claimants, the urban poor, black/minority ethnic youth and disabled people. The 'weaponisation' of stigma and social blame in relation to marginalised and excluded groups (Scambler, 2018), who are constructed as the source of social ills (itself an act of institutional violence [Cooper and Whyte, 2017]), is integral to the crafting of 'technologies of consent' under neoliberalism (Jensen and Tyler, 2015).

The restructuring of welfare and criminal justice systems to achieve convergence around the principles of disciplinary proletarianisation has intensified in the wake of the Financial Crisis of 2008 and is visible in a range of policy areas. For instance, within the benefits system, enforcement of labour market engagement has intensified since the 2012 Welfare Reform Act through mechanisms such as conditionality, sanctioning and disentitlement, that aim to disincentivise claiming support and thereby engender re-entry into paid employment (Fletcher and Wright, 2018). Another arena of disciplinary proletarianisation is prison expansion, with enlargement of this system utilised as an alternative means for managing rising levels of inequality (Corporate Watch, 2018). There has also been a recent related increase in the use of detention centres for managing migrant populations (Silverman and Griffiths, 2018). Moreover, the expansion of punitive modes for managing marginalised populations across these sectors is transparently geared towards the creation of opportunities for corporate profit maximisation through outsourcing of state provision (Tombs and Whyte, 2015).

The lens of the integral state, introduced above, enables contextualisation of this shift from social protection to disciplinary proletarianisation as an instance of the recalibration of the balance between force and consent. We have highlighted a small number of these strategies through which this is implemented from *administrative domination* (Davies, 2014: 3222), that is, the deployment of force through an array of coercive techniques to inculcate behavioural compliance (e.g. welfare-to-work reforms) (see Peter Beresford's Chapter 5, in this volume; also Moth and McKeown, 2016), to the divisive and stigmatising rhetoric deployed in government and media discourses to stoke popular fears and resentments towards marginalised groups (the weaponisation of stigma noted above). These responses represent an attempt to resolve economic crises in favour of capital and shore up weakening systemic legitimacy through repressive policy measures. This lens enables an understanding of the possibilities for flexible implementation by the integral state of different modalities of power along the force/consent continuum as political exigencies demand.

CRISES OF SOCIAL REPRODUCTION UNDER NEOLIBERALISM

In the chapter so far, our focus has been the transition from Keynesianism to neoliberalism as a political strategy from above by the integral state to resolve recurrent crises of capitalism since the 1970s. However, core elements of this neoliberal reform agenda, such as the retrenchment of the welfare state, involve not only reconfiguration of the background conditions for capital accumulation but also, by extension, an assault on the very conditions of social reproduction that enable wider human needs to be met. This has significant implications for modes and levels of class struggle because these social, political and economic transformations generate particular crisis tendencies. As Fraser notes, such crises are not simply economic or financial but multidimensional involving a host of harmful social consequences which encompass '"non-economic" phenomena [such] as global warming, "care deficits" and the hollowing out of public power' (Fraser, 2014: 56). Moreover, many of the activist campaigns and social movements that will be described in the subsequent chapters of this book have their genesis in the punitive restructuring of systems of reproduction in areas such as housing, health care, mental distress or disability. We argue, therefore, that crises of social reproduction have become increasingly significant, both as an important driving force for resistance and a terrain of political struggle. This section will therefore begin with an overview of production and social reproduction and an exploration of crises of reproduction and their implications for contemporary political contestation in the current period.

Marx's *Capital* rigorously conceptualises the circuits of capitalist production. However, while Marx does note the background conditions vital for the system's ongoing reproduction, these are relatively underdeveloped in his work. Later theorists, in particular Marxist-feminists, have therefore built upon Marx's insights in order to expand our understanding of the processes through which the 'front story' of exploitation under capitalism (private ownership, free labour markets and accumulation) rests upon a 'back story of expropriation' constituted by (mostly) unpaid reproductive labour (Fraser and Jaeggi, 2018: 28–9). These processes of social reproduction[2] serve three main functions: the maintenance and renewal of the current workforce; the sustenance and regeneration of those outside the labour force such as children, older people, (some) people who are disabled or experiencing mental distress and individuals with health conditions; and the replenishing of populations of workers to replace those who leave the labour force due to old age, illness and disability (Barker, 2017; Bhattacharya, 2017a).

This back story of reproductive labour enables important light to be shed on both the historical development of capitalism and its operation as an organic totality. However, in doing so, it also reveals deep contradictions between the capitalist mode of production and the conditions for the reproduction of social and personal life under this system. For instance, in its current form, capitalism is dependent on the family unit as the primary site of the reproduction of labour power through processes of care which are unpaid and primarily carried out by women, though boundary struggles have also led to the emergence of reproductive welfare institutions such as health and welfare systems (Fraser and Jaeggi, 2018: 174). However, crises of social reproduction are further precipitated and intensified by contemporary reforms, that externalise 'care' responsibilities onto families while simultaneously recruiting women into the workforce and thereby reducing their capacities to perform such labour (Fraser, 2017). Moreover, the supply of productive and reproductive labour has been replenished and regenerated not only by processes of expropriation in the domestic sphere but also, at a global level, through slavery (in capitalism's early stages of development) and more recently through immigration. Indeed, sources of racialised labour from Africa, South America and Asia have become a key means for addressing labour shortages in reproductive sectors such as nursing and domestic work in the Global North. However, as this discussion suggests, though the various forms of unwaged and now increasingly waged labour within the circuit of reproduction play an essential role as a foundation for capital accumulation, their historical trajectories mean they are deeply gendered and raced. Consequently, labour in both its productive and reproductive forms is fundamentally entwined with experiences of oppression which are conditioned by the structures of capitalism. By demonstrating how production and reproduction are parts of a unified process, social reproduction theory (SRT) offers a basis for an *integrative* analysis of both exploitation in the workplace and the production of forms of oppression. Furthermore, SRT facilitates a form of contemporary class analysis that reflects diverse socio-political realities and thereby enables a clearer understanding of strategic potentials for oppositional politics in the current conjuncture.

An important implication of the SRT framework is that the reproductive sphere, like the productive sphere, should be understood as a site of class struggle (Bhattacharya, 2017b). This is based on SRT's analysis of the way in which class relations articulate with various forms of oppression. This is not an argument for the reduction of race or gender to class, but is instead a framework for understanding capitalism as a concrete totality, in other words a unity comprised of many diverse determinations and relations (including gender and ethnicity) which are co-constitutive within an organic whole (Bhattacharya, 2017a). For instance, under neoliberalism in its most recent austerity phase, a multiplicity of processes of subjugation (including gendered, racialised and disablist forms of oppression) are deeply implicated in the creation of a specific classed social order (i.e. bolstering the power of capital). This understanding of the interrelationship between class dynamics and other relations of domination underpins a more expansive definition of class struggle that incorporates those engaged in productive *and* reproductive labour, both formal and informal. Consequently, the terrain of such struggle should be understood as not only within the workplace but also beyond it in spaces of contestation that include everyday life, welfare services and 'civil society'. In this way, SRT facilitates recognition of, and more effective political responses to, the twin assault on rights and conditions in the workplace and the wider social reproductive needs of the working class in areas such as housing, education and health care during the neoliberal period (Bhattacharya, 2017b: 92).

Contesting Exploitation in Shifting Sites of Class Struggle

In this section, we highlight the changing locus of workplace contestation with some of the most visible and militant disputes taking place within reproductive sectors such as education and health care. This also draws attention to the shifting class structure in terms of its occupational dimensions, gender and racial characteristics and the organisation of reproductive work. We conclude this section by considering the political implications and potentialities of these recomposition trends for processes of resistance.

In the USA, one of the most militant sections of the working class over the last decade has been in the education sector, with a high-profile strike wave by teachers' unions against the privatisation, cuts and closures of state schools across the country including Chicago and more recently Los Angeles (Henwood, 2019). The most significant features of these struggles have been on the one hand democratisation, with frontline teachers prising a leadership role from conservative trade union bureaucracies by means of teacher–activist caucuses, and on the other, the development of ongoing alliances and campaigns alongside parents, students and wider communities. These alliances were particularly successful in building bridges between the teachers' struggle and the needs of marginalised minority ethnic groups in poorer neighbourhoods whose children were set to lose most as a result of these school closures and reforms. As a result, strong support and solidarity for the strikes was forthcoming from these communities, a factor which has underpinned the relative success of these disputes (McAlevey, 2016; Bhattacharya, 2017b: 93). This broader approach to workplace struggle has been described as 'social justice trade unionism' (Weiner, 2012). In a similar vein, two of the most significant industrial disputes of recent years in the UK have been the junior doctors' and lecturers' strikes. In terms of scale, the NHS junior doctors' strike was the biggest dispute of 2016, accounting for 40 per cent of the total strike days during that year (Clegg, 2017). While the dispute was nominally concerned with changes to doctors' contracts and conditions, it attracted widespread popular support in part as a result of framing of the strike in terms of maintaining access to universal health care against a backdrop of austerity-related retrenchment and marketisation of NHS services and, within this, the evocation of shared interests between medical professionals, patients, activists and wider publics in resisting these developments (Pushkar, 2019). Similarly, the 2018 strike by university workers, the longest ever sustained strike action in UK higher education (HE), arose as a result of proposed cuts to one of the sector's pension schemes. While the dispute acted as a channel for a number of grievances over job insecurity and work intensification, it soon came to represent wider political significance in the context of HE marketisation. One symbol of this was the emergence of a student movement in support of the strike. Students organised a wave of university occupations in solidarity with lecturers, but in doing so, they also articulated wider concerns and needs in the form of demands for the reinstatement of free education and student grants as part of a wider critique of consumerist education reforms (Bergfeld, 2018; see also Tombs and Whyte, Chapter 3 in this volume). These developments illustrate the extent to which institutions of social reproduction now constitute an increasingly vital arena of class struggle both for the workers delivering them and those utilising their services.

However, these examples highlight not only the changing terrain of twenty-first-century class struggle, but also shifting dynamics within it. One aspect of this is the 'proletarianisation' of professionals engaged in social reproduction such as teachers and lecturers who might once have been considered middle class (Mooney and Law, 2007). Far from underlining the end of the working class, as some theorists have argued, this underlines instead its recomposition due to changing capital–labour relations (Mathers, Upchurch and Taylor, 2019). Consequently, such professional groups represent an increasingly large proportion of the total workforce in the UK, with their numbers doubling over two decades to become the largest single occupational category. Another important and related dimension is the changing gender and racial composition of this workforce. For example, the second and third largest professional groups within the UK labour force are now teaching and medicine and, in both cases, women constitute over 60 per cent of the total (Office for National Statistics, 2018). This reflects a wider and continual growth in the proportion of UK women in employment over the last 40 years from 57 per cent to 78 per cent in 2017 (Roantree and Vira, 2018). The working class in countries such as the USA and the UK has also become more ethnically diverse, with BME groups constituting one-third of the US population (Moody, 2017) and 13 per cent in the UK (Office for National Statistics, 2013). This increasingly diverse workforce composition, and the attendant racial diversification and feminisation of labour, means that struggles to address racial and gender inequalities have become a central aspect not only in developing wider political consciousness but also in the more immediate tasks of building unity and solidarity within workplace struggles (Moody, 2017; Molyneux, 2019). These inequalities are shaped by historical divisions of labour and the relations of exploitation that structure production and reproduction in capitalist society. Under such conditions, various forms of sexual and racial violence have become institutionalised. However, recent years have seen the emergence of significant challenges to these forms of oppression from campaigns such as #MeToo and Black Lives Matter. The tactic of women's strikes against gender violence in places such as Argentina and Spain has also garnered widespread support, and demonstrated the potential of radicalising impulses emerging from social movements against oppression to spill over into and cross-fertilise with struggles in the workplace (Garcia, Alabao and Perez, 2018).

In all these examples, we see the development of politics which bridge issues around reproduction and production. Demands which start as narrow workplace-based concerns can quickly become explicitly about the systems of welfare on which whole sections of society are dependent, such as education and health care. Contemporary struggles against exploitation are also often concerned with gendered and racialised oppression, especially depending on which group of workers or 'service users' in question are affected. Both the funding of 'welfare' services (i.e. in its broadest term, inclusive of education, housing, health care or pensions), and the rights and entitlements of those who work in these services are increasingly important issues of class struggle.

OPPOSITIONAL CURRENTS AND RESISTANCE

We have so far examined economic crises of capitalism and repressive political interventions, as well as the political challenges and opportunities arising from crises of reproduction, and the changing composition, terrain and dynamics of working-class struggles from below. These emergent crises and possibilities have prompted a number of recent theoretical contributions from the Left, which seeks to assess the current conjuncture and offer recommendations for political strategy. In this section, we will offer a brief overview and critique of a selection of these.

As we noted above, a number of neoliberal trends and associated punitive policy agendas and narratives intensified following the 2008 Financial Crisis. Consequently, the last decade has seen a slew of theoretical contributions by activists and critical theorists who have sought to understand how neoliberalism has managed to survive and stabilise following this economic shock. Our focus in this section will be on two widely read texts which have offered diagnoses of the purported failures of the Left and progressive movements to capitalise on this crisis situation and/or develop alternative proposals for building oppositional activities with the aim of securing systemic transformations. We will offer an overview and evaluation of these interventions before turning in the following section to an outline of our own strategic perspectives and proposals.

One prominent contribution to the debate has been by ultra-realist criminologists Winlow and colleagues (2015). The main focus of their argument is the capacity of liberal capitalism to appropriate and domesticate oppositional currents because of the tendency of contemporary protest movements to frame their political interventions *reactively* on the failures of global capitalism. Instead, these authors propose a *reconstructive* approach based on the articulation of 'realistic' utopian alternatives. In order to achieve the latter, they recommend withdrawal from immediate events (Winlow *et al.*, 2015: 5) and 'the pseudo-activity of campaigning' (Winlow *et al.*, 2015: 197) to enable political contemplation, 'critical reflection' and 'deep thinking' that facilitates the design and elaboration of models for a realist utopia. They diagnose flaws in the politics of the contemporary Left arising from excessive attention to micro-resistance (i.e. prefigurative politics) and cultural insubordination rather than addressing the real locus of power at the level of global political economy. Though they coruscate the failures of this somewhat ill-defined 'Left', they do not outline an alternative political practice nor offer detailed strategic proposals that articulate their realist utopia beyond arguing for a shift from 'identity politics' towards policies underpinned by a philosophy of universalism (Winlow *et al.*, 2015: 197), and commending the building of pragmatic[3] leftist electoral coalitions (using the example of Syriza in Greece) oriented to taking state power. This suggests their utopian vision is effectively a more radical iteration of social democracy though they assert that their transformative horizon exceeds this.

In another widely read intervention, Srnicek and Williams (2015), like Winlow and colleagues, engage in a critique of prefigurative or autonomous horizontalist approaches (for an example of the latter orientation, see Haiven and Khasnabish, 2014),[4] which seek to create and expand alternatives within the interstices or 'cracks' in the system. For Srnicek and Williams, prefiguration is a form of 'folk politics', which, they argue, privileges the local and small scale and thereby evades questions both of seizing and transforming state power/market economy[5] and of formulating large-scale policy alternatives to challenge capitalist hegemony. Such an orientation is, in their view, highly problematic in an increasingly globalised and networked world. In its place, they offer the kind of detailed utopian blueprint which Winlow and colleagues demand but do not deliver. Srnicek and Williams' outline an 'accelerationist' post-capitalist agenda which embraces full automation and an associated universal basic income to supplement or replace wages in a 'post-work' context. They identify a 'populist' broad left, cross-class alliance as the primary agent of these transformations, and advocate a diverse and wide-ranging eco-system of activist institutions including political parties and social movement organisations as the means of its delivery. Though relatively pessimistic about the role of labour and workplace struggles, Srnicek and Williams (2015) commend an eclectic range of disruptive tactics from road blockades to rent strikes and propose a broader and longer-term strategy of developing counter-hegemonic projects such as repurposing technological and economic infrastructures to popularise, strengthen and embed a new post-capitalist 'good sense'.

These interventions offer a useful overview of the theoretical and strategic terrain encountered by activists resisting the punitive state–corporate nexus.[6] In responding to them, our intention is to mark out areas of agreement and difference as a means to locate our own proposals more effectively. For instance, we agree with Winlow and colleagues that new political imaginaries which embody the hope that 'another world is possible' are necessary and urgent. However, we fundamentally reject their proposal for a scholarly utopian blueprint 'from above' that is detached from the lived experiences of the exploited and oppressed and everyday political struggles. For us, it is essential that strategy emerges from and draws upon democratic political practice 'from below'[7] and, in one sense, the deliberative element of the assemblies of Occupy embodied such an ethos. Nonetheless, in practice, the strategic orientation of Occupy also imposed significant limits on political intervention. We share with Srnicek and Williams the view that the rejection by horizontalist movements of the idea of articulating determinate demands because of the potential for division and co-optation is problematic (Srnicek and Williams, 2015: 33). Demands play an important role both in supporting processes of collective mobilisation and assisting participants to gauge progress in the achievement of strategic aims and assess their recalibration if and when necessary. Similarly, the refusal by horizontalists of any form of organisational verticality has the potential to undermine possibilities for coordinated activities that serve both to defend movements from attack by the state and to engage in transformative collective action. An example of the latter is the support for Tahrir Square protestors from textile workers organised in trade unions during the Egyptian movement in 2011. It was intervention by these vertically organised workers in support of a more horizontally structured protest movement that proved a tipping point in the struggle to bring down the Mubarak dictatorship (Srnicek and Williams, 2015: 33–4). This also highlights the continued relevance of the institutional power of workers' struggle at the point of production for transformative projects. However, it is common for contemporary activist interventions to downgrade the importance of trade union resistance in the workplace and foreground alternative sites of struggle. For instance, Srnicek and Williams point to the growing importance of new repertoires of contestation related to movements of precarious workers and issues of social reproduction (Srnicek and Williams, 2015: 173). While, as we have noted, resistance around reproduction is increasingly significant, we consider the attendant theoretical and practical marginalisation of the potential of organised workers' struggle to be mistaken. Moreover, we consider the domains of production and reproduction to be fundamentally interconnected with significant implications for how we understand and build political challenges and resistance to state–corporate harms, both inside and outside the point of production. Finally, and importantly for the arguments to follow, while we commend Srnicek and Williams' basic intention to begin to develop leftist demands which are essentially post-capitalist in their orientation, we believe that there is an under-emphasis in their approach on the transitional dimension. In particular, there is a question of the extent to which key elements of their post-work political demands arise organically as a response to the crises and contradictions of contemporary capitalism and in the context of emergent social and labour movement struggles. In the next section, we will outline our own alternative strategic perspective in greater detail.

RESISTING THE PUNITIVE STATE–CORPORATE NEXUS: STRATEGIES FOR TRANSFORMATION

We noted earlier some significant demographic shifts and their implications for the relationship between production and social reproduction. In our view, these changes also have significant consequences for political contestation. We therefore seek to develop this line of argument by elaborating our own strategic proposals for strengthening and enhancing social struggles and resistance. We use the term *integrative transitional approach* (ITA) to describe this proposed framework.

Building Resistance: Notes Towards an Integrative Transitional Approach

We begin this section by building on our earlier discussion of Gramsci's conception of the state. As we noted, the 'integral state' is a framework for understanding the counterbalancing of coercion and consent in this context (Thomas, 2009: 164). In order to build oppositional currents to contest these dynamics, Gramsci advocated the development of an assembly of social forces from below (what he termed a counter-hegemonic historical bloc) (Sotiris, 2018: 59). However, while the implications of this Gramscian strategic proposal are the creation of cross-sectional alliances and united fronts (Thomas, 2009: 197–241), the specific nature of neoliberal political economy and its shifting class dynamics necessitates a relative renewal and adaptation of this strategic orientation to fit changing contemporary realities.

Integrative Considerations

In the earlier sections of the chapter, we described the emergence of a 'punitive turn' in public policy during the neoliberal era. This involved economic reforms that undermined labour rights and reconfigured class composition in the productive sphere alongside welfare retrenchment and coercive workfare agendas that responsibilised reproductive tasks to individuals, households and communities. These policy developments have, we argue, several important implications for political contestation. First, punitive neoliberal reforms have created interrelated crises that have led to a closer alignment of experiences across both productive and reproductive spheres. While reinforcing inequalities, this process also has the potential to create shared material interests across diverse constituencies (Moth and McKeown, 2016: 380) (such as those between workers in and users of public services that were articulated in the course of the NHS and education struggles outlined above). However, second, in a context in which difference has been weaponised (Arruzza, Bhattacharya and Fraser, 2019), the recomposition of both the workforce and wider society means the success of oppositional currents seeking to resist these crises both in and beyond the workplace will depend on the prefiguring of anti-oppressive, egalitarian and democratic relations (Boggs, 1977) in the course of collective political action. Third, organising to build diverse cross-sectional coalitions of resistance will therefore be imperative, and articulating determinate political demands that reflect these shared interests and address concrete practical needs arising in *both* productive and reproductive spheres offers an important foundation for alliance building and a means to embody this inclusive stance. This illustrates the strategic importance of the interconnected nature of the domains of production and reproduction for contemporary political organising and constitutes the first 'integrative' (i.e. integrating productive and reproductive political demands) element of the ITA framework.

Transitional Demands

The second 'transitional' component of ITA refers to the form in which the determinate demands of movements should be made. Political demands adopt a transitional[8] form when they transcend the narrow horizons of extant (in this case neoliberal) policy. A transitional strategy involves stretching 'static' political demands (i.e. those that merely seek to ameliorate conditions or restore earlier equilibrium) in a 'dynamic' or ruptural direction to foreground the need for broader societal transformation (Gindin, 2012). These are sometimes referred to as 'non-reformist reforms',[9] which, unlike 'reformist reforms' that buttress capitalism, incorporate utopian and anti-systemic intent though are *grounded* in emergent tendencies within current conditions.

An example of a set of transitional demands gaining traction in the current political context is the Green New Deal (GND) (Hockett and

Gunn-Wright, 2019).[10] GND simultaneously addresses the pressing requirement to reduce carbon emissions with the need for greater socio-economic inequality by creating millions of high-wage 'green/climate' jobs in sectors such as renewable energy, home insulation and low-cost public transport in order to rapidly facilitate the transition to a low carbon society. While GND implicitly articulates the centrality of improved conditions of social reproduction (i.e. less-polluted environments, better homes, transport, etc.), it also explicitly notes the need to address class, race and gender inequalities through its mechanisms of implementation.[11] However, the scale of state intervention, direction and economic redistribution that will be required to deliver GND is likely to place its advocates in direct conflict with powerful capitalist interests negatively impacted by its proposals (e.g. oil, gas and automobile multinationals) and thereby become an arena of political struggle. In this way, GND represents an exemplar of ITA by illustrating the necessity and potential of demands that integrate productive and reproductive needs (in order to build alliances of support) while, at the same time, engendering the conditions to stretch forms of political contestation in more fundamentally socially transformative directions. Other recent examples where integrative and transitional demands are combined include Selwyn's strategy for labour-centred economic and social development in the Global South (Selwyn, 2017), and the (notes for a) Sedgwickian 'psychopolitical' manifesto oriented around transformative changes in work, welfare and wider society to address endemic societal stress and distress (Moth and McKeown, 2016), while the feminist manifesto for the 99 per cent (Arruzza, Bhattacharya and Fraser, 2019) also implicitly reflects elements of this approach.

We now turn to a more detailed description of the theory/practice elements of ITA. We begin by examining the potential of counter-hegemonic 'subversive concepts' for building and strengthening alliances of resistance before highlighting the central role of praxis, in the form of strikes and other forms of direct action, in this ruptural strategic approach.

Subversive Concepts

Subversive concepts are abstractions, ideas or generalisations, in short, forms of deviant knowledge (Walters, 2003), which represent novel critical frameworks for understanding restrictive, exploitative or oppressive conditions. Moreover, these are also transformative insofar as they offer *cognitive liberation* (Barker and Cox, 2002: 4–6) by mapping new ways of thinking that undermine the dominant 'common sense' and/or providing resources for imagining alternative ways of organising social relations. In order to illustrate this notion, we will offer two examples. We begin with what we consider the paradigmatic subversive concept: the social model of disability.[12] This concept emerged in the 1970s as a result of the debates and grassroots campaigning of disabled activists within the Union of the Physical Impaired Against Segregation (UPIAS), the pioneering self-organised social movement of disabled people in the UK. UPIAS activists challenged the medicalisation of their experiences and, through the social model, developed an alternative analysis that made the crucial distinction between impairment (as physical limitation) and disability as social oppression. This model of oppression reframed the causes of the restrictions experienced by disabled people as arising from the structural barriers they faced in society, such as lack of accessibility of buildings, rather than physical impairment. This proved liberatory, not only politically by providing a basis upon which to make strategic demands on society and government, but also psychologically by raising the self-esteem and removing the sense of individual fault associated with traditional accounts of disability (Shakespeare, 2013, see also Williams-Findlay, Chapter 7 in this volume).

Another more recent example of a subversive concept is 'psychocompulsion' (Friedli, and Stearn, 2015). This concept, developed by activists involved in the Boycott Workfare campaign who are critical of the recent and highly punitive welfare reform programme of the UK government,[13] reveals two mutually interacting dimensions of this policy agenda. The first is the promotion of psychological explanations for unemployment, which reframe out of work status or 'worklessness' as a product of individual maladjustment while suppressing the role of structural economic factors in this process. The second aspect refers to the policy prescriptions implemented to address this purported condition. These mobilise forms of coercive conditionality including the imposition on benefit claimants of mandatory activities and interventions, underpinned by the threat of sanctions, with the aim of changing their beliefs, attitudes and dispositions in order to enhance 'job-readiness' and 'employability'. This concept has cognitive liberatory effects in the sense that it problematises the governmental framing of welfare-to-work interventions as benign and supportive, while simultaneously exposing and challenging the responsibilisation and attendant sense of shame and self-blame experienced by those subjected to this agenda. Moreover, it has contributed to the cohering of a campaigning alliance of survivors, mental health workers and other activists to challenge this aspect of welfare reform (see McKenna, Peters and Moth, 2019).

As these particular examples illustrate, subversive concepts can play an important role in articulating concerns around issues of social reproduction and sharpening the narrative coherence of counter-hegemonic proposals for social reform. We argue that these can usefully contribute to the development and utilisation of wider strategic interventions that are consistent with our ITA proposals.

Collective Action

However, it is important to emphasise that we do not privilege the task of theoretical elaboration. Instead we understand the development of subversive concepts, and the wider ITA strategic programme of which they form a part, as a process arising from, responding to and rooted in the *collective* practices, experiences and experiments of social struggles, movements, parties and grassroots organisations (Sotiris, 2018: 112).[14] In this sense, social movements and radical political parties function as historical laboratories (Sotiris, 2013) for class struggle in which the theory and practice of 'worker-intellectuals' are dialectically integrated (Gramsci, 1971: 141). Moreover, we advocate the articulation of 'non-reformist reforms', which means ITA demands must necessarily be located within a wider 'ruptural' (Wright, 2010) or transformative anti-capitalist rather than reformist strategy.[15]

Our intention in emphasising the emergent possibilities of mobilising around issues of social reproduction is not thereby to de-emphasise workplace struggle. On the contrary, we view the latter as an essential component in processes of systemic transformation, and concur with Rosa Luxemburg's view that, 'where the chains of capitalism are forged, there must the chains be broken' (Luxemburg, 1918). But, as we noted earlier, recent history has indicated an increasing strategic importance for extra-workplace struggles and non-traditional strikes (e.g. feminist mass strikes) as forms of class struggle. The potential for the militancy of these struggles to be harnessed together with, and to infuse and radicalise workplace contestation is an exciting possibility. The alliances between trade union activists and the anti-capitalist/global justice movements, Occupy and anti-austerity formations have already pointed to such potentials (Mathers, Upchurch and Taylor, 2019). And so an essential component of ITA is the creation of bridges between workplace and community struggles, drawing on the inspiration of recent teachers' and junior doctors' strikes through the articulation of inclusive demands and forms of direct action.

In summary, we believe the crucial task and challenge for social movements, networks and radical parties[16] is to develop a strategy which spans needs in both productive and reproductive spheres while combining the prefiguring of egalitarian relations in practice, the strengthening of resistance currents in the present *and* the development of future-oriented sets of demands and programmes that 'stretch' activism towards the realization of transformative social change. We offer these initial notes on ITA as a modest contribution towards that goal. In doing so, our intention is not to be prescriptive or didactic. Instead, we see ITA as a tactical distillation that draws upon an analysis of contemporary integral state–capitalist power and class recomposition as a condition of possibility for emergent forms of activism. However, in order to realize this potential, the formulation and implementation of ITA must necessarily involve a thoroughly inclusive, egalitarian and democratic form of political practice.

CONCLUSION

We have argued in this chapter that neoliberalism and recent austerity policy has engendered a shift away from the social protection functions of the state. We explored diverse examples of welfare and criminal justice policy transformation that illustrate this in relation to a broader reconfiguration of the 'background conditions' of capital accumulation. Unlike the welfare settlements through which its Keynesian predecessor maintained consent, neoliberalism as 'hegemonic regime' has in many areas of provision effected a regressive rebalancing of processes of social reproduction from state to household. We noted the coercive policy techniques and divisive and stigmatising rhetoric deployed by the integral capitalist state in order to secure consent in this new context. However, these processes have also generated reproductive crises. The scales on which these contradictions are visible range from the intra-personal level, where escalating levels of mental distress are engendered by endemic labour and societal precarity, insecurity and inequalities, to the global level where unrestrained demands of capital for resource extraction and inter-imperialist rivalries interact to produce the displacement of people and simultaneous degradation of the natural environment (Haiven and Khasnabish, 2014). Consequently, the need to push against the limits of the possible is a pressing one. Moreover, these altered conditions have also produced the potential for reconfigured and more expansive forms of working-class political agency. We have offered our proposals for an ITA strategy in the hope that these can make some small contribution to building and strengthening the alliances necessary to realize projects of resistance and social transformation.

NOTES

1. We distinguish societal reproduction, the processes underpinning reproduction of the *entire* capitalist system (i.e. relations *and* forces of production), from social reproduction, a narrower definition concerned with the range of institutions inside and outside the market that ensure the maintenance of human populations. We utilise this latter definition in the rest of the chapter. See Brenner and Laslett (1991).
2. This concept is differentiated from societal reproduction which Marx understood as the reproduction of the totality of the capitalist system including both public and private spheres.
3. This feels somewhat contradictory as one of their primary criticisms of the Left is its purported shift from utopianism to pragmatism.
4. Haiven and Khasnabish argue that social movements are alternative modes and spaces of social reproduction within which the radical imagination, or capacities to envision better futures, may be fostered in order to prefigure these alternatives in the present. However, the authors identify a 'double crisis' of social reproduction that constitutes a barrier to this. These twin crises are, first, the failure of capitalist society to provide secure material and affective conditions of life for its citizens and, second, in this context the challenge for social movements in creating and sustaining supportive infrastructures of activism. In response to these urgent challenges, they foreground the need for the cultivation of collective forms of insurgent knowledge production, informed by the radical imagination as part of broader prefigurative movement building projects underpinned by a reflexive and therapeutic ethos. While we are sympathetic to a number of these authors concerns, we broadly concur with Srnicek and Williams' more general critique of horizontalist approaches of the type articulated here by Haiven and Khasnabish.

5. These authors regard Holloway (2010) as the exemplar of folk politics.
6. Whether or not these books have actually been read by activists is not essential to our argument, our point is that these texts stake out some key orientations prominent within activist debates and interventions.
7. This is the problem with the rather abstract 'top down' formulations developed by Winlow and colleagues (2015), which do not feel organically connected to and rooted within extant political and social movements. Instead, we highlight and draw upon the notion of socialism 'from below' made in Draper (1966).
8. The idea of the transitional demand was originally developed by Trotsky, see Hallas (1979).
9. The term is originally from Gorz (1964), but has been used more recently by Srnicek and Williams (2015: 108).
10. For an earlier version containing similar proposals developed in the UK, see Neale (2014).
11. This includes marginalised groups such as prisoners, with GND explicitly calling for decarceration.
12. For a detailed examination of the disabled people's movement, see Williams-Findlay Chapter 7 in this volume.
13. This concept is introduced in Friedli and Stearn (2015). The punitive nature of this welfare reform programme is described in more detail in the Beresford, Chapter 5 and Williams-Findlay, Chapter 7 in this volume.
14. This bottom up approach is in sharp contrast with Winlow and colleagues 'top down' advocacy of withdrawal from campaigning in order to engage in utopian reflection.
15. For instance, Williams-Findlay's Chapter 7 in this volume makes a strong case for the need to stretch social model of disability demands in a more revolutionary/ruptural direction.
16. The three authors have subtly divergent perspectives on the role of radical political parties and their relationship with social movements, which there is not space here to develop.

REFERENCES

Arruzza, C., Bhattacharya, T. and Fraser, N. (2019) *Feminism for the 99 Percent: A Manifesto*. London: Verso.

Ashman, S., and Callinicos, A. (2006) Capital Accumulation and the State System: Assessing David Harvey's The New Imperialism. *Historical Materialism*, 14(4): 107–31.

Bergfeld, M. (2018) 'Do you Believe in Life After Work?' The University and College Union Strike in Britain. *Transfer*, 24(2): 233–36.

Barker, C. (2017) Social Reproduction Theory: Going Beyond Marx's Capital. *rs21*, 9 December, www.rs21.org.uk/2017/12/08/social-reproduction-theory-going-beyond-marxs-capital/.

Barker, C. and Cox, L. (2002) What have the Romans Ever Done for Us? Academic and Activist Forms of Movement Theorizing. In 8th Annual Conference on Alternative Futures and Popular Protest, April. Manchester: Manchester Metropolitan University, http://eprints.nuim.ie/428/1/AFPPVIII.pdf.

Bhattacharya, T. (2017a) Introduction: Mapping Social Reproduction Theory. In T. Bhattacharya (ed.), *Social Reproduction Theory: Remapping Class, Recentering Oppression*. London: Pluto Press, 1–20.

Bhattacharya, T. (2017b) How Not to Skip Class: Social Reproduction of Labor and the Global Working Class. In T. Bhattacharya (ed.), *Social Reproduction Theory: Remapping Class, Recentering Oppression*. London: Pluto Press, 68–93.

Boggs, C. (1977) Marxism, Prefigurative Communism, and the Problem of Workers' Control. *Radical America*, 11(6): 99–122.

Brenner, J. and Laslett, B. (1991) Gender, Social Reproduction, and Women's Self-Organization: Considering the US. *Welfare State. Gender and Society*, 5(3): 311–33.

Clegg, R. (2017) Labour disputes in the UK: 2016. Office for National Statistics, 30 May, www.ons.gov.uk/releases/labourdisputesintheuk2016.

Cooper, V. and Whyte, D. (2017) Introduction: The Violence of Austerity. In V. Cooper and D. Whyte (eds), *The Violence of Austerity*. London: Pluto Press, 1–34.

Corporate Watch (2018) *Prison Island: Prison Expansion in England, Wales and Scotland*. London: Corporate Watch Cooperative Ltd.

Davies, J. (2014) Rethinking Urban Power and the Local State: Hegemony, Domination and Resistance in Neoliberal Cities. *Urban Studies*, 51(15): 3215–32.

Doogan, K. (2009) *New Capitalism? The Transformation of Work*. Cambridge: Polity.

Draper, H. (1966) The Two Souls of Socialism. *New Politics*, 5(1): 57–84.

Esping-Andersen, G. (1990) *Three Worlds of Welfare Capitalism*. Princeton, NJ: Princeton University Press.

Ferguson, I., Lavalette, M. and Mooney, G. (2002) *Rethinking Welfare: A Critical Perspective*. London: Sage.

Fine, B. (2012) Financialisation & Social Policy. In P. Utting *et al.* (eds), *The Global Crisis and Transformative Social Change*. Basingstoke: Palgrave, 103–22.

Fletcher, D.R. and Wright, S. (2018) A Hand Up or a Slap Down? Criminalising Benefit Claimants in Britain Via Strategies of Surveillance, Sanctions and Deterrence. *Critical Social Policy*, 38(2): 323–44.

Fraser, N. (2014) Behind Marx's Hidden Abode: For an Expanded Conception of Capitalism. *New Left Review*, 86: 55–72.

Fraser, N. (2017) Crisis of Care? On the Social Reproductive Contradictions of Contemporary Capitalism. In T. Bhattacharya (ed.), *Social Reproduction Theory: Remapping Class, Recentering Oppression*. London: Pluto Press, 21–36.

Fraser, N. and Jaeggi, R. (2018) *Capitalism: A Conversation in Critical Theory*. Cambridge: Polity.

Friedli, L. and Stearn, R. (2015) Positive Affect as Coercive Strategy: Conditionality, Activation and the Role of Psychology in UK Government Workfare Programmes. *Medical Humanities*, 41(1): 40–47.

Garcia, B., Alabao, N. and Perez, M. (2018) Spain's Feminist Strike. *New Left Review*, 110: 35–7.

Gindin, S. (2012) Rethinking Unions, Registering Socialism. In L. Panitch, G. Albo and V. Chibber (eds), *Socialist Register 2013: The Question of Strategy*. Pontypool: Merlin Press, 26–51.

Gorz, A. (1964) *A Strategy for Labor*. Boston, MA: Beacon Press.

Gramsci, A. (1971) *Selections from the Prison Notebooks*. New York: International Publishers.

Haiven, M. and Khasnabish, A. (2014) *The Radical Imagination: Social Movement Research in the Age of Austerity*. London: Zed Books.

Hallas, D. (1979) *Trotsky's Marxism*. London: Pluto Press.

Harman, C. (2009) *Zombie Capitalism: Global Crisis and the Relevance of Marx*. London: Bookmarks.

Henwood, D. (2019) There Are So Many Things That We Can Learn From This Strike: An interview with Alex Caputo-Pearl and Jane McAlevey. *Jacobin*, 8 February, https://jacobinmag.com/2019/02/caputo-pearl-mcalevey-henwood-interview-la-teachers-strike.

Hockett, R.C. and Gunn-Wright, R. (2019) The Green New Deal: Mobilizing for a Just, Prosperous, and Sustainable Economy. *Cornell Legal Studies Research Paper*, No. 19-09.

Holloway, J. (2010) *Crack Capitalism*. London: Pluto Press.

Jensen, T. and Tyler, I. (2015) 'Benefit Broods': The Cultural and Political Crafting of Anti-Welfare Commonsense. *Critical Social Policy*, 35(4): 470–91.

Jessop, B. (2008) *State Power: A Strategic-Relational Approach*. Cambridge: Polity.

Luxemburg, R. (1918) On the Spartacus Programme. *Marxist Internet Archive*, 31 December, www.marxists.org/archive/luxemburg/1918/12/30.htm.

McAlevey, J. (2016) Everything Old is New Again. *Jacobin*, 1 August, https://jacobinmag.com/2016/08/everything-old-is-new-again-mcaveley.

McKenna, D., Peters, P. and Moth, R. (2019) Resisting the Work Cure: Mental Health, Welfare Reform and the Movement Against Psychocompulsion. In M. Berghs *et al.* (eds), *The Routledge Handbook of Disability Activism*. London: Routledge.

Mathers, A., Upchurch, M. and Taylor, G. (2019) Social Movement Theory and Trade Union Organising. In J. Grote and C. Wagemann (eds), *Social Movements and Organized Labour: Passions and Interests*. London: Routledge, 22–42.

Molyneux, J. (2019) The Future of Marxism. *Irish Marxist Review*, 8(23): 5–14.

Moody, K. (2017) *On New Terrain: How Capital is Reshaping the Battleground of Class War*. Chicago, IL: Haymarket.

Mooney, G. and Law, A. (2007) *New Labour/Hard Labour? Restructuring and Resistance Within the Welfare* Industry. Bristol: Policy Press.

Moth, R. and McKeown, M. (2016) Realising Sedgwick's Vision: Theorising Strategies of Resistance to Neoliberal Mental Health and Welfare Policy. *Critical and Radical Social Work*, 4(3): 375–90.

Neale, J. (ed.) (2014) *One Million Climate Jobs*. Bexleyheath: Marstan Press.

Office for National Statistics (2013) 2011 Census: Key Statistics and Quick Statistics for Local Authorities in the United Kingdom. 11 October, www. ons.gov.uk/peoplepopulationandcommunity/populationandmigration/ populationestimates/bulletins/keystatisticsandquickstatisticsforlocal authoritiesintheunitedkingdom/2013-10-11.

Office for National Statistics (2018) EMP04: Employment by Occupation. 11 September, www.ons.gov.uk/employmentandlabourmarket/peopleinwork/ employmentandemployeetypes/datasets/employmentbyoccupationemp04.

Pushkar, P. (2019) NHS Activism: The Limits and Potentialities of a New Solidarity. *Medical Anthropology*, 38(3): 239–52.

Roantree, B. and Vira, K. (2018) *The Rise* and *Rise* of *Women's Employment in the UK*. IFS Briefing Note BN234. London: Institute for Fiscal Studies.

Roulstone, A. (2015) Personal Independence Payments, Welfare Reform and the Shrinking Disability Category. *Disability & Society*, 30(5): 673–88.

Scambler, G. (2018) Heaping Blame on shame: 'Weaponising Stigma' for Neoliberal Times. *The Sociological Review Monographs*, 66(4): 766–82.

Selwyn, B. (2017) *The Struggle for Development*. Cambridge: Polity Press.

Shakespeare, T. (2013) The Social Model of Disability. In L.J. Davis (ed.), *The Disability Studies Reader*, 4th edn. Abingdon: Routledge, 214–21.

Silverman, S.J. and Griffiths, M.E.B. (2018) *Immigration Detention in the UK*. Migration Observatory briefing, COMPAS, University of Oxford.

Sotiris, P. (2013) Hegemony and Mass Critical Intellectuality. *International Socialism Journal*, 137.

Sotiris, P. (2018) Gramsci and the Challenges for the Left: The Historical Bloc as a Strategic Concept. *Science & Society*, 82(1): 94–119.

Srnicek, N. and Williams, A. (2015) *Inventing the Future: Postcapitalism and a World Without Work*. London: Verso.

Thomas, P. (2009) *The Gramscian Moment: Philosophy, Hegemony and Marxism*. Leiden: Brill.

Tombs, S. and Whyte, D. (2015) Counterblast: Crime, Harm and the State-Corporate Nexus. *Howard Journal of Criminal Justice*, 54(1): 91–5.

Wacquant, L. (2009) *Punishing the Poor: The Neoliberal Government of Social Security*. Durham, NC: Duke University Press.

Walters, R. (2003) *Deviant Knowledge: Criminology, Politics and Practice*. Collumpton: Willan.

Weiner, L. (2012) *The Future of Our Schools: Teachers Unions and Social Justice*. Chicago, IL: Haymarket.

Winlow, S., Hall, S., Treadwell, J. and Briggs, D. (2015) *Riots and Political Protest: Notes From the Post-Political Present*. London: Routledge.

Wright, E.O. (2010) *Envisioning Real Utopias*. London: Verso.

2

Prefigurative Politics as Resistance to State–Corporate Harm

Fighting Gentrification in Post-Occupy New York City

Laura Naegler

INTRODUCTION

The US Occupy movement famously started with the occupation of Zuccotti Park in New York City's Financial District on 17 September 2011 and soon spread across the country, leading to hundreds of occupations in large and small US cities alike. Occupy Wall Street (OWS) was inspired by the global 'movement of squares' – the Egyptian revolution of 2011 and anti-austerity movements in, among others, Spain and Greece – and inspired, too, further protest against the political and financial elites. Emerging in reaction to the global financial crisis of 2007–2009 and its devastating consequences for the national economy, the Occupy movement expressed people's frustration and growing disillusionment with the existing political system and their desire for alternatives (Harvey, 2012). It had opened up a newly ignited discourse on social and economic inequality: the semantics of the '99 per cent' versus the '1 per cent' brought forward a language of inequality intrinsic to the capitalist system, thus turning away from a perspective of poverty as an individual problem. Allowing for discussions on political participation outside of institutionalised politics, the movement re-introduced a wide range of political practices with a long tradition in autonomous and anarchist movements.

Echoing the strong impact of anarchism on OWS, the movement's politics were those of prefiguration and direct action. Direct action is any autonomous action that does not appeal or take recourse to any external authority (Franks, 2003); 'acting as if one is already free' and proceeding, as far as possible, 'as if the state does not exist' (Graeber, 2009). Prefiguration, or prefigurative politics, describes the conscious attempt to build, if only temporarily and on a limited scale, 'utopic' alternative social relationships in the present. To engage in prefiguration means 'to anticipate or enact some feature of an "alternative world" in the present, as though it has already been achieved', or to engage in modes of organisation that prefigure how they 'might normally be performed in the future' (Yates, 2014: 3-4). This can happen through building 'movement alternatives', 'community', or by the creation of egalitarian, non-hierarchical 'counter-institutions', which, if viable, would eventually replace dominant institutions and power structures (Shantz and Williams, 2013). Furthermore, prefiguration can be understood as a dynamic underlying protest and political mobilisation (Yates, 2014) based on the equivalence of means and ends. The means-ends-equivalence, a further key element in prefigurative politics, describes the belief that any political tool has to be in accordance with the aims and goals of those enacting it, in rejection of political consequentialism or revolutionary vanguardism (Springer, 2014). By engaging in prefiguration, activists in the Occupy movement aimed to enact a society without the state and private property by taking matters of self-sustenance into their own hands, and by 'stepping out' of the commodification of every aspect of living. Here, prefigurative politics are seen as creating situations in which alternatives are not only imaginable, but can be experienced and lived, thus demonstrating their feasibility. Furthermore, prefigurative endeavours are framed and intended as 'resistance' by activists themselves: targeted, like OWS, at fighting economic and social inequality in its many and everyday manifestations.

The encampments in Zuccotti Park were evicted in November 2011 and OWS was forcibly broken up by a massive police operation. The supposed 'failure' of OWS had been subject to much debate; a debate often dismissing the networks of political organising that continued to bring forward the movement's critique of systemic inequality after OWS disappeared from the international headlines. However, there was no way of denying that, in the years after OWS, New York City – place of not only the first but also the internationally most observed occupation in the USA – had consolidated its position as one of the most segregated and unequal cities in the United States.[1] This was not least shown in the city-wide gentrification, skyrocketing of rents and the lack of affordable living space, which, strongly exacerbated by the impacts of the financial crisis, lead to the displacement of whole ethnic and working-class communities and record numbers of homelessness.

In this chapter, I explore activists' endeavours to build upon the prefigurative politics of OWS, and to use 'prefigurative resistance' (Naegler, 2018) to fight the housing crisis in NYC. My argument is based on ethnographic research taking place from 2013 to 2015 with NYC's 'post-Occupy movement', or the decentralised multi-layered networks and non-formal organising structures that emerged out of OWS and continued political organising and implementation of anarchist(-inspired) politics. In this chapter, I will focus on anti-gentrification resistance and the Anti-Eviction Networks (AEN), emerging in NYC in late 2013. Here, enquiry focuses on prefigurative politics as a form of creative resistance that aims to build the 'new society in the shell of the old' (Breines, 1989: 52), but at the same time strives for 'taking away' power from authority by rejecting its legitimacy, thus making authority obsolete.

During fieldwork, I adopted the role of the researcher-activist (Juris, 2007; Haiven and Khasnabish, 2014) working with a variety of groups and collectives. I collaborated with anti-gentrification collectives and activists engaged in local community organising and participated in organising meetings, workshops and events as well as protests, marches, and actions. In my role as both activist and researcher, I actively contributed to the activists' collective knowledge production and theorising that emerges from, and results in, concrete political practice (Naegler, 2018). At the same time, I used my ethnographic data collection to participate in collective reflection and analysis. I conducted semi-structured in-depth interviews with 28 activists that extended from discussions among activists and facilitated two group interviews, which were simultaneously reflections on collectives' practices.

As I have argued elsewhere (Naegler, 2018), an understanding of prefiguration as resistance must start from a concept of creative or 'constructive resistance' (Sørensen, 2007). Resistance is commonly defined as an action or practice enacted in opposition to a certain order, situation, condition or behaviour (Hollander and Einwohner, 2004; Johansson and Vinthagen, 2014). 'Opposition' is seen as a core element: the notion of resistance as 'acting against' is inherent in the term's etymological roots (Hayward and Schuilenburg, 2014) and results in the concept being framed as mostly reactive (Vinthagen and Lilja, 2007: 1215–17). Concepts of creative resistance, however, emphasise the positive imaginative capacities of resistance, and the proactive, future-oriented elements that come with the creation of alternative. These, built or carried out independently of structures of dominant power (Sørensen, 2007: 57), either 'facilitate resistance' or create new, resistant subjectivities. In this understanding, resistance is not limited to practices of contentiousness and confrontation but can 'transcend the whole phenomenon of being-against-something' (Naegler, 2018: 12). The concept of constructive resistance allows for an understanding of prefiguration as a means to facilitate more conventional forms of opposition. Prefigurative spatial and organisational practices can create the physical and/or conceptual 'safe' spaces (Naegler, 2018) in which organising and processes of imagining alternatives take place and which allow for the creation of networks of affinity and solidarity (Yates, 2014). In addition, similar to the concept of constructive resistance, the aim of prefigurative politics is to replace the 'undesired' with an alternative, turning this alternative into 'the norm, thus resulting in a complete collapse of the previous dominant structure' (Sørensen, 2007: 58–9).

In the following, I will start by outlining the conditions in which the activism centring around post-Occupy is situated, introducing the Anti-Eviction Networks (AEN), which, inspired by the national Occupy Homes movement, started organising against gentrification in 2013. This will set the context for the analysis of both the political strengths and limitations of 'prefigurative resistance'. As I will argue, using the data from my fieldwork, rather than entering into an antagonistic relationship with dominant power, prefigurative resistance follows a 'logic of subtraction', in which the resistant potential is found in the creation of alternatives. Through prefigurative politics, activists create spaces in and through which collective egalitarian power relationships are built, realized and lived. Here, resistance moves from being purely reactive to being creative. Accordingly, prefigurative politics as creative resistance are not remaining at the level of critique and 'raising awareness'. Rather, they emphasise the necessity for immediate alternatives and solutions, whose direct experience holds the potential to spark an imagination capable of seeing beyond the omnipresent capitalist reality. Prefigurative resistance, however, brings with it several challenges that raise questions on its effectiveness and potentials of achieving aims of social change. This includes the question on the limitations of prefiguring alternative social relationships within current capitalist relations, as well as of how to form a mass movement inclusive of a broader population, including those not yet organised but most affected by economic and social inequality, and people outside of activist circles.

'ORGANISING THE CITY' IN POST-OCCUPY NEW YORK

OWS had raised the issue of 'space' in several ways and reinvigorated the debates of the just accesses to and distribution of urban space. Activists used spatial strategies of disruption that challenged the increasing control and privatisation of the city (Pickerill and Krinski, 2012). By choosing places like parks and squares close to the centres of power, protestors emphasised the symbolic importance of these locations. They made the 'spatial dimensions of exclusion and inequality' visible 'by forcing society to recognize that capitalist accumulation happens in certain places' (Pickerill and Krinski, 2012: 280). As Harvey points out, the 'distinctly urban manifestation' of the Occupy movement in its display of the 'collective power of bodies in public space' and the forceful reaction by authorities did not only demonstrate how spatial organisation and control is used as a political weapon, but revealed the effectiveness of disrupting urban economies (Harvey, 2012: 120–35). To the extent that 'the city' constitutes one of the prime sites of capital accumulation and is produced by the labour of thousands of workers, the workers' central role indicates their capacity to disrupt the circles of capital at their core. The state reacted aggressively to OWS as it held the possibility of the 'unorganised urbanisation producers' to explore these revolutionary capacities. Accordingly, to 'organise a city' becomes one of the central tasks for the anti-capitalist resistance to figure out.

For many activists from the Occupy movements, this question of how to 'organise a city' continued as a central question in the aftermath of the uprisings of 2011/2012. For this aim, moving forward from the occupation of public spaces to reclaim private property, and hence, to formulate an inherent critique of the dominant ideology of private ownership (Roos, 2011), seemed to be a logical next step. This included fighting the housing crisis in NYC that was exacerbated with the recent financial crisis. While profits on Wall Street had dropped dramatically in 2008, the financial bailout of banks through the Federal Reserve allowed them to rebound already by 2011. The vast majority of New Yorkers, however, did not benefit from this recovery and suffered increased unemployment – during the recession, 375,000 New Yorkers lost their jobs – as well as underemployment through the rapid increase of low-wage industries (Vanden Heuvel, 2014). In 2013, over 22 per cent of people in NYC lived below the federal poverty line and another 20 per cent of workers live in 'near poverty' (Fiscal Policy Institute, 2012).

This came together with the increasing impact of a decade-long political and economic project aimed at fostering city-wide gentrification since the 1960s (Zukin, 2012; Angotti, 2008). Gentrification describes the process in which working-class neighbourhoods, often after experiencing a period of conscious disinvestment, are restructured by means of government policies, targeted investments and the influx of capital through middle-class tenants and homeowners, and transformed into middle-class neighbourhoods (Smith, 1996). In NYC, gentrification was significantly pushed forward by the local administration and the real estate market in the early 2000s. An extensive re-zoning of previously commercial or industrial areas into residential neighbourhoods took place, allowing, among others, for the building of new luxury condominiums on the desired, previously working-class waterfront districts of Brooklyn (Zukin, 2012). From 2001 to 2011, NYC lost 39 per cent (385,300 units) of affordable housing (Coalition for the Homeless, 2014: 14), which resulted in rents skyrocketing: from 2000 to 2012, the median apartment rent rose by 75 per cent; with some former low-income neighbourhoods experiencing a 50 per cent increase in average rent prices (Bureau of Fiscal and Budget Studies, 2014). This coming together with the severe impact of the recession meant that the rising rents dramatically outpaced New Yorkers' average income. This led to housing costs, which were hardly manageable for many low-income households, in particular for elderly people, multi-child families and the working poor. By 2012, low-income renters spent up to 49 per cent of their income on rent; among the poor, up to 80 per cent spent half their income – some even up to 65 per cent (Naegler, 2018). This city-wide gentrification and skyrocketing of rents eventually lead to the displacement of whole ethnic and working-class communities and increasing numbers of homelessness, which, with over 50,000 homeless people including more than 20,000 children, had reached the highest number in the city's history by 2013 (Coalition for the Homeless, 2014).

It was in this context that post-Occupy activists aimed for a radical transformation of the housing system in order to stop gentrification. This included fighting its material consequences and highlighting the class and race dimensions (Smith, 1996) of the process. It also included fighting politicians and the real estate industry's ideological paraphrasing of gentrification as 'up-grading' and 're-vitalisation', or euphemistically promoted as the inevitable progress of the contemporary city (Naegler, 2018). Here, prefigurative politics, as enacted in OWS, played a significant role in achieving these political aims.

Prefigurative politics as enacted in anarchist-inspired movements such as OWS start from the position that desired future structures and social relationships have to be created in the present (Franks, 2003; Springer, 2014) and have to be lived on the micro-level prior to any macro-level transformation. The aim is to eventually overcome the totality of current conditions and dominant power: those engaging in prefigurative politics 'actively seek alternatives that provide a point of alterity or exteriority that calls the limits of the existing order into question' (Springer, 2014: 3) through which alternatives can emerge that otherwise could not be imagined. Creating these alternatives demonstrates that this point of exteriority to dominant power already exists in the present, making overcoming its totality possible (Ferrell, 2001). For this reason, the kitchen, tents, clinics, media centre and library that activists built during OWS, for example, served a purpose beyond the provision of basic needs. Similar to the direct democratic organising practices, they were expressions of the movement's desire to create egalitarian alternatives to the status quo entailing the hope that these would eventually exceed the confines of Zuccotti Park. Following the notion that the ideology of anarchist movements is expressed in its modes of organisation and political mobilisation (Graeber, 2002), prefigurative politics entails what can be understood as an 'ideological separation' from dominant power. This is achieved by creating situations and spaces based on egalitarian relationships, in which the validation of dominant power is not meant to be given. Without this ideological separation, the means-ends-equivalence cannot be achieved without significantly compromising its underlying principles. An equivalence of means and ends can only be achieved when the structures of inequality permeating the dominant order are – even if only temporarily – displaced (Ince, 2012).

This aim of achieving an ideological separation from dominant power reveals one of the strengths of prefiguration: an understanding of resistance as a creative force. As argued above, the concept of constructive resistance allows for an understanding of prefiguration as a means to facilitate resistance. However, 'prefigurative resistance', if conceptualised from an anarchist perspective, does not stop at the facilitation of opposition. The resistant potential of prefiguration must be seen as located in the creation of alternatives outside of dominant power. It is, in the words of activist Jessica,[2] resistance as defined 'as the building of alternative power relationships, egalitarian power relationships, that are not in opposition to, but separate from the state.' This is in contrast to the common understanding of resistance as caught in a cyclical relationship with power, which eventually reproduces power instead of dissolving it (Hollander and Einwohner, 2004).

Here, a clear distinction is made between resistance and 'protest'. Conventional protest relies on what activist Simon called a 'logic of antagonism': by 'making demands', seeking recognition and engaging with structures of representative politics, these legitimise existing power relations rather than meaningfully transforming them. 'Real' resistance – direct action and prefiguration – seeks to overcome dominant (state) power. In this understanding, prefigurative resistance refuses to recognise and to be recognised by authority as this is seen as a legitimisation of the dominant power's grasp on actors' endeavours (Day, 2005). Rather, resistant prefiguration relies on a 'logic of subtraction': it is 'taking away' power from authority by rejecting its legitimacy and acting 'as if' the political, social and/or economic structures perceived as unjust and harmful have already been invalidated (Graeber, 2002). Prefiguration is seen as resistance precisely because it is *not* antagonistic, but as creative resistance that transcends the 'phenomenon of being-against-something' (Vinthagen, 2007: 12) – a notion challenging the understanding that opposition constitutes a core element in resistance (Hollander and Einwohner, 2004).

The housing movements that emerged in the years after OWS demonstrate how prefigurative resistance is implemented in practice. Facing the prevailing, devastating conditions which the housing crisis of 2007 to 2009 had caused throughout the country, a number of pre-existing anti-foreclosure organisations, together with people from the Occupy movements in Boston, Detroit, Chicago, Atlanta, Minneapolis and several cities on the West Coast joined under the banner of *Occupy Homes*. Homeowners, community organisers, activist groups, lawyers and unions and the newly built Occupy Homes coalitions began to fight evictions and foreclosures in targeted on-the-ground campaigns, and soon achieved successes. They prevented evictions and foreclosures, blockaded auctions, conducted sit-ins and protests at banks like Wells Fargo, and engaged in public pressure campaigns (Jaffe, 2014; Gottesdiener, 2012). They utilised a community-oriented strategy which instead of simply exposing economic injustice and raising awareness engaged in direct action enacted by those affected. Given the pressing need for fighting the current housing situation in the city, activists in post-Occupy NYC were eager to develop a similar housing movement. In 2013, the newly founded Anti-Eviction Networks (AEN) based on the model of the Occupy Homes started their organising meetings. The aim was to create an autonomous city-wide direct action network of activists, radical academics and people engaged in local community organising, while centring anti-gentrification resistance in the neighbourhoods most affected. This should happen by the support of direct action in local communities and the engagement in prefigurative resistance.

THE POLITICAL STRENGTHS OF PREFIGURATIVE RESISTANCE

As the Occupy Homes movement showed, defensive direct actions such as eviction-blockades can be very effective. Also in NYC, people engaged in various direct actions, such as a group of residents of three apartment buildings in a gentrifying working-class neighbourhood in Southwest Brooklyn, who had initiated a rent strike in 2010. Over the years, the owner of the buildings had refused repairs and maintenance with the aim to harass the residents out of the apartments. The buildings deteriorated until reaching inhospitable conditions: broken rooftops led to the flooding of cellars and apartments, rotten garbage was not collected leading to infestations, heating did not work, and the decayed electricity system exposed the tenants to life-threatening risk of electrocution, or of fire breaking out. The residents, supported by other community members, eventually decided to become organised and to collectively refuse to pay rent until conditions improved. In 2013, this group of community organiser started to collaborate with the newly founded AEN. At this point, the rent strike was still ongoing.

As Luis, an activist in the AEN emphasised, direct actions such as rent strikes require building 'community power' first. Any successful organising against the impacts of gentrification had to start with immediately securing living space – keeping people in their homes – and with dealing with the at hand, pressing needs to ensure everyday provision of housing, food, health care and education. In Southwest Brooklyn, the community provided practical support for the rent strikers, helping out with repairs but also offered the emotional assistance and solidarity necessary for residents to keep up the year-long, tiresome struggle. Only if this basic level of security is provided, as Luis put it, can people have the full capacity to imagine and realize 'new forms of non-speculative community ownership' – or, in other words, have the necessary resources to engage in resistance.

The building of 'community power', or 'power-to' is what makes this resistance prefigurative and as such creative rather than reactive. In the process of subtracting power from the state, capital or any other external authority that is central to prefigurative resistance, the aim is to render the dominant power obsolete and replace it, as Jessica put it, with 'a different kind of power'. This power is 'power-to' rather than 'power-over': it is not 'a form of power held by a subject and institution, over another subject or institution' (Sitrin, 2012: 103), such as the state. Rather, it is 'power as potential and capacity' (Sitrin, 2012: 102); a power that is inherently social and collective, 'something that one creates, uses, and shares' (Holloway, 2002: 102). This power-to eventually manifests in people's growing ability to self-organise everyday and political life without having to resort to the capitalist market or representational politics, the state and its institutions.

During meetings with the AEN, community organisers in Southwest Brooklyn, this power-to was expressed in the emphasis of formulating a positive vision of resistance that was not, as activist Gabriela put it, about 'always fighting *against* something, but is also fighting *for* something.' The neighbourhood struggled, next to rising rents and increased homelessness due to gentrification, with various social problems such as unemployment, lack of welfare provision and the police harassment of the predominantly Latina/o population. Concrete steps were necessary to help people with the 'immediate pains', as activist Sara put it. These steps included the provision of legal aid in community meetings through lawyers recruited within the networks of the AEN, which could help people dealing with evictions or legal difficulties they faced due to their immigration status.

Further, strategies included prefiguring alternative social relationships by means of mutual aid, self-organising and 'care'. The voluntary and reciprocal exchange of services or resources, commonly referred to as mutual aid, have a long tradition in anarchist politics going as far back as the early formulations by Kropotkin (2006 [1892]). Post-Occupy activists made a strong distinction between mutual aid and 'charity' – similar to the way a distinction was made between 'protest' and 'resistance'. The former, which was strongly objected to by activists, was based on the capitalist state holding the monopoly over care activities. Mutual aid rejects this monopoly and is an act of solidarity among people striving for a self-organised, egalitarian society – and who were prefiguring a society without the state and private property by taking matters of self-sustenance into their own hands, and by 'stepping out' of the commodification of every aspect of living.

In the Southwest Brooklyn community, examples of mutual aid included the help with repairs, which was central when landlords refused these to harass people out of their apartments. In addition, community members had started take matters of the neglected garbage disposal in the neighbourhood into their own hands. Others had created a food co-op that provided affordable organic and sustainable vegetables they received from a farm in upstate New York. People were organising non-commercial childcare, and engaged in alternative forms of conflict management. Given the risk of police brutality the Black and Latina/o residents were facing, and the necessity to protect undocumented immigrants in the community, creating alternative ways of dealing with drug issues or domestic violence that did not involve the authorities was a central concern. This happened, for example, through community accountability process mirroring models of restorative justice.[3]

These examples demonstrate the political strengths of prefigurative resistance. Prefigurative practices are aimed not only at helping each other to meet material needs, but also at creating physical and/or conceptual safe spaces and networks of solidarity and affinity. These enable direct actions and allow for both protecting and empowering community members. The 'logic of subtraction' in resistant prefiguration manifests in acting 'as if' dominant political, social and/or economic structures are already invalid. By securing living space through direct action, the autonomous provision for everyday needs, or the refusal to engage with and share information with the police, the power of authorities or the capitalist market is 'taken away'. At the same time, this puts people in a position of power that would also allow for facilitating more 'offensive' actions. These were not just reacting to eviction and displacement but aimed at taking space directly, such as squatting and establishing alternatives to the capitalist housing system through collective forms of organising land and property on a larger scale.

Within these processes, prefiguration creates resistant subjectivities. The creative potential of prefigurative resistance fundamentally lies in transforming understandings of power and values that eventually delegitimises the capitalist (housing) system. Through the engagement in collective prefigurative practices, new solutions and situations become 'thinkable'. This includes the de-naturalisation of notions of private property and critical examination of gentrification as a 'natural' and inevitable process in the neoliberal city. People experience directly that private ownership, and the power to displace and evict that stems from it is nothing 'natural', that it is not grounded in an invulnerable legitimacy that simply has to be accepted 'the way it is'. As such, people in a community coming together and engaging in prefigurative resistance do not only experience immediate, practical benefits such as keeping people in their homes, or making repairs that the landlords fails to provide. Through these actions, people create new forms of self-organised community and demonstrate to themselves (as well as to landlords, banks or private developers) that they are willing and capable of taking matters into their own hands. Here, dominant power, represented by landlords, banks or private developers acting upon the seemingly invulnerable legitimacy of private property, becomes contestable and changeable.

THE LIMITS OF PREFIGURATIVE RESISTANCE

There are inevitably several challenges that come with prefigurative resistance. Prefigurative politics are hardly ever fully autonomous as there is currently no 'outside' of dominant power and capitalist relations (Duncombe, 2007). Acting 'as if the state does not exist' has it limits, as the state does still exist. For the AEN's aim to support building 'community power', the difficult question was how to do this in the context of a condition under which the possibilities of taking space become increasingly difficult. The real estate market in NYC holds tremendous economic power and exists in an interwoven relationship with political power making it difficult to challenge in the first place. In a city in which 80 per cent of people are renters, the Occupy Homes movement's strategies in fighting foreclosures of privately owned property, widely successful through their utilisation of narratives of the individual right to homeownership deeply embedded in the US culture, were difficult to apply. A further challenge consists in the difficulty to transcend the hyper-local struggles and often closed 'ecosystems of resistance' of like-minded radical activists that is associated with anarchist and prefigurative politics. This indicates a central difficulty of prefiguration that is found in negotiating the aim of forming a mass movement inclusive of a broader population while maintaining the commitment to prefigurative principles.

For example, for many activists, the Non-Profit Industrial Complex (NPIC) (INCITE!, 2007) was seen as impeding efforts to implement direct action and prefigurative politics in the communities. As one of the financial epicentres of the country, the NPIC – understood as the relationship between state, private and corporate foundations and Non-Profit Organisations and NGOs – is particularly strong and powerful in NYC. For activists in the post-Occupy movement, the NPIC is seen as allowing for the control and monitoring of social movement activity by 'managing dissent' (INCITE!, 2007). This happened partly though the channelling of activist energies in career-based trajectories that mirror capitalist structures and strengthen people's dependence on them rather than challenging them. Furthermore, the more established NGOs reinforced community groups' and grassroots movements' dependence on external funding provided by foundations or state institutions allows for influencing their work. This turned activists and community organisers into mere consultants for the work that the foundations decided to pay for, making the use of direct action, such as in Occupy Homes, difficult to implement.

Accordingly, especially the anarchist and autonomous activists in the post-Occupy movement were hesitant to have the AEN cooperate with NGOs. There was a central contradiction, as activist Robert put it, in 'working with those forces that are oppressing us, the very same foundations that we look up to when we wait for the next check to come in.' There were examples in which cooperation between community groups and NGOs worked successfully, as in some of the local Tenant Associations that formed in gentrifying neighbourhoods in Brooklyn. The cooperation was managed in a way in which careful attention was paid to ensure that paid organisers would not dominate or compromise decisions made by volunteers, while NGOs provided many resources and support. Still, many activists in the post-Occupy anti-eviction work refused to work with NGOs, or even were reluctant to work with community groups that were connected to NGOs. These decisions have to be understood in light of the logic of prefigurative politics: the aim is an ideological separation from dominant power that allows for the realization of egalitarian and anti-authoritarian principles in the present without compromising on the ideals and visions underlying prefigurative politics. However, given the strong NGO sector in NYC, a clear-cut separation is practically unfeasible, as many of the community groups and grassroots organisations are supported by NGOs. In a city as expensive as NYC, external funding is necessary for many groups to survive. An insistence with not compromising on political practice – upholding the means-end equivalence and ideological separation – comes with the risk of being exclusive to a broader population in political organising. Prefigurative politics holds the risk of reproducing what activist Susanna called 'ecosystems of resistance': closed, self-sustaining systems carefully preventing any outside influences in order to retain their internal stability. For the AEN, this soon resulted in issues of capacities: unable to recruit members beyond activist circles leading to the dissolving of many of the organising attempts of the post-Occupy period.

A further challenge for prefigurative resistance arises from the fact that the risk of the reproduction of structures of domination in daily practices of organising is not erased by the mere commitment to prefigurative principles. The systematic destabilisation of communities through displacement and the results of economic and social inequality limits in particular the resources of the people that are most affected. As argued above, it is this systematic destabilisation that is the target of prefigurative resistance. However, prefigurative politics require a significant amount of time: a difficulty of direct democratic organising models consists also in the unresolved question of who was actually able to engage in neighbourhood assemblies in terms of time and capacity, and who is able to be heard in terms of societal privilege. This comes together with the creation of internal hierarchies in activist circles, in which status is often derived from time-intensive engagement. This makes organising easily appear closed and alienates people outside of activist circles; thus, contradicting their aim of 'scaling up' and creating inclusive mass movements.

Last, the vision of prefigurative politics must face the reality that social, political and economic equality does not yet exist, and that tensions that derive from class and race divisions among activists cannot be ignored. This does not only mean the confrontation of privilege that comes with the involvement of, for example, white, middle-class activists aiming to cooperate with Black or Latino/a working-class communities. It also requires preventing the fetishisation of the 'local community' as 'the real site of struggle' (Thompson, 2010: 84), which is located outside of the experience of white middle-class activists. In the case of the neighbourhood in Southwest Brooklyn, this led to (white) post-Occupy activists' denial, or ignoring, of internalised divisions and racialised conflicts taking place within the community, for example, between the local Latino/a and Chinese population, whereas the latter was often perceived as those 'better off' as they frequently owned property. Here, a fetishisation (and romanticising) of the community of the 'oppressed Other' (Haiven and Khasnabish, 2014) homogenises differences, occludes power relations and risks obscuring forms of oppression taking place within communities.

CONCLUSION

The use of prefigurative resistance in housing activism post-Occupy raises questions of its effectiveness and potentials in achieving aims of social change. An insistence on ideological separation and upholding the equivalence of means and ends resulted in the dissolving of autonomous organising attempts, despite the pressing need for fighting gentrification and the lack of affordable housing in NYC. It also mirrors a common dilemma of anarchist politics: the necessity to negotiate between 'scaling up' anarchist principles while at the same time seizing opportunities to engage in hyper-local struggles and community organising that are inclusive of a broader population, especially those most affected by the issues at stake. Nevertheless, prefiguration can be a very important, if not crucial aspect for resistance. The concept of prefigurative resistance is fundamentally proactive. The inherent understanding of resistance as a creative and constructive force, demonstrates its political strength. Here, prefigurative resistance is not only reacting to a need of remaining at the level of critique and 'raising awareness', but also emphasises the necessity for immediate alternatives and solutions; prefigurative resistance aims to create situations in which alternatives are not only thinkable and imaginable, but can also be experienced and lived. By means of this direct experience, it holds the potential to spark an imagination capable of seeing beyond the omnipresent capitalist reality, overcoming the cynical distance that contributes to the all-pervading belief that 'there is no alternative' (Winlow et al., 2015).

For radical movements, the challenge remains to utilise the creative and constructive potential of prefigurative politics, without these resulting in an overemphasis on means at the expense of ends which is less likely to achieve a broad, collective basis of support outside of activist circles. As such, what is required is scepticism of prefigurative politics and what it can achieve on its own. With this scepticism, prefiguration's inherent creativity might allow for tapping into the revolutionary potential that lies in the construction of alternatives in the here and now.

NOTES

1. Based on the data of the American Community Survey (ACS) from 2009 to 2011, NYC, with a Gini index of 0.539, was the most unequal of the 25 largest US cities.
2. Pseudonyms are used for all participants.
3. For more information on community accountability processes, see, for example, INCITE, https://incite-national.org/community-accountability/.

REFERENCES

Angotti, T. (2008) *New York for Sale: Community Planning Confronts Global Real Estate*. Cambridge, MA: MIT Press.

Breines, W. (1989) *Community and Organization in the New Left 1962–68: The Great Refusal*. New Brunswick, NJ: Rutgers University Press.

Bureau of Fiscal and Budget Studies (2014) *The Growing Gap: New York City's Housing Affordability Challenge*. New York City: New York City Comptroller.

Coalition for the Homeless (2014) *State of the Homeless 2014*. New York City: Coalition for the Homeless.

Day, R. (2005) *Gramsci is Dead: Anarchist Currents in the Newest Social Movements*. London: Pluto Press.

Duncombe, S. (2007) *Dream: Re-Imagining Progressive Politics in an Age of Fantasy*. New York: The New Press.

Ferrell, J. (2001) *Tearing Down the Streets: Adventures in Urban Anarchy*. New York: Palgrave Macmillan.

Fiscal Policy Institute (2012) *Pulling Apart: The Continuing Impact of Income Polarization in New York State*. New York: Fiscal Policy Institute.

Franks, B. (2003) Direct Action Ethic. *Anarchist Studies*, 11(1): 13–41.

Gottesdiener, L. (2012) We Win When We Live Here: Occupying Homes in Detroit and Beyond. *Waging Nonviolence*, 28 March.

Graeber, D. (2002) The New Anarchists. *New Left Review*, 13: 61–73.

Graeber, D. (2009) *Direct Action: An Ethnography*. Edinburgh: AK Press.

Haiven, M. and Khasnabish, A. (2014) *The Radical Imagination: Social Movement Research in the Age of Austerity*. London: Zed Books.

Harvey, D. (2012) *Rebel Cities: From the Right to the City to the Urban Revolution*. London: Verso.

Hollander, J. and Einwohner, R. (2004) Conceptualizing Resistance. *Sociological Forum*, 19(4): 533–54.

Holloway, J. (2002) *Change the World Without Taking Power*. London: Pluto Press.

Ince, A. (2012) In the Shell of the Old: Anarchist Geographies of Territorialisation. *Antipode*, 44(5): 1645–66.

INCITE! (2007) *The Revolution will not be Funded: Beyond the Non-Profit Industrial Complex*. Cambridge: South End Press.

Jaffe, S. (2014) Post-Occupied. *Truthout*, 19 May.

Johansson, A. and Vinthagen, S. (2014) Dimensions of Everyday Resistance: An Analytical Framework. *Critical Sociology*, 42(3): 1–19.

Juris, J. (2007) *Practicing Militant Ethnography with the Movement for Global Resistance in Barcelona*. Oakland, CA: AK Press.

Kropotkin, P. (2006 [1892]) *The Conquest of Bread*. Alberta, GA: Black Cat Press.

Naegler, L. (2018) 'Goldman-Sachs Doesn't Care if you Raise Chicken': The Challenges of Resistant Prefiguration. *Social Movement Studies*, 17(5): 507–23.

Pickerill, J. and Krinski, J. (2012) Why Does Occupy Matter? *Social Movement Studies*, 11(3–4): 279–87.

Roos, J. (2011) Occupy Homes Lauds a Radical New Phase for the Movement. *ROAR* magazine, 3 December.

Shantz, J. and Williams, D. (2013) *Anarchy and Society: Reflections on Anarchist Sociology*. Chicago, IL: Haymarket Books.

Sitrin, M. (2012) *Everyday Revolutions: Horizontalism and Autonomy in Argentina*. London: Zed Books.

Smith, N. (1996) *The New Urban Frontier: Gentrification and the Revanchist City*. London: Routledge.

Sørensen, M. (2007) Constructive Resistance: Conceptualising and Mapping the Terrain. *Journal of Resistance Studies*, 1(2): 49–78.

Springer, S. (2014) Space, Time and the Politics of Immanence. *Global Discourse*, 4 (2–3): 159–62.

Thompson, A.K. (2010) *Black Bloc, White Riot: Anti-Globalization and the Genealogy of Dissent*. Baltimore, MD: AK Press.

Vanden Heuvel, K. (2014) No More Tale of Two Cities? How de Blasio's 2015 Budget Could Make New York More Equal. *The Nation*, 12 May.

Vinthagen, Stellan (2007), *Understanding 'Resistance': Exploring Definitions, Perspectives, Forms and Implications*. www.resistancestudies.org/files/VinthagenResistance.pdf.

Winlow, S., Hall, S., Treadwell, J. and Briggs, D. (2015) *Riots and Political Protest: Notes from the Post-Political Present*. Abingdon: Routledge.

Yates, L. (2014) Rethinking Prefiguration: Alternatives, Micropolitics and Goals in Social Movements. *Social Movement Studies*, 14(1): 3–4.

Zukin, S. (2012) *Naked City: The Death and Life of Authentic Urban Places*. Oxford: Oxford University Press.

3

Struggles Inside and Outside
the University

Steve Tombs and David Whyte

INTRODUCTION: GRAMSCI AND HEGEMONY

Critical academics are generally very proud that they work in universities. We may not like the marketised, neoliberal university, and we may despise the way that academic freedom and learning have been commodified, but we generally see universities as places that we are still able to work in, in ways that oppose the dominant ways of thinking and doing things. Critical academics are often proud to describe themselves as 'counter-hegemonic'. In the past, we have probably both described our own work in precisely these terms. However, as the cracks begin to show in the financialised model that dominates the UK university sector now, one of the traps that we fall into when we see our role as 'counter-hegemonic' in the context of the university is that we overestimate our own autonomy and we underestimate the ability of universities to incorporate social criticism into the neoliberal project. After all, as we teach our courses in power, capitalism, feminism, decolonising the curriculum and so on to undergraduates, we are always at the same time reproducing class inequalities. The process of teaching university students is a key mechanism of class sorting; we are producing university-educated workers that will have a class advantage over all the people that didn't go to university. Those students may or may not listen to us; and they may or may not turn out to be critical thinkers – but this is not really the point. We are implicated in a process of class sorting, no matter how critical or mainstream our teaching. Similarly, as critical academics, we think that our radical analyses, set down in academic journals or impact statements, are capable of challenging power. And all the while, our papers are by and large ignored and the world becomes more unjust, less equal, more violent and less sustainable. Why should we be surprised? As this chapter argues, the university is a hegemonic apparatus. It is one of the key institutions that enables hegemonic power to be reproduced. A key question that this chapter will ask, then, is whether we as critical academics are completely deluded. Is the university a place that 'counter-hegemonic' work can develop from? Are universities worth 'saving' from neoliberalism? And if so, how?

The Italian Marxist Antonio Gramsci argued that a social order becomes 'hegemonic' when a leading faction of the class that plays a key role in the extraction of the surplus in 'the decisive nucleus of the economy' successfully develops a leadership that is capable of dominating a society through a combination of force (whether this means legal, economic or military force) and ideas (through the domination of news media, literature, the arts and other cultural channels) (Gramsci, quoted in Morera, 1990: 168). This is achieved through the formation of what Gramsci called a 'historical bloc'. A historical bloc involves a complex and often contradictory formation of a politico-economic alliance that is capable of persuading other members of a particular social class, other dominating classes and other professional groupings, to accept its moral and political leadership and to both accept and contribute to its mode of governance. The historical bloc must be constituted, to some extent, in and through the state.

Members of a historical bloc expect their ideas, their understanding of the world and their specification of historical possibilities to become the general 'common sense' so that subordinate classes can formulate their interests with reference to the ideas, concepts, analytical categories, and to some extent within the ontology, of the dominant ideology (Gramsci, 1971: 180–95). The ability of the members of the historical bloc to set this agenda will depend upon their degree of dominance over mainstream social institutions, including those involving education, communication, mental and physical health, political organisation, the means of production (all involving disciplinary practices through which subjects are socially constituted, distributed to different tasks, and empowered to fulfil these in an appropriate manner) and apparatuses of repression. Thus, hegemony involves: 'the entire complex of practical and theoretical activities within which the ruling class not only justifies and maintains its dominance, but manages to win the active consent of those over whom it rules' (Gramsci, 1971: 244).

From a Gramscian perspective, the construction of hegemony always relies not just on material power (the ability of capital and national states to distribute wealth, to police, to grant or prevent access to services etc.), but also on a moral and intellectual leadership. The latter aspect of hegemony building involves the promotion of ideas to the extent that they seep into popular consciousness, ruling out alternatives and integrating into the ranks of the (relatively) advantaged and 'subordinate' groups while also consigning many of these latter groups to economic and social marginalisation (Pearce and Tombs, 2006). In particular, moral and intellectual leadership both proposes ways of thinking about the world and also silences and renders invisible alternative ways of thinking about the world (Tombs and Whyte, 2002).

The capitalist historical bloc deals with the threat of counter-hegemonic movements through this process of neutralising criticism and alternatives. It also seeks to fragment resistance, through repression, through limited progressive reforms and through the selective incorporation of personnel, of organisations and of the counter-culture into its ideology. Hegemony always involves the fragmentation of both hegemonic and counter-hegemonic groupings.

The university plays a highly significant role in the process of reproducing both material and moral/intellectual power, in constructing 'feasible' or 'acceptable' views of the world (Snider, 2000; Pearce and Tombs, 1998), but also in the process of incorporating critical voices and neutralising or diminishing the strength of alternative ways of thinking.

This chapter addresses the role of the 'academic' and the struggle for the contemporary university in the context of some of these Gramscian claims. Further, it considers universities as state-ideological apparatuses, sketching the key role of university education and research in reproducing class power before asking how academics can challenge this role and can support counter-hegemonic struggles. We develop this discussion in the context of the 2018 University College Union (UCU) dispute over attacks on members' pensions. We first contextualise the historical context for this offensive by the employers' federation, Universities UK (UUK). Then we discuss the nature and potential of the apparently radical demand that emerged within the dispute on the part of university workers to 'reclaim' the university from the clutches of neoliberal managers (since, as the hashtag claimed #wearetheuniversity). We argue that such demands remain based upon a mystification of what the university is, as a site of a 'pure' form of knowledge production that is insulated from economic or political demands (Tombs and Whyte, 2003). The need therefore is not to seek to 'save' the university, or even maintain our professional autonomy, but to deepen our organic connections to social struggles.

THE ROLE OF INTELLECTUALS WITHIN UNIVERSITIES

For Gramsci, all humans have the capacity to be intellectuals: 'All men are intellectuals, but not all men have in society the function of intellectuals' (Gramsci, 1996: 9). For those who 'achieve' the function of being intellectuals, this means that their status and position as an intellectual becomes something distinct, valorised by the institutional context in which they work, or by the purpose of their intellectual labour.

Gramsci distinguishes between two types of *functional* intellectuals: organic and traditional (Gramsci, 1996: 3–23). He describes the former as those who emerge to give the dominant hegemonic group 'homogeneity and an awareness of its own function' in the economic, social and political spheres (Gramsci, 1996: 5). The latter are the intellectuals who, despite the emergence of a new hegemonic order, retain their social position as intellectuals. For traditional intellectuals, their *apparent* disconnection from the dominant social group, or from other economic groups – added to the apparent historical continuity that they retain – is what enables them to claim their political neutrality and ability to produce value-free intellectual work. Denying their role in the class warfare of position and manoeuvre, traditional intellectuals are idealised as organically linked to the institutional context within which they work. In the case of universities, the institutional context that ensures historical continuity is the 'academy'. For many university teachers and researchers, the 'academy' – the institutional location of academic study – represents a higher loyalty that keeps them above the affray of class struggle (Tombs and Whyte, 2002; 2003).

There are two points to make here. First, academic research has a crucial role in the construction, manipulation and presentation of 'common sense' views of the world. As the dominant ideas of a society are promoted, disseminated and reproduced, they bid, through a variety of means (not least, universities and research institutions) to reach popular consciousness. When these ideas gain popular acceptance beyond the confines of groups of intellectuals, they are said to have become part of 'common sense' (Gramsci, 1996: 423). Second, academic research also plays a key role in providing the means for particular social and economic groups to respond to particularly threatening situations/conditions as they arise. This role becomes acutely significant during moments of crisis for the hegemonic bloc, or at a micro level, during moments of exposure for particular fractions of capital and state institutions/departments. It is during those phases that the reapportioning of moral and intellectual authority place even greater premium on the production of ideas that can be rehearsed to legitimise state strategies and assume a *decisive* role in class struggle.

We emphasise the word struggle here, since, although the universities construct, present and reproduce the 'common sense', and act as a moral and intellectual resource for dominant groups, they are also places where social struggles and struggles over ideas also take place. We find critical and counter-hegemonic ideas in universities just as we find intellectuals who are closely connected to counter-hegemonic groups. That said, in general, academic intellectuals play a central role in *both* the long-term process of common sense construction and manipulation, and in reproducing the forms of power and social relationships required by the state and the hegemonic order.

Moreover, as Poulantzas reminds us, the separation between the public and private realm (and indeed state and civil society) is purely a juridical one: its distinction is established by law (Poulantzas, 1970: 305). This is not to underestimate the importance of the formal legal separation between public and private spheres, since the demand for juridical separation itself is often the site for protracted and bitter class struggles; however, it is to recognise that many of the ideological apparatuses (including the universities) have no essence as public or private entities, or as part of civil society, but are part of the complex web of state ideological apparatuses. This applies to universities.

Thus, although some institutions are idealised as 'autonomous', part of 'civil society', or even 'private', they may in reality be *state* ideological apparatuses. They may only be regarded as 'autonomous' or 'private' in that they enjoy some measure of formal autonomy from the state. Universities are in this category. This means that they are as vulnerable to – and significant in promoting – the dominant material and ideological tendencies of the hegemonic bloc, as part of a process of (perpetual) hegemonic reconstruction. In this neoliberal period, this has meant the reshaping of the universities through the ideas and practices of 'marketisation' and 'financialisation' that we go on to discuss below.

For 600 years, universities have been marked by a continual process of change, always in some relation to developments in the mode of social organisation. The industrial revolution and the rise of a new ruling class ensured that universities would, to some extent, be impelled to produce the science and technology required by new industries for organising and developing production. But this transformation of the universities did not occur without a protracted struggle, and resistance to a full takeover by the industrialists from within the universities and beyond was largely successful. John Stuart Mill's inaugural lecture as rector of the University of St Andrews in 1867, summed up the position of the traditionalists, at that time:

> There is a tolerable agreement about what a university is not. It is not a place of professional education. ... Their object is not to make skilful lawyers and physicians or engineers, but capable and cultivated human beings.
>
> (cited in Sanderson, 1972: 5)

The struggle between the increasingly powerful industrial capitalists on one hand and the traditionalists on the other cannot be simplified as a pure distillation of the organic–traditional dichotomy. The traditionalists were not only defending the right of universities to provide a liberal education but were also defending the social structure that this university system maintained: one that sustained the prominence of the propertied class. Thus, the successful co-option of the universities to provide the teaching and research that could be utilised directly by the industrial merchants and manufacturing classes (as opposed to the traditionally dominant subjects such as the classics or philosophy that were deemed to be vocationally useless) did not appear in a fully developed form until well into the nineteenth century. When the role of the university did begin to transform, it was based upon the rising acceptance of the utility value of education (and, of course, the expansion of industrial production, transportation and latterly consumption) as a social good. Education that was relevant to industry had to be introduced into the universities if capitalism, and British society, was to advance and flourish (Sanderson, 1972: 5).

All this being said, the popular conception of universities is abstracted from hegemonic struggle; an abstraction which enables its claims to objectivity, the pursuit of knowledge, promotion of learning and so on. The romantic ideal of the 'ivory tower' – where research is conducted which is neutral, value free and divorced from the partisan imperatives of economic forces – has always been a highly fetishised but very powerful one. In short, then, universities – and many academics within them – are part of a liberal illusion of 'free' movement of critical ideas and knowledge, not least contributing to 'progress', and at the same time legitimising certain forms of class exploitation and hegemonic domination. The university, then, emerged as yet another institution where class struggle is mediated, contained and transformed, as well as having the more immediate function in production and reproduction of dominant hegemony. This immediately marks out the university as a seemingly contradictory place – a source of radicalism, dissent and critique just as it is a source of the maintenance of capitalist domination.[1]

NEOLIBERALISM, MARKETISATION, FINANCIALISATION

Writing in the 1970s, Ralph Miliband charted the evolving relationship between corporations, the state and universities and noted the growing influence of the state and business interests. The state was not only becoming more involved in the direction of the university, but 'academics are also immeasurably more involved than ever before in the life of the state' (Miliband, 1973: 249). This was evident in both the production of material that can be used in the formulation of policy and also in the involvement in those processes so that senior academics become increasingly embroiled in grappling with the problems of government (they become 'officialised'). Miliband argued that not only had the expansion of corporate activity and power intensified – and with it the (quantitative) demand for trained and morally prepared subjects – but that universities and students at universities are increasingly (qualitatively) tailored to those demands. It is this latter point that is of the utmost significance, since it is the structural development of the mode of production that underpins all other aspects of the university–business relationship. Specialisation and technological development, moral justification and the training function all have a changing requirement as capitalism advances and university research adapts to the changing environment around it.

Over the past four decades, links between university departments and corporate/state sponsors have developed in the context of a rapid expansion of the higher education sector and, at the same time, steady cuts in state funding. Structurally, the marketisation of research has been encouraged (and indeed deemed necessary) by political reforms to the funding regime for Higher Education. The end of the binary divide prompted by the Education Reform Act (1988) abolished the old Polytechnic Board and the UGC, which had tended to act as a buffer between the financial autonomy of the universities and government policy. Local accountability was also discarded by taking polytechnics out of Local Education Authority control. Now the universities, old and new (the former polytechnics) were placed in the hands of the new Higher Education Funding Councils. This effectively tied the higher education system more closely to centralised administrative control and meant the end of the binary divide, encouraging greater competition for student and research income between institutions. In the prelude to this seismic shift in the governance of higher education, in the first term of the 1979 Conservative government, the University Grants Committee (UGC), the central funding body for the universities, had its grant cut by 17 per cent. Around 4,000 university posts were lost to a government early retirement scheme. From 1985 onwards, universities were to see their grants cut on average by between 2 per cent and 4 per cent in real terms every year for the next decade (Monbiot, 2000; Slaughter and Leslie, 1990).

This period simultaneously witnessed a huge expansion in student recruitment to universities, largely as a result of the financial restructuring project that (under changes to the Universities Funding Council formula in 1988) linked government grants directly to student numbers, thus stimulating a market in student recruitment. Between 1988/89 and 1993/94, the total number of full-time students in higher education had increased by 65 per cent and part-time students by 35 per cent. In the same period, staff numbers increased by less than 17 per cent (Hillyard and Sim, 1997: 51-2).

Higher Education policy in 'UK Plc' in the Blair and Brown years accelerated those trends. By 2006, 48 per cent of 18-30 year olds had participated in higher education (Callinicos, 2006), signalling that the 'massification' of the university sector in the UK reached a high point in the mid-2000s. In many ways, though, 'massification' was only part of the strategy. The drive to increase student numbers was coupled to a broader process of neoliberal reform. After decades of austerity, universities were forced to drive down costs yet further, in a process of academic 'strip mining' (Callinicos, 2006: 17), that sharply intensified university teaching productivity on one hand and on the other, used universities to boost commercial forms of research and development. Meanwhile, the market in student recruitment was carefully honed by successive governments, seeking to prepare the sector for a fully-fledged process of financialisation (McGettigan, 2013). Mair has noted a paradox, whereby the system for privatising debt and asset stripping future generations has been publicly financed:

> Huge amounts of government money have flowed into British universities since the introduction of tuition fees by Tony Blair's New Labour administration in 1998. The fees were initially set at £1,000 per year, were raised to £3,225 in 2009, then £9,000 in 2012 and reached their current level of £9,250 in 2015.
>
> (Mair, 2018a)

In other words, this has been a process of *market-making*. The newly inflated fees on one hand aimed at a further driving down of costs and the intensification of market discipline. On the other hand, the new fee economy sought to encourage a kind of limited financial autonomy. We say limited, because the long neoliberal march had ensured that universities were more than ever forced to respond to the research demands of the state and the private sector, while the student market was to be wholly demand-led, rather than shaped by traditional specialism or any commitment to maintaining disciplines for the sake of maintaining discipline. In this sense, the 'traditional' autonomy of the universities, particularly the pre-92 universities, was fatally weakened. The lifting of the cap of student numbers in 2015 (although the limits on student recruitment had been progressively loosened for a number of years) was a key moment that ensured any residual brake on 'massification', even in the majority of the elite 'Russell Group' universities was to be futile in a fee-driven hyper-aggressive student recruitment market.

This moment also made it more obvious that the burden of this indi-vidualised system does not lie wholly with graduates who are charged with paying back their interest. A combination of publicly acknowledged high default rates and an exceptionally favourable deal with the invest-ment firms financing the loan book means that the UK taxpayer is now subsidising higher education more than at any point in the history of the universities. Indeed, the fee economy has proven to be a bonanza for the financial sector. There have been successive sales of the student loan book on terms highly favourable to investors. One analysis by the *Financial Times* (29 November 2017) of the sale of the latest tranche in late 2017 suggests that because that the government sold assets worth £2.5 billion to raise £1.7 billion, the sale will have cost the taxpayer £800 million. The sheer scale of the market so-created by the introduction of student loans is staggering. As a recent House of Commons report summarised:

> Currently more than £16 billion is loaned to around one million higher education students in England each year. The value of out-standing loans at the end of March 2018 reached £105 billion. The Government forecasts the value of outstanding loans to reach around £450 billion (2017–18 prices) by the middle of this century. The average debt among the first major cohort of post-2012 students to become liable for repayment was £32,000. The Government expects that 30% of current full-time undergraduates who take out loans will repay them in full.
>
> (Bolton, 2019: 3)

The story of the student loan book is not merely a story of privatisation and marketisation. It is a story of *financialisation* because, in Epstein's terms, it is based on the 'increasing role of financial motives, financial markets, financial actors and financial institutions' in the political economy of higher education (Epstein, 2005: 3). Of course, this is not merely a logic that permeates higher education, but now dominates in many areas of the public sector. The UK had been one of the 'earliest adopters' of financialisation, leaving it in the position of being 'one of the most financialized economies in the world' (David and Walsh, 2017). The financialisation of goods and services, which had been publicly provided, was therefore a logical step since access to such goods and services, including higher education, are easily 'privatized and mediated by the financial system' (Lapavitsas, 2013: 800).

As part of this process of financialisation, the market-making fee economy has made the obscene inflation of senior management remuneration possible. The latest *Times Higher* survey puts the average Vice-Chancellor remuneration in the UK at over £280,000 per year, a figure that is probably larger than any other public sector equivalent. As well as enabling the advent of private sector CEO pay levels in the university, the fee economy has also enabled the rapid expansion of the sector into some highly profitable spheres of activity and influence, perhaps most prominent being the exponential growth of the international market – with many UK universities now opening new campuses in locations such as Singapore, China and India, training police officers in Bahrain and offering qualifying law degrees in tax havens such as the Cayman Islands. This has been coupled with a rapidly expanding domestic economy of public–private partnerships in university provision: partnership degree accreditation; the proliferation of consultancy and licensing deals with the private sector. At least as significant as these other developments has been the growth of the involvement of universities in property development and as big players in property markets. It is estimated by the university workers' union UCU that in 2016/17 the aggregated surplus earned by the sector was £2.27 billon; in the same year, the sector invested £4.2 billion in property, building and infrastructure (UCU, 2018). By 2017, the value of student property across the UK was estimated to be in excess of £45 billion (Ward, 2017; Adventum, 2017).

Neoliberal discipline claims to ensure responsiveness to the market. On one hand the aim is to introduce the rigour of the (internal) market and ensure that universities are ever more responsive to the demands of the (external) market. On the other hand, the aim is to stimulate the technological requirements of British industry in a university system that was deemed to have over-valued generalised, arts-based, non-vocational education for too long. The end point of this is a much bigger and more significant project: a project to fully financialise universities, to ensure that they operate according to the logic of maximising financial return on investment.

The expansion of higher education in the UK in the 1990s was largely a result of successive governments' unflinching political allegiance to the neoliberal project as a means of bringing the universities to the market. And the expansion of the sector under a bonanza fee economy in the 2010s has been the logical end point of the neoliberal strategy with financialisation as its motor-force. In the context of the evolving processes described in this section, it is therefore accurate to say that the hegemonic assimilation of the universities into the neoliberal project is getting close to completion. As this project gathers momentum, it becomes ever more difficult to present alternatives to the creeping processes of entrepreneurialisation and marketisation that are unfolding in our universities.

STRIKE AGAINST FINANCIALISATION!

In spring 2018, university workers in the UK were involved in the biggest campaign of strikes and industrial action ever seen in the sector. The strike made major unexpected gains in pushing back an audacious attempt by UUK to drastically devalue university workers' pensions. Since 1997, UUK coordinated a unilateral cut in their pension contributions to the pension fund, because, they argued, the scheme was in such good financial health (Otsuka, 2018). In 2017, UUK began to argue that the scheme was in deficit and therefore it could not afford to guarantee pension benefits. UUK's sudden pessimism was confirmed by a now widely discredited evaluation of the pension published in November 2017 as part of the statutory monitoring of the health of the pension scheme. UCU had its own expert assessment that showed that the pension fund 'deficit' was concocted as a convenient narrative to justify the wholesale transfer of risk from employers to the employees. The mechanism to do this was to change pension remuneration from a 'defined benefits' system to a 'defined contributions' system. This meant that instead of pension benefits being guaranteed by employers, they would now be linked directly to the value of the fund's investment portfolio – that is, they would be fully financialised. Losses to the value of academic pensions were estimated at between 20 per cent and 40 per cent depending on individual circumstances. The 2018 strike was organised in response to the employer's proposal for this wholesale transferal of risk and the full-scale financialisation of pensions.

In effect, the strike was a defensive action against a significant attack on wages, via a proposed pensions theft. But it soon took on wider dimensions, as university workers developed a broader narrative that raised issues far beyond the defence of their pensions. Senior management remuneration packages and the proliferation of vanity capital projects were juxtaposed with the clear and unremitting deterioration of teaching and learning conditions. At the same time, the pressures on fees alongside a bloated, socialised loan book were also soon highlighted. These became readily visible and easily comprehensible manifestations of what might otherwise have remained the somewhat esoteric phenomenon of financialisation; this very soon became the target of critical attention, which then inevitably encompassed related processes of the managerialism, marketisation and neoliberalisation of Higher Education.

In many places, the most casualised university workers (around 50 per cent of university staff in the UK are on precarious 'zero-hours' or temporary contracts) played leading roles in the strike, while emphasising that they were not eligible for pensions, so that their action was one of solidarity with and a commitment to challenging the financialisation of higher education as an end in itself. Alongside this, here was an unprecedented wave of student militancy, not least student occupations at more than 20 universities around the country, all echoing our demands and all explicitly declaring the importance of worker–student solidarity. Again, non-commodified education was the focus of student demands. This solidarity was often further developed and related to wider progressive struggles, through bottom-up designed 'teach-outs' in which teaching and learning was explicitly divorced from the instrumentalism and credentialism of contemporary Higher Education in the UK, perhaps in small ways prefiguring other ways of organising university education.

In other words, and as was widely acknowledged, very quickly the strike stopped being about pensions and started being about a bigger imperative: the need to sweep away the principles of neoliberalism and marketisation that have strangled the life out of our universities. As the arrogance of UUK began to waver in the face of trade union and student solidarity, the widespread demands of striking academics shifted beyond the abandonment of the pension proposals and towards an articulation of a range of demands for progressive change across the sector (Mair, 2018b). Perhaps the most widely used slogan to come out of the strike was the disarmingly radical *#WeAreTheUniversity*.

The strike was an expression of a much bigger fightback against the competitive metrics, against the performance indicators introduced as part of the national Research and Teaching Excellence Frameworks (REF and TEF), against the escalating and accumulating micro-management of working conditions, and against the instrumentalism of education and students as consumers or clients as opposed to learners. One of the most common complaints heard by university staff is that they are 'infantilised', their academic autonomy undermined by an endless stream of patronising and disciplinary techniques and demands imposed by management, and that this process, too, requires the infantilisation of students who face more micro-forms of surveillance in terms of progression and attendance. It seems clear to us that a key reason for the strike being so successful is that it became a way of galvanising opposition to the neoliberal university.

That this was a strike against the *neoliberal* university was explicit. Yet, what was hidden was the end point of the story we have told above. The struggle over pension risk, after all, is really a struggle over financial capacity. If the universities can transfer future financial risk from themselves to employees (who, under the employers proposals, were to become reliant on the health of financial markets rather than university reserves), then they can free up capital reserves for the capital-intensive project of international expansion, domestic expansion in collaboration with the private sector and property development. This was the real reason that UUK provoked this strike.

In this context, the question about whether 'we are the university' and the associated demands to 'reclaim' the university assume a major significance. How can we reclaim the university from an advanced stage of financialisation? What will it take to reverse the process of neoliberal reform? Clearly, in the sense that the pension strike sent a shot across the bows from a professional group that is angry about both the undermining of their autonomy and the conditions that the most casualised among them face, and in the sense that it sought to slow down the process of financialisation, this strike was an assault on financialisation, marketisation and neoliberalism – phenomena which are inextricably linked within the sector, but which are not synonymous (Davis and Walsh, 2017).

Of interest for us is the way in which the strike targeted the newly constructed 'common sense' around the nature, purpose and organisation of Higher Education in the UK. Thus, it was a material struggle, but one infused with moral and intellectual critique. With marketisation had come not simply new politico-economic modes of organisation but a new cultural political economy as well (Wiegratz, 2013). Market logics had proliferated and become the norm across non-economic areas of social life. Marketisation is, then, far more than institutional – it has normalised, in a very Gramscian sense, a market populism and imagery which achieves a 'partial colonisation of common sense' (Clarke, 2010: 381).

Most fundamentally, then, we have lived through a period in which a new common sense has circulated: business interests – which are by definition sectional (class) interests arising out of activity conducted for clear motives – are increasingly represented as 'general' or 'national' interests (Tombs, 2016). And this affects all institutions of 'state' and civil society, 'public' and private. The university is not immune from these processes of hegemonic reconstruction – and these tendencies have made anti-marketisation and anti-financialisation voices and demands much less articulable within a university context.

In these contexts, then, counter-hegemony means resisting the tendencies of both marketisation and financialisation – and, more broadly, neoliberalism. The 2018 actions were seeds of such counter-hegemonic resistance. Yet we also need to be realistic. Counter-hegemonic struggle that takes place inside the university is only ever going to have a very limited impact on hegemonic power. Counter-hegemonic struggle is made much more possible, within institutions where there are already strong forces of resistance outside the university. For example, counter-hegemonic research on economy and society is stronger when it is linked with intra- and extra-university popular movements (workers movements, community organisations and social movements). On the other hand, universities in which managements act relatively unfettered, where unions are relatively weak, where casualisation, instrumentalism and intra-workforce division are easily fostered are those least likely to allow let alone support counter-hegemonic research – and vice versa. At the same time, struggles against the financialisation of the university are made stronger when those struggles are supported by popular movements that have strong community links and are international.

This means being engaged in struggles within the university which resist both processes; and it means supporting wider struggles which seek to do the same. Engaging in the former in the absence of the latter means that academics as university workers will perpetuate the illusion of the university as a free-floating site of critical enquiry, relatively untouched by wider social struggles defined by class, 'race' and gender; it also means that any gains that might be made in teaching, learning and working conditions are always vulnerable, only focused around, and indeed contingent upon, the balances of forces within institutions – while the dominant factors which structure universities operate well beyond them. Marketisation and financialisation are pervasive, within of course but well beyond universities, and need to be exposed (not least through counter-hegemonic research) and challenges through industrial and direct action, as well as through formal political processes. Albeit in perhaps fragmented and often small ways, each of these tendencies were present in the 2018 strikes.

On the other hand, counter-hegemonic practice, whether it takes the form of strikes or critical scholarship in the university becomes immeasurably weakened when popular forces remain under-utilised and under-galvanised. To return to our earlier discussion of Gramsci's theory of hegemony, the point about hegemony is that it seeks to develop resources for power in ways that galvanise a leading fraction in the economy. The leading fraction in the UK economy is finance capital. Indeed, the UK economy has been one in which finance capital has long held a peculiar dominance therein (Ingham, 1984). It is for this reason that we need to be aware that when we are challenging the universities over financialisation, we truly are involved in a counter-hegemonic struggle because we are dealing with a historical bloc in which the finance sector is the leading fraction of capital. This means our fight is not just with UUK or with the USS; our fight is also with the logic and practices that have embedded the principles of financialisation in the university.

Put this way, we clearly have a long way to go if we are to 'reclaim the University'. For all kinds of reasons (not least, for the survival of critical space in the university, and for mounting an effective challenge to financialisation) it is increasingly important for researchers to be organically linked to counter-hegemonic struggle outside the university: to workers organisations, political and social movements, to pressure groups and community organisations that are committed to challenging state and corporate power. For academics, this work begins, of course, within the university, but it cannot stop at the campus gates.

CONCLUSION

For all the deterioration in working conditions, the pernicious rise in casualisation and the relative decline in academic pay in higher education in recent years, university academics, particularly those (albeit a diminishing number) on full-time, permanent contracts, are in a relatively privileged position, with access to skills and resources. Because of this, we have a duty to fight for access to those resources for those groups and individuals who are denied access to, or lacking, such privileges.

Our duty is to imagine, and to struggle for, how things could be otherwise; but this imagination cannot be based on experiences within the university. It is an imagination that has to be nurtured by, and in turn has to nourish, struggles outside of the university. Experience of involvement in counter-hegemonic struggles which fed into 'teach-outs' organised by UCU at the University of Liverpool during the strike included opposition to prison-building as part of a wider abolitionism, demands for accountability in the context of the Grenfell Tower fire, and the campaign against the global arms trade through focusing on the role within it of the University of Liverpool Plc (Liverpool Friends of Palestine and Campaign Against the Arms Trade, 2015).

The neoliberal assault upon the universities has, in one sense, raised the stakes for critical research in terms of a choice of open partisanship, and revealing the truly organic nature of our work as intellectuals. Researchers who refuse to pursue large grants or engage in policy evaluations are increasingly vulnerable to disciplinary mechanisms within universities. This degree of vulnerability means that it is ever more important for critical academics to be involved with organisations that can give them some organic strength and collective credibility, and also raises the importance of being involved in international networks of counter-hegemonic academics.

This is not to romanticise or fetishise the idea that the university nor critical research within it can autonomously act as a force for progressive social change. As we have argued in this chapter, this is not a particularly useful way to conceptualise the purpose or function of higher education or research more generally in capitalist social orders. The fact that critical and counter-hegemonic work emerges from the ideological apparatuses is not a function of the institutions themselves but is always a result of protracted struggles (either within or beyond the institution) that create the space for this work.

Thus, what *can* change the university is the process of struggle: how we struggle as workers – with organic links across workforces within the sector and also links to wider social struggles outside the university (Alvesalo-Kuusi and Whyte, 2017; Tombs and Whyte, 2002). The strikes within the sector in 2018 were instructive in these respects. Members mobilised on an unprecedented scale in UK higher education, and many were no doubt radicalised (Hart, 2018). It is clear that industrial action changes things and can change things quickly, and indeed can change what we ourselves believe is possible. But this process of change cannot be fleeting and intermittent, nor, therefore, can it be confined within the sector. To change the university means we must struggle within it – but, this struggle will come to nothing if we don't develop a lasting, organic, struggle side by side with workers, community struggles and social movements outside the university.

NOTE

1. We are grateful to an anonymous reviewer for summarising our argument so succinctly here.

REFERENCES

Adventum (2017) Student Property Value in the UK: £45 Billion in 2017. www.adventumoffshore.com/blog/student-property-value-in-the-uk-45-billion-in-2017/ (accessed 30 October 2018).

Alvesalo-Kuusi, A. and Whyte, D. (2017) Researching the Powerful: A Call for the Reconstruction of Research Ethics. *Sociological Research Online*, 23(1): 136–52.

Bolton, P. (2019) Student Loan Statistics. House of Commons Library Briefing Paper, Number 1079, 18 July, http://researchbriefings.files.parliament.uk/documents/SN01079/SN01079.pdf (accessed 19 October 2018).

Callinicos, A. (2006) *Universities in a Neo-Liberal World*. London: Bookmarks.

Clarke, J. (2010) After Neo-Liberalism? Markets, States and the Reinvention of Public Welfare. *Cultural Studies*, 24(3): 375–94.

Davis, A. and Walsh, C. (2017) Distinguishing Financialization from Neoliberalism. *Theory, Culture and Society*, 34(5–6): 27–51.

Epstein, G. (2005) Introduction: Financialisation and the World Economy. In Gerald Epstein (ed.), *Financialisation and the World Economy*. Cheltenham: Edward Elgar, 3–16.

Gramsci, A. (1971) *Selections from the Prison Notebooks*. London: Lawrence and Wishart.

Gramsci, A. (1996) *Selections from the Prison Notebooks*. London: Lawrence and Wishart.

Hart, E. (2018) The UK University Strikes and the Marketisation of Higher Education: The State of Play and Why We Must Fight on with Hope. *Brave New Europe*, 17 April, https://braveneweurope.com/emily-luise-hart-the-uk-university-strikes-and-the-marketisation-of-higher-education-the-state-of-play-and-why-we-must-fight-on-with-hope (accessed 5 July 2019).

Hillyard, P. and Sim, J. (1997) The Political Economy of Socio-Legal Research. In P. Thomas (ed.), *Socio-Legal Studies*. Aldershot: Dartmouth.

Ingham, G. (1984) *Capitalism Divided? The City and Industry in British Social Development*. Basingstoke: Macmillan.

Lapavitsas, C. (2013) The Financialization of Capitalism: 'Profiting without Producing'. *City*, 17(6): 792–805.

Liverpool Friends of Palestine and Campaign Against the Arms Trade (2015) Get Your Bombs Off Our Lawn the Arms Industry and the University of Liverpool. *Labout Net*, www.labournet.net/other/1510/livarmsall.pdf (accessed 30 October 2018).

McGettigan, A. (2013) *The Great University Gamble: Money Markets and the Future of Higher Education*. London: Pluto.

Mair, M. (2018a) The UK's University Strike. *Brave New Europe*, 25 February, https://braveneweurope.com/michael-mair-the-uks-university-strike (accessed 19 October 2018).

Mair, M. (2018b) Fateful (Dis)Junctures: An Update on the UK's University Strike. *Brave New Europe*, https://braveneweurope.com/michael-mair-fateful-disjunctures-an-update-on-the-uks-university-strike (accessed 19 October 2018).

Miliband, R. (1973) *The State in Capitalist Society*. London: Quartet.

Monbiot, G. (2000) *Captive State: The Corporate Takeover of Britain*. London: Macmillan.

Morera, E. (1990) *Gramsci's Historicism: A Realist Interpretation*. London: Routledge.

Otsuka, M. (2018) USS Deficit Traced to 1997 Employer Contribution Cut by 4.55% of Salaries. *Medium*, https://medium.com/@mikeotsuka/uss-deficit-traced-to-employer-contribution-holiday-47828757a8e4 (accessed 9 May 2019).

Pearce, F. and Tombs, S. (1998) *Toxic Capitalism: Corporate Crime and the Chemical Industry*. London: Routledge.

Pearce, F. and Tombs, S. (2006) Hegemony, Risk and Governance: 'Social' Regulation and the US Chemical Industry. *Economy and Society*, 25(3): 428–54.

Poulantzas, N. (1970) *Fascism and Dictatorship*. London: New Left Books.

Sanderson, M. (1972) *The Universities and British Industry 1850–1970*. London: Routledge and Kegan Paul.

Slaughter, S. and Leslie, L. (1990) *Academic Capitalism: Politics, Policies and the Entrepreneurial University*. Baltimore, MD: Johns Hopkins University Press.

Snider, L. (2000) The Sociology of Corporate Crime: An Obituary (Or: Whose Knowledge Claims have Legs?). *Theoretical Criminology*, 4(2): 169–206.

Tombs, S. (2016) *Social Protection After the Crisis: Regulation Without Enforcement*. Bristol: Policy Press.

Tombs, S. and Whyte, D. (2002) Unmasking the Crimes of the Powerful. *Critical Criminology*, 11(3): 217–36.

Tombs, S. and Whyte, D. (2003) Unmasking the Crimes of the Powerful: Establishing Some Rules of Engagement. In Steve Tombs and David Whyte (eds), *Unmasking the Crimes of the Powerful: Scrutinising States and Corporations*. New York: Peter Lang, 3–48.

Ward, R. (2017) UK's Purpose-Built Student Accommodation Market Valued at £45.8bn. StuRents online, https://sturents.com/news/2017/01/06/uk-s-purpose-built-student-accommodation-market-valued-at-45-8bn/948/ (accessed 19 October 2018).

Wiegratz, J. (2013) The Neoliberal Harvest: The Proliferation and Normalisation of Economic Fraud in a Market Society. In Simon Winlow and Richard Atkinson (eds), *New Directions in Crime and Deviancy*. Abingdon: Routledge, 55–70.

PART II

RESISTING THE PUNITIVE WELFARE STATE:
HOUSING, MENTAL HEALTH, DISABILITY
AND IMMIGRATION

4

Class, Politics and Locality in the London Housing Movement

Lisa Mckenzie

INTRODUCTION

Legitimacy is important within any organised political activist group or professional political campaign, especially having a connection and reach into what we might call the 'grassroots'. In terms of political campaigning, the 'grassroots' means those that are situated closest to a particular issue. These types of bottom-up campaigns often start out as last resort attempts in saving or changing or ending local or national government policy and/or practice. Grassroots campaigns can also grow in opposition out of unwanted private industry interference that may be having a negative effect on a community or group. Communities, groups and individuals in society that have little legitimate institutional or political power start campaigns often out of desperation and through feelings of embattlement, when other forms of complaint have come to a dead end. Grassroots campaigners are mostly made up of people that have little to no personal power as individuals and are not practised or confident in fighting against institutional power. Consequently, they come together as a collective, even if it is for only a short period of time, in an attempt to make their voices heard together. In any democracy, peaceful protest and political campaigning are considered as part and parcel of the democratic process, and an example of 'good citizenship'.

In this chapter, I argue that citizenship is not simply the struggle for rights and legal norms, but also involves more lived and affective dimensions such as values, feelings and the need for social solidarity. Questions of citizenship are not simply settled by issues of power and status; rather, within contemporary democratic societies, discussions around citizenship are the subject of a considerable amount of contestation, debate and disagreement (Stevenson, 2003). Here, with specific reference to questions of inequality, social class and locality in relation to the grassroots housing movement in London, I will argue that the power maintained within an institutional political sphere too often puts out the precarious flames rising from a grassroots movement. This argument belongs to a tradition of critical cultural sociology that looks to explore how citizenship and the civil domain remain marked by questions of power, thereby obscuring 'realities' and viewpoints that can inform wider forms of public debate and dialogue. In this respect, the chapter contributes to the wider discussion on class and its relationship to the development of neoliberalism (Skeggs, 2004), linking how institutional 'official' politics deal with local and grassroots movements with a deeper ethnographic understanding by contextualising small protest groups within the wider issues of class inequality and especially within a housing crisis.

This chapter focuses upon recent grassroots housing campaigns in London that have been predominantly led by working-class women forced into struggle. These small campaigns took on the daunting position of resisting government and for-profit organisations, global and local institutional power. The chapter uses ethnographic data collected over three years by the author and during two campaigns in east London; both campaigns were set up by women attempting to save the communities where they lived. These types of campaigns are not rare despite 'official' and organised campaigning structures that often complain and report that they cannot engage with local communities, or that local people particularly those in working-class communities are difficult to engage in politics. Yet social media is filled with small, local campaigns using Twitter and Facebook, creating their own websites, in addition to the more traditional organising. These small-scale, grassroots groups usually start up by engaging their communities and bringing attention to local issues, such as the closing of a community centre, school or hospital, however, not all local grassroots campaigning is seen as 'legitimate'. Following Stephanie Lawler's research (2005) in relation to working-class women campaigning and protesting in Portsmouth against what they believed was a local government initiative in rehousing convicted sex offenders into their neighbourhood, there had been a widespread national media response to the protests, which Lawler (2005) argued used the narrative of 'the mob' to delegitimise the campaign. Although the protests caused wider debate throughout the general public and media relating to British criminal law and the rehabilitation of sex offenders, Lawler was not critiquing the protest or aims of the protest – rather, the ways that the women's campaign had been delegitimised:

> What I am concerned with here is, first, the way in which the concept of 'the crowd' or 'the mob' is strategically used to legitimate some forms of protest and to pathologize others, and, second, the ways in which class and gender are built into the heart of notions of 'the mob'.
>
> (Lawler, 2005: xxx)

What Lawler (2008) later highlights through her book *Identity* is the marked class difference between women protesters: middle-class women are seen as 'concerned' and their concerns are therefore legitimised through their class positions, while working-class women's protests are conversely read as 'not knowing the right things', 'not doing the right things' and not 'looking right' (Lawler, 2008: 139–41). Consequently working-class concerns, that are on the outside of a political party or an organised trade union are delegitimised (Mckenzie, 2015).

Consequently, very few of the many small-scale local campaigns are picked up by the national media or supported by organised political parties as their 'local social capital' is seldom recognised by professional and party political activists as legitimate (Mckenzie, 2015). Yet grassroots groups find their 'fight back' has emerged organically out of anger and frustration against organised and institutional power. This chapter, therefore, argues that party politics, charities, and non-governmental organisations (NGOs) in addition to local and national government are part of the Marxist concept of a cultural and political super structure that works with the capitalist economic base which creates and maintains unequal and oppressive social structures.

SOCIAL HOUSING NOT SOCIAL CLEANSING

Families who live in social housing are particularly vulnerable to rising levels of unemployment caused by the contraction of the public sector and the global crisis of capitalism. Poor families were also rendered vulnerable following the loss of the manufacturing industries in the early 1980s under the Thatcher Government. This has led to a situation whereby some families living on council estates have been outside regular and stable paid work since the early 1980s. Consequently, there has been a significant change in the ways council estates and working-class people are represented within the wider culture. Typically, council residents are now seen as social 'failures', unable to participate in the wider consumer-orientated economy. Yet before the rise of neoliberalism, being a resident of a council estate in the UK was to be connected to the employed working class, where extended families were kept close together, and where communities could grow around work, local politics and local services (Coates and Silburn, 1970; Pahl, 1984; Rogaly, and Taylor, 2009). Today's working-class residents of poor estates are not a homogenous group; and differing localities around the country mean the housing situation for working-class people varies widely. In London, as in many large global cities, the value of land is high, and competition for space is fierce. The consequences of this competition to have somewhere to live has left the poorest residents in extremely vulnerable and precarious situations.

THE GLOBAL CITY: AGGRESSIVE LANDSCAPES

At the heart of the campaigns discussed within this chapter is gentrification and displacement, which are vital issues in relation to providing a critical account of whether local campaigns can either win or lose. The concepts of victory and defeat can often be a complicated outcome to decide upon when grassroots movements take on powerful institutions. The centre of contention, and consequently the flash points around these conflicts of housing in London that have arisen between local and national government policy and those being displaced by these policies. This chapter argues that the very act of resistance should not be underestimated.

Urban working-class resistance movements have been set up in all global and large cities in opposition to the gentrification process that is a form of class cleansing, displacement and dispossession (Watt, 2012). The debates around gentrification have been around for more than 50 years, when Ruth Glass linked housing and class struggle together in London during the early 1960s where she lived in Islington, North London. Ruth Glass's research focused upon her concerns over the rehabilitation of Victorian lodging houses, but also how the community was moving away from renting and towards owning of property, leading to property price increases and the displacement of working-class occupiers by middle-class incomers (Glass, 1964). Hence, she created the term 'gentrification' with the intention to capture the class inequalities and injustices created by capitalist urban land markets and policies that lead to a rising house expense burden for low-income and working-class households. At the same time, she captured the devastating experiences of displacement, eviction and homelessness, which she argued are the outcomes of when capital accumulation takes priority over family and community.

Tom Slater (2015) has argued of the importance in retaining this level of critical commitment in studying 'gentrification' and also of retaining its focus on class inequality, which over time has begun to disappear from the debate. Slater (2014) responded to an article in the *Guardian* newspaper (2014) that suggested gentrification was a 'natural process' in an urban environment; Slater was indignant in his response that 'there is nothing natural about gentrification', arguing vociferously why we need to ensure that the language of gentrification stays true to Glass's original concept that is centred upon class struggle.

However, Butler and Hamnett have put forward the notion that processes of de-industrialisation and professionalisation have had an intense impact upon working-class Londoners, as London's 'old' traditional, industrial manual working class is being replaced not displaced by professional and managerial groups with the concomitant effect that 'the middle class is the biggest (but not the only) class in town' (Butler and Hamnett, 2009: 226).

While others, including Davidson and Wyly (2008), have challenged this 'evolutionary narrative' by attacking the way 'professionalisation' downplays ongoing social and political struggles over space in contemporary London' (Davidson, and Wyly, 2012), London remains a city with extensive multi-ethnic, working-class areas and populations, while class struggles over the uses and appropriation of space in London continue. Even if the notion of an ethnically homogenous, manual working class is anachronistic: 'we should not mistake the changing appearance of class structure with the disappearance of class antagonism' (Davidson and Wyly, 2012: 396). Gentrification is, however, increasingly noticeable in East London, partly caused via the 'collective social action' of clusters of middle-class gentrifiers in areas such as London Fields in Hackney (Butler and Robson, 2003), but also via large-scale capitalist processes of new-build developments connected to rounds of regeneration, as in London Docklands (Butler and Robson, 2003; Minton, 2012). This logic has had severe consequences for working-class people in contemporary Britain through the current crisis of underfunding in social housing, deals between local councils and property development companies and social cleansing: the process that removes poorer residents from a community in favour of higher earning people.

In order to legitimate aggressive 'for profit and for-shareholder' logic which mostly damages and hurts local communities, neoliberal organisations are increasingly undertaking their own research which is then used by local and national governments. An example of this is how the London mayor's office works closely with several property developers, and estate agents with the research used interchangeably on both local government and company websites (Savills, 2018). Not to mention the increasingly revolving door between the property developers and local government executive employment. Research undertaken by the estate agent Savills in 2016 calculated that London is now the most expensive city to live and to work in the world and measured the cost of space an individual needs for accommodation, together with the space needed to work in through office rental costs totalling a figure of £80,700 a year per person. Thus, reducing people to a market value figure of their wealth, as Skeggs says, and thus only seeing value from within the blinkers of capital's logic and removing all recognition of the values that live beyond value (Skeggs, 2014). This connection between an individual's market value and their moral and social value have been central in producing new ways of exploitation through the fields of culture and media, strengthening established forms of class differentiation but also inventing new forms of class prejudice. Consequently, even the ways working-class people try and organise themselves against power is judged as legitimate or illegitimate, depending upon who or what they have on their side.

The poorest people and the neighbourhoods where they live within the UK have already been established and been conceptualised and known through many forms and the definitions constantly shift. Those definitions have led to specific and often negative understandings of those communities, and it is through this negative baptism that there has been a growing stigmatisation of the poorest people in the UK. Levels of symbolic violence towards working-class people and in particular those that live in council housing are unprecedented.

QUESTIONS OF VALUE

Defining working-class people as valueless has taken on new forms in recent years, in often very negative ways. Since the 2008 banking crash and especially since 2010, there has been a development in working-class women's representation.

However, for the local working-class communities that live within these spaces that are highly valued as investment interests to global capital, what they see are multimillion pound housing developments rising from familiar places that seem to be inexhaustible in their grab for space, and creating a place that is foreign to them. This process of gentrification that is dispossessing local and established communities in London works on two levels, by forcibly removing existing communities and also by making them feel unwelcome in a community they have lived in for generations. Many residents that are suffering this form of dispossession describe themselves as living on 'reservations' or on 'islands' as one elderly woman told me in 'a sea of hipsters'.

It seems that social cleansing, social apartheid and social inequality have been accepted as 'common sense' by the political elites of London through the notion that London is a special place where the special people live, and if you cannot afford to live in London you need to leave. However, the unintended consequences of this hard-line neoliberal thinking is that there have become political movements growing in working-class communities around a class consciousness of struggling in London. This grassroots activism is thriving among those groups who are being treated harshly and have very little or no power; they are fighting for their lives and for the futures of their children as local mining communities did in 1984 against pit closures. This fight has become especially apparent among working-class mothers, who were not politically active, until they were faced by eviction like the Focus E15 women. There are now campaigns all over London from Hendon to Lewisham fighting forced evictions, and the unfair inequality and struggles that Londoners are now experiencing in their everyday lives.

It is important to note how stable working-class communities in the global city are no longer seen as a resource for the future, or indeed as being capable of acting as a critical citizenry. As the radical educationalist Henry A. Giroux (2012) has argued in relation to young working-class people, rather than treating them as democratic citizens in the making who need jobs, opportunities and rights to a democratic voice, under neoliberalism, they are increasingly treated as disposable citizens by a punishing state. Here we mourn the loss of a previous era's social liberalism where critical educationalists such as Raymond Williams (2016) and Richard Hoggart (2009) spoke of the need to connect a politics of class, education and critical citizenship in the context of social justice and democracy.

Missing from the discussion thus far is a more critical engagement with the impact of neoliberalism. If neoliberalism is an ideology that seeks to shrink the social state, promote entrepreneurialism, cut taxation for the wealthy, attack trade union rights and promote market-led solutions and insecurity at work, it concomitantly creates a society built upon huge social divisions. Pierre Bourdieu argues that neoliberal social policies create a dual economy built upon overworked and stressed professions alongside those who have a life on benefits or who are poorly paid and in insecure employment (2003: 29). As David Harvey notes, most cities today are less governed by an inclusive citizenship than they are by the needs of capital and an 'individualistic neoliberal ethic' (2012: 15). The increasing segregation of cities into rich zones of consumption, exclusive schools and privileged sites of leisure adjacent to areas where there is a lack of affordable housing as well as low wages and poverty means that grassroots protest should be seen in the context of social division.

As Loic Wacquant (2010) argues, what is missing from the debates about neoliberalism is the idea that economic deregulation requires a new kind of state to manage social instability at the bottom of society. The move from the social (or welfare) state to the security state requires state policies to push workers into low-paid jobs and a much more punitive state to deal with rapidly rising levels of social inequality. Wacquant has provocatively suggested that neoliberalism is best thought of as the configuration of an emphasis upon the free market, welfare cuts and workfare strategies, the notion of individual responsibility and an expansion in the use of incarceration as a means of social control (Wacquant, 2010: 213). These features cut across notions of Left and

Right and convey neoliberalism as a practice and philosophy that offers freedom for capital but repression for those at the bottom of society. Wacquant (2008) has noted that the halt in social mobility and the structures of 'new poverty' are far from fully understood by social researchers. However, poor neighbourhoods and working-class people need to be understood in the context of long-term joblessness, the proliferation of low pay and part-time employment and the build-up of multiple deprivations within the same households and neighbourhoods. There has also been a widening gap between rich and poor, and an entrenched disillusionment with mainstream politics. This level of distrust and disenfranchisement, particularly within working-class neighbourhoods, has led to the undermining of the legitimacy of the social order, and as Loic Wacquant (2008) argues, hostility directed towards the state organisation of power.

A WAVE OF HOUSING ACTIVISM

Between 2013 and 2015, there was a wave of activism in London focused upon the lack of social housing and the process of 'class cleansing' and 'redevelopment' among council estate residents. London, on one level, was and still is an oppressive, aggressive and hard to survive in place. Despite the global elite setting up camp and becoming ever-prevalent in London Renting in the private sector, making it almost impossible for most middle- and working-class people in London, there was a sense of hope and a real resistance coming from the grassroots. Between 2013 and 2015, there were almost 200 different grassroots housing campaigns, mostly led by young, working-class women (Mckenzie, 2015).

I was involved in several local housing campaigns and the London-wide fight for social housing that was gaining traction. One such campaign was the New Era Estate in Hoxton. Its previous owner had run the estate as social housing for low-paid, working-class Londoners. Several generations of the same families have lived on this estate, and it has been a safe and stable community that has thrived: one of the mothers leading the campaign described the estate as being 'in her blood', it was much more than bricks and mortar, it was her home. However, once the American property firm Westbrook Partners bought the estate from its previous owners (a philanthropic trust), Westbrook planned to treble the community's rents and 'uplift' them from a social rent to a market rent. This would mean that the existing tenants would have been forced out. At the time, property prices in the capital had risen by 25 per cent and were selling at an average of £450,000, while wages had drastically failed to keep pace.

Hackney in general, but the areas surrounding Hoxton in particular, have been at the sharp end of this dramatic change. This part of London has been at the forefront of a gentrification process that has – without mercy – displaced communities that could not keep up with the rising cost of living in the trendy Shoreditch area of London.

After a very public campaign that was supported by a wide spectrum of political views, even the then Conservative Mayor of London Boris Johnson spoke in support of the campaign. The *Guardian* newspaper on the Liberal left, and even the *Daily Mail* on the Conservative Right ran stories in support of the campaign that had hit a nerve with the general public, that this was unfair. This was an easier case to make because the residents of New Era were the working class, employed in service work, and care assistants for the NHS, and in the building trade for men.

The actor and comedian Russell Brand took a starring role alongside the mothers who were at the forefront of this campaign, after meeting them as they collected signatures for a petition in their local neighbourhood where Russell Brand also lived at the time. The campaign, which had been quite small – consisting of the residents and a few local housing activists – grew very quickly once the media attention started to shine upon it. The organising committee consisted of local trade unions, members of the Socialist Worker Party, residents and activists that met in the local pub and organised a march to the member of parliament's office. I was part of this committee for a short time, and soon realised there was a two- or even a three-tier campaign happening between the actual residents, the experienced campaigners and Russell Brand.

The campaign came to an end at the end of December 2015 and after a hard year where the New Era community had no idea from day to day whether they would be evicted, and what would happen to them. The unprecedented media attention had forced both the local Conservative MP and the Westbrook Partners to relent and they decided to sell the housing estate to another social housing scheme 'Dolphin Living. The deal was brokered by the local Labour Mayor of Hackney, Labour councillors and members of parliament who had been reluctant at best and obstructive at worst to support this campaign in its early days. The *Inde-*

pendent newspaper ran the story with the headline: 'New Era Housing Estate Saved by Russell Brand Becomes First to Introduce 'Means-Tested Rent' (Milmo, 2015). The result for the New Era residents was that the community kept their homes, although they did proceed onto a means tested rent system that had no assurances that as properties became vacant, they would continue to be rented as 'social housing' with a genuinely affordable social rent.

I first met the Focus E15 campaign in 2013 when a group of very young mothers living in a local homeless hostel had set up a street stall in order to garner support from their local community in Stratford east London. At this point, they were fighting eviction from 'Focus E15', which was the name of a rundown temporary hostel for homeless young people (and their babies, in the case of the young mums) that they were living in. In 2013, the coalition government in the UK was taking harsh and draconian measures to cut the national deficit by cutting spending that ultimately affected public services. Local governments, as part of these austerity measures, were told to cut their own budgets and make 'efficiency savings'. Newham council in East London decided to cut the £41,000 that it paid towards support for the young people in the Focus E15 hostel. When the funding cut was announced, the East Thames Housing Association, which manages Focus E15, said that it could not continue to house the women and their young children. Consequently, the women were served notices to leave. Although living in this temporary accommodation was not what the women really wanted, as one mother told me, 'it's not ideal but it's not on the street either'. The young mothers hoped and believed that sticking it out in the hostel would mean, at some point, they would be offered a permanent home in the borough.

Undoubtedly, this was not a good situation for families and the women had mixed feelings about the Focus E15 hostel; the mothers had to live under very strict rules as woman told me at the time: 'You're only allowed to have someone stay for three nights a week, even if it is your mum coming around to help.' The women said that the rooms were tiny, with fold-out beds and in truth the accommodation was supposed to be temporary, equipped for a few months at the most – a bed and basic facilities for a short space of time for young homeless people – but some of the women and their children had been there several years. Jasmin Stone, who was at the time only 19-years old and her daughter was

18-months old, had lived in the hostel for just over a year. She told me: 'It's not fit for a mother and a baby, there's damp and the repairs don't get done.' The mothers complained about mould and broken rubbish shutes; they also noted that they had problems with rodents. However, the hostel had become a home of sorts for the women, and they had certainly built and created a close-knit community out of their struggle, and as they constantly said: 'it's better than being on the streets with your baby in care'; this was the mothers' worst fear.

All of the mothers, while they were living in the hostel, hoped and prayed for an offer of social housing, at an affordable rent and near their friends and family. They were desperate to start their lives in stable homes. These offers never came. The women were terrified of being pushed into the highly unstable, unaffordable private rental sector and they knew even this was unlikely, because they were on benefits. The added worry for these mothers was to beat the benefit cap, now and in the future, Newham council would send them to live miles away in some distant town like Hastings, Sheffield, Birmingham and Liverpool, where private rents were cheaper and tenants on benefits could still be placed. That would remove young mothers from their families and friends in Stratford, who they relied on and who could provide all-important free childcare when the women went into training and work – which they all wanted to do. They also knew that other towns also didn't want them; they would be added pressure to any council. Consequently, out of frustration, anger and pure desperation the Focus E15 campaign began. Initially, the young mothers held a street stall that asked passers-by to sign their petition for decent, reasonably priced social housing for people on low incomes and benefits in the borough. The women wanted social housing in particular. They wanted social housing for everyone. They readily walked up to Broadway shoppers, explained their housing problems and asked people to sign.

Thousands signed and many spoke of their own housing troubles – steep and fast-rising rents, bullying landlords, scandalous overcrowding, slow repairs when things broke, mould, damp and maggots, and short-term tenancies which left people vulnerable to sudden homelessness. There was a general understanding, as well there should be, that people on low incomes were as entitled as anyone to basics like housing. By February 2014, several thousand people had signed the Focus E15 petition, which the women planned to take to Boris Johnson the then

Mayor of London. Jasmin Stone became a key spokesperson in this campaign, a very shy young mother of only 19-years old that found her voice by speaking directly to local people and their shared fears when she said from the start that: 'we just want to know where we're going to live. It's been really horrible, because they [the local council] says they don't know where any properties [for us are]' (Mckenzie, 2015). Newham council had recently changed its housing allocation policy to prioritise people who were in work ahead of people who were not. The Focus E15 mothers were a 'difficult' demographic, young, poor, working class, mostly single mothers and homeless. They did not have the 'respectable' working-class narrative that the New Era residents had been awarded by the wider media and the wider political sphere.

Jasmin told me at the time: 'We've been to see the mayor, Robin Wales … and he was really negative about everything. He said to us that he was "cross with our campaign".' Jasmin went on to explain to me that the response from the local political representatives, MPs and councillors, and the mayor of Newham that Focus E15 had approached, had been the same to their questions about homelessness and social cleansing, that: there is 'no housing'.

However, the campaign continued with a hopefulness and resilience that is very rare among those who are most marginalised. This group of young women were defiantly drawing strength and support from each other. One of the women's most inspired actions came in mid-January when the group occupied a showroom flat in the East Thames building and then Newham council's housing offices. The local council, politicians and the media started to take them seriously as they were becoming a nuisance. The Labour Mayor and councillors ran a campaign against the mothers, accusing them of being 'trouble makers' going about this 'the wrong way' being 'unreasonable' and of course always within the subtext of the old underclass tropes of them being 'rough, lazy, and promiscuous' (Mckenzie 2015; Shildrick and MacDonald 2013).

The campaign is still going, and the mothers still meet for their weekly street stall outside Wilkos on Stratford High Street. They are supported by local families and other housing campaigns, however, none of the original Focus E15 mothers still live in this part of Newham; they have been moved further and out of the Borough, and in some cases out of the City.

MANAGING AND LEGITIMATING OUT RESISTANCE

Both New Era and Focus E15 campaigns were undoubtedly grassroots campaigns; neither one was connected or affiliated to any official political group or party, although many supporters of both campaigns had affiliations. None of the campaigns were being directly or indirectly 'managed'; they were community led and organised. Both campaigns were led by women, who had clear and connected stakes in the fight they had been forced into. None of the campaigners before their campaigns had been involved in any type of mainstream political or social movement previously. Some of the Focus E15 mothers are still active in the housing campaigns in Newham and across London, and can be seen on the street stall in Stratford and on the various rallies and demonstrations that continue in the City, despite being 'cleansed' out of the neighbourhood. However, the New Era campaign and campaigners are not involved in the wider housing movement in London, and the campaign is closed.

Although I have focused on two campaigns during this period, I was part of and supported many other grassroots housing campaigns in London. In the years between 2013 and 2015, these campaigns and supporters often met up and integrated supporting each other through strategic methods of resistance. In January 2015, all of the housing campaigns in London and others from outside of London joined forces and were brought together by the Focus E15 group with support from trade union branches, local Labour Party supporters and interested academics. Meeting in East London, they marched over Tower Bridge to City Hall – the place where the London Assembly meet and where the Mayor of London's office is based. At the beginning of the march, there were speeches from campaigners and a few Labour members of parliament, although there was opposition even then to politicians that sat in seats where there was social cleansing and council estate regeneration happening. Although most campaigns agreed hesitantly to politicians being given a platform, for the sake of building the housing movement, the day felt like the end of the beginning for social cleansing, as 5,000 housing campaigners sang 'We've got to get rid of the rich' marching over Tower Bridge and towards the strip of land on the Southbank of the Thames walkway that is owned by the Qatari Royal Family. None of us knew at the time that was a high point in terms of numbers and solidarity in regards of the Housing Movement.

As the 2015 General Election approached, the Labour Party supporters and the Trade Union support became reluctant to put pressure publicly on Labour Party councils and members of parliament that had become focused on the general election rather than the local and grassroots battles. Instead, they used their positions inside the campaigns to encourage campaigning for the Labour Party rather than opposing social cleansing. This became a source of contention over time, as parliamentary politics and Westminster power grabs sucked out the support from seasoned and 'professional' political campaigners.

From the start of the 2015 General Election, the housing campaigns right across London were finding it increasingly difficult to garner support wider than their community. The Labour Party and the trade unions were in election mode, and the housing campaigns in London that had direct battles with Labour councils became inconvenient and politically difficult.

The campaigns found that they had to fight their local councils, MPs and mayors which amounted to overwhelming pressure for those communities. Party politics appear to always trump local, grassroots campaigns as organised party political activists and party machines focus upon electioneering. Local, grassroots campaigns were being asked to 'wait' and were encouraged to put their own campaigning on hold and join the party election campaigning. This had a devastating effect on the London Housing Movement in particular because most of the grassroots housing campaigns were fighting against local government decisions that were predominantly being made by Labour Party councillors and mayors. Following the 2015 election, where the Conservative Party won and formed its first government in 20 years, divisions within the Labour Party opened with the left-wing candidate Jeremy Corbyn overwhelmingly winning and becoming leader of the Party. Following this left-wing victory, the grassroots housing campaigns were asked again to 'wait' and support a Jeremy Corbyn-led Labour Party. Two further years of turmoil ensued within the Labour Party as they fought among themselves, and again the housing campaigns were asked to wait. The negative attention about Labour councils social cleansing their working-class tenants out of London were unwelcome by a party as it struggled within itself.

In January 2018, I was contacted by some of the New Era residents: they had been given notice that Dolphin Living planned to demolish the New Era estate. The landlord wrote to residents in August 2017 to say it was considering a number of options for the estate, including refurbishing existing homes and rebuilding the entire estate. The landlord said the best option would be to demolish and rebuild the estate adding into the development a substantial amount of 'for sale' market rate apartments as the 'only way' to deliver all the improvements it wants to carry out without residents having to pay more in rent. Meetings were held in January 2018 with residents and Dolphin Living said 84 per cent of residents supported the demolition and rebuild plan, one of the residents told me 'we are exhausted, we can't go through all that again'.

None of this is surprising; the emotional and physical effort, time and resources that is needed in taking on institutional power is immense, and most grassroots campaigns have little if any of those resources, by their very nature. Most local grassroots campaigns are thrown reluctantly into positions of constant negotiating with institutional power initially with the agency/organisation they have issue with, and then later with local government officials. Eventually, as in both cases, here the negotiation of power continued through elected government officials. Both campaigns faced similar problems. Initially, elected officials ignored them and then patronised them. The Labour MP for the constituency where the New Era estate was had been invited to a meeting held by the campaign. The residents were clearly upset that their estate was under threat and were upset that the Labour Party were not supporting them – the MP told them she didn't have time 'for this' and left. The Mayor of Newham tried to physically attack the campaign and had to be held back by Labour councillors at a 'Family Fun day' (Focus E15, 2015). However, he later made a public apology of sorts in a national newspaper where he excused his behaviour as about 'London's housing crisis', yet still insisted that the initial decision to close the hostel and offer the mothers 'alternative' housing in places hundreds of miles away 'was the right one'.

Political time moves slowly, it moves in parliaments and elections; community time moves very differently, the people who are fighting for their communities become very easily exhausted over a few months of campaigning – they have little or no resources. They do not have two years or five years of resources in them. The campaigns fold, or the residents are moved out or make concessions that are not beneficial to them because they simply cannot fight on. It is unrealistic and quite arrogant that Labour Party activists expected grassroots community campaigners to either wait for five or ten years for a successful power grab, and to join alliances and even support local politicians that have not supported them.

MISSED AND MANAGED NARRATIVES

The poorest people often have no choice but to resist, the structure of a neoliberal society pushes towards resistance, success or annihilation; it is the capitalist model. The restructuring of urban space that Harvey (2008) identifies as accumulation by dispossession is producing increasingly antagonistic class relations that are in turn making such relations and their accompanying social injustices more apparent to those whose right to the city is being threatened. In turn, this is leading to greater class resentment and in some cases anger against 'them' – corporate wealth and power – a resentment and anger whose political consequences are as yet unforeseen, but are no doubt being played out on the streets and estates of London. Class struggle in itself is resistance, and campaigns that start from local communities that build up a sense of collectivist ideas, and actions are successes within themselves, despite the outcome of the campaign. However, these small-scale resistances find it difficult if not impossible to fight institutionalised power independently of institutionalised power. The grassroots London housing campaigns that are in direct struggle with their local council officials that are part of local government and wider national party politics, are easily suffocated and the fire in their anger can be put out by organised politicians and their supporters, if the campaigns aims are in direct opposition to their elected officials, especially when the political cycle has moved into election time.

CONCLUSION

To conclude, it is important to ask what we can gain from these stories of housing campaigns in London and about the process of resistance. Resistance does not necessarily mean winning; we need to understand victory in many ways when we are considering the constant uphill fight that grassroots campaigns have. Their campaigns start through hurt, and anger and desperation. They have little to no resources but their very act of resistance is a victory in itself. What happens too often is their campaigns are co-opted by well-meaning outsiders that sometimes have their own agendas, sometimes they don't; often they are well meaning but naive to the struggle that working-class people face that is structural and systematic. If social democracy or social liberalism has been historically associated with ideas of equality, the same can be said for ideas of a more active citizenship. Here, we can point to the interconnection between social rights that offer security and a stake in the community and political rights that only become meaningful within a social setting. If the lives of citizens are too precarious, then political engagement and critical citizenship becomes increasingly difficult to achieve. Therefore, the opportunities to engage in protest or movement building becomes only for those who have enough stability and capital to cope with both party politics and neoliberal organisations. If there are to be genuine strategies of resistance against an economic and political system that most now agree is not serving the greatest number of people, asking or expecting those that are at the very sharp end of the system to wait and wait and wait until their needs are eventually addressed by the very people who have been part of taking away the social resources that they need is arrogant and only further represents a system that they know is not working for them.

REFERENCES

Bourdieu, P. (2003) *Firing Back: Against the Tyranny of the Market 2*. London: Verso.

Butler, T. and Hamnett, C. (2009) Walking Backwards to the Future – Waking Up to Class and Gentrification in London. *Urban Policy and Research*, 27(3): 217–28.

Butler, T. and Robson, G. (2003) Negotiating Their Way In: The Middle Classes, Gentrification and the Deployment of Capital in a Globalising Metropolis. *Urban Studies*, 40(9): 1791–1809.

Coates, K. and Silburn, R. (1970) *Poverty: The Forgotten Englishman*. London: Penguin.

Davidson, M. and Wyly, E. (2012) Class-Ifying London: Questioning Social Division and Space Claims in the Post-Industrial Metropolis. *City*, 16(4): 395–421.

Focus E15 (2015) Blog, July. https://focuse15.org/2015/07/.

Giroux, H.A. (2012) *Disposable Youth: Racialized Memories and the Culture of Cruelty*. London: Routledge.

Glass, R. (1964) *Aspects of Change*. London: MacGibbon & Kee.

Harvey, D. (2008) The Right to the City. *New Left Review*, 53: 23–40.

Harvey, D. (2012) *Rebel Cities from the Right to the City to the Urban Revolution*. London: Verso.

Hoggart, R. (2009) *Uses of Literacy: Aspects of Working-Class Life*. London: Penguin Classics.

Lawler, S. (2005) Disgusted Subjects: The Making of Middle-Class Identities. *The Sociological Review*, 53(3): 429–46.

Lawler, S. (2008) *Identity: Sociological Perspectives*. Cambridge: Polity.

Mckenzie, L. (2015) *Getting By: Estates Class and Culture*. Bristol: Policy Press.

Milmo, C. (2015) New Era Housing Estate Saved by Russell Brand Becomes First to Introduce 'Means-Tested' Rent. *Independent*, 18 August. www.independent.co.uk/news/uk/home-news/new-era-housing-estate-saved-by-russell-brand-becomes-first-to-introduce-means-tested-rent-10461178.html.

Minton, A. (2012) *Ground Control: Fear and Happiness in the Twenty-First-Century City*. London: Penguin.

Pahl, R.E. (1984) *Divisions of Labour*. London: Wiley-Blackwell.

Rogaly, B. and Taylor, B. (2009) *Moving Histories, of Class and Community*. London: Palgrave Macmillan.

Savills (2018) Insight and Opinion, Blog. www.savills.co.uk/insight-and-opinion/research.aspx?rc=United-Kingdom&p=&t=&f=date&q=&page=1.

Skeggs, B. (2004) *Class Self* and *Culture*. London: Routledge.

Skeggs, B. (2014) Values Beyond Value? Is Anything Beyond the Logic of Capital? *Sociology*, 65(1): 1–20.

Slater, T. (2014) Unravelling False Choice Urbanism. *City*, 18(4–5): 517–24.

Slater, T. (2015) There is Nothing Natural about Gentrification. *New Left Project*, www.newleftproject.org/index.php/site/article_comments/there_is_nothing_natural_about_gentrification.

Stevenson, N. (2003) *Cultural Citizenship: Cosmopolitan Questions*. Maidenhead: Open University Press.

Wacquant, L. (2008) *Urban Outcasts: A Comparative Sociology of Advanced Marginality*. Cambridge: Polity Press.

Wacquant, L. (2010) Crafting the Neoliberal State: Workfare, Prison Fare and Social Insecurity. *Sociological Forum*, 25(2): 197–220.

Watt P. (2012) 'Seeing Olympic Effects Through the Eyes of Marginally Housed Youth: Changing Places and the Gentrification of East London'. *Visual Studies*, volume 27, no. 2, pp. 151–60.

Williams, R. (2016) *The Country and the City*. London: Vintage Classics.

5

Mad Studies

Campaigning Against the Psychiatric System and Welfare 'Reform' and for Something Better

Peter Beresford

> You never change things by fighting the existing reality. To change something build a new model that makes the existing model obsolete.
>
> R. Buckminster Fuller, American architect,
> inventor and visionary

INTRODUCTION

This is not only a story of resistance. It is a story of the creation of alternatives and the advancement of people's own visions. It is also a story of changes in forms and *patterns* of collectivity and resistance. It reveals how service users/survivors of the psychiatric system have attempted to critique existing forms of 'care' and forge alternative models through the formation of their own movement and cooperative political alliances.

There are long-term changes in alliances, with the emergence of both new reactionary and new progressive alliances, as well as the apparent weakening of some traditional ones. Reflecting this, the chapter is organised in three sections, which relate to changing dynamics in the pattern of alliances affecting people experiencing distress and on the receiving end of services, linked with the psychiatric system and the broader politics under which both exist. This reveals the emergence of powerful reactionary alliances, the emergence of new user-led alliances of resistance, and also most recently, the introduction of a new positive praxis for renewal – Mad Studies – which seeks to put service users and their organisations at the helm.

REGRESSIVE AND DAMAGING ALLIANCES

This first section sets out the significant detrimental and harmful impact on mental health service users and disabled people of three particular developments during the neoliberal era. The chapter begins by looking at these political forces. They are the emergence of three reactionary alliances: (i) the new political right and psychiatry/big pharma; (ii) right-wing politicians and anti-welfare corporate institutions (and their academic/policymaker supporters); and (iii) the weakening of older progressive alliances (between the UK Labour Party, voluntary sector and service user movements).

The Neoliberal/Psychiatric Alliance

We begin with the growing alliance that has developed between psychiatry and prevailing right-wing politics. This key informal and possibly unintended alliance – which has its origins in Western societies, including the UK since the late 1970s, and had global implications – has been that between psychiatry and prevailing neoliberalism. This alliance has become increasingly strong and significant, beginning with the emergence of the political new right and culminating in the continuing dominance of neoliberal politics internationally. Not only do neoliberal ideology and the psychiatric system share a common individualising and medicalising analysis and response to human distress and madness, this relationship is also one to the advantage of market-driven politics more generally. It benefits the huge multinational pharmaceutical industry – 'big pharma' – which is also related to other enormous global chemico-industrial projects, like agribusiness and the munitions and arms trade (Moncrieff, 2008; Burstow, 2015). We can see this informal but increasingly important and influential alliance being advanced on a global scale (Mills, 2018).

A further expression of this informal alliance between neoliberalism and the psychiatric system is the growing international importance of the concept of 'recovery'. At first glance, this idea can seem to be a progressive one; rejecting assumptions that mental health service users/ survivors are inherently and permanently damaged and incapable of ever contributing to their communities and societies. But as it has been rolled out by government and policy makers in the UK and beyond, for all its social and humanistic rhetoric, 'recovery' is inherently a term lodged in medicalised thinking – essentially based on a medical model – 'getting better'. Thus, recovery suggested that it would be possible to withdraw support as people 'recover'. This ignores the reality for many mental health service users/survivors, that their need for help and support may be varied, continuing or recurring. It fits well with welfare reform policy committed to getting people 'off benefits' and into employment. Increasingly, a key criterion of recovery has been people entering or re-entering employment, with little consideration given to the nature, quality or suitability of such employment (Harper and Speed, 2012).

Over this period, there have been big changes in the psychiatric system. As Moncrieff (2008) has highlighted, these changes have extended its operation far beyond the old asylums and institutions, 'into the community' and people's homes. Neuroscience research committed to finding the biological origins of distress has burgeoned; psychiatric diagnostic categories have dramatically expanded in range and quantity. Use of psychiatric drugs has increased massively. Growing numbers of social problems, from children's difficulties with school to older people's problems in residential institutions, are being framed in psychiatric terms and treated with psychiatric medication. Psychiatry has become more normalised in society. Thus, its individualising biomedicalisation of people's experience, emotions and difficulties has been reinforced at the very time that the social pressures increasing personal problems have magnified under neoliberalism (Pellizzoni and Ylönen, 2012; Moncrieff, 2008). While mental health service users can still expect to encounter major barriers and discrimination, the official rhetoric is of 'telling your story' and being open about your feelings and experience. Yet mental health policy and provision is still the poor relation of physical health care. Internationally, the trend is for its control provisions – for compulsory medication and detention – to be extended. It is still significantly underfunded and does not match either the innovations or the success stories associated with physical health care.

Yet the psychiatric system continues unimproved, without qualification. The prevailing counter-narrative is that people are not receiving its support who need it, in terms of diagnosis and treatment, because it is unfairly neglected, *not* that it has a record of systemic failure, abuse and multiple discrimination and neglect. There have been numerous campaigns based on this analysis, for example, highlighting the neglect of children and young people and BME service users, some involving service users, but generally they have failed to secure more resources or priority for mental health services or greater regard for their users.

The Neoliberal/Anti-Welfarism Alliance

This alliance is committed to pulling back the post-war welfare state, where policies aimed to support citizens and groups disadvantaged by the unstable and unequal workings of the market. While its focus is a broad one – seeking to undermine and transform all welfare state services, from health and housing, to education and public transport, one particular area for attack has been welfare benefits, particularly for those on low income, who are marginal in the labour market and who identified as disabled. This includes mental health service users and people experiencing distress as well as people with physical, sensory, intellectual and other impairments. This informal neoliberal, anti-welfare alliance, which has focused on attacking their benefits, includes right-wing politicians and ideologues, fellow traveller theorists, academics and policy makers, international corporations and their lobbyists.

Perhaps the most detailed and thoroughly evidenced account of this alliance in the UK has been developed by Mo Stewart, a disabled veteran, who was driven to research this development after she experienced it first-hand (Mo Stewart Research, 2018). What emerged from her studies was evidence that governments formed by all major parties supported a system of managing long-term sickness and disability benefit claims driven by a giant US insurance corporation. This was based on a 'work capability assessment' (WCA) process, which has subsequently been shown to be fundamentally flawed and associated with many deaths and suicides, as well as a disproportionate rate of successful appeals. As Mo Stewart has highlighted, this assessment has been based on a so-called 'biopsychosocial' model of disability. This is framed in terms of the disabled person adopting a 'dependent maladaptation' and being unwilling to accept employment. This takes no account of: labour market exclusions and discriminations against disabled people and mental health service users; the difficulties they may face in unsupported employment; often poor employment services and the fact that the employment available to them tends to be some of the most unpleasant and devalued available. The assessment process tends particularly to discriminate against people with 'mental health problems' because assessors are not confronted with the more familiar cues of wheelchairs, white sticks or missing limbs (Mo Stewart Research, 2018; Stone, 2017). However, the scale and nature of routine abuse and misrepresentation in the service of reducing the number of successful disabled claimants only becomes fully apparent when we examine examples of what actually happens in the interview room, for example, in the volume of evidence submitted to the parliamentary committee investigating the assessment process. Thus, from one qualified social worker with 28 years' experience, who reported on disabled people, being told:

- even if they have pain 'it must be remembered that activities do not have to be performed without any discomfort or pain and that suffering from pain is not reason in itself to be found to have Limited Capability for Work'
- it is possible to type with one hand (if they can't use the other hand)
- Mr M. could get a wheelchair from the NHS to get to work and then it is the employer's responsibility to provide a space to keep the wheelchair
- it does not matter if they are waiting for test results around their condition because lots of people in work are waiting for test results.

(House of Commons, 2018: 1)

The social worker also reported these cases:

... J ... in her early 60s. She was in the support group for Employment and Support Allowance but has had her benefit stopped after she was called to a face-to-face assessment. She has severe anxiety and cannot leave the house. She is convinced that everyone she comes into contact with, will be harmed in some way because she gives off an 'evil aura'. She is on medication for her anxiety but no longer sees a psychiatrist as her medication is now managed by her GP. She has been unable to leave the house to attend the Job Centre and claim Job Seekers Allowance and so has been living off her Disability Living Allowance. The decision maker commented that she had no proven or long term connection with mental health services.

(House of Commons, 2018: 3)

And:

> Mr D, who has serious arthritis and back problems reported that the assessor dropped her pencil. There was a pause and he realised she was waiting for him to pick it up. However he is not able to bend so after a short silence she picked it up. This 'trick' has been reported to me over and over again by clients attending their face-to-face assessment. Some have picked the pencil up out of politeness – at great effort – and then seen on the letter explaining their benefit is to be stopped that they were observed as being able to bend and pick something up.
>
> (House of Commons, 2018: 4)

While the United Nations has accused the British government of violating the rights of disabled people (United Nations, 2018), including mental health service users, this policy is essentially continuing unchanged and is associated with early deaths of people passed as fit to work, numerous suicides and frequent suicidal thoughts.

The Ending of Older Alliances

Neoliberal politics have also led to a weakening of old alliances that have traditionally helped protect mental health and other welfare state service users from discriminatory media, policy and political pressures. Thus, the UK Labour Party, creator of the welfare state and traditional ally of impoverished and disadvantaged groups, under Tony Blair, talked of a 'hand up' not a 'hand out'. Once seen as the defender of the poor and oppressed, when in government, the Labour Party began the calls to 'get a million people off incapacity benefits' (Brewer, Clark and Wakefield, 2001). Blair's New Labour supported neoliberal tenets of welfare reform, reflecting in a focus on 'work first', expanding means testing, downgrading of contributory benefits. It was not until Jeremy Corbyn was elected leader of the Parliamentary Labour Party that it returned to challenging the identification of disabled people with scroungers and even then it remained divided over welfare cuts (BBC, 2015).

Once voluntary organisations that claimed to represent mental health and other long-term health and social care service users would have been seen as another bastion for their defence, speaking up on their behalf and representing their interests. However, significant changes in their nature and relationships with government and the state have seriously challenged this.

The large traditional charities seem to have become increasingly concerned with their own interests and advancement. While often piggybacking disabled people's own campaigns, for example, Leonard Cheshire Disability and Scope claiming they are committed to their rights and access, they are anxious not to lose existing government contracts as service providers and to secure new ones in welfare reform. PR exercises seem to be replacing active campaigning. Increasingly corporate and indistinguishable from other sectors, some big charities seem to be moving in the same direction as the large multinational corporations – seeing the marketing of a brand name as more important than actually doing much. The direction of travel of the UK voluntary sector, for example, has been towards fewer, larger, metropolitan-based voluntary organisations; what has come to be called 'big charity'. Operating in a contract culture, where government policy has increasingly been to divest itself of state provision and move instead to the charitable and for-profit sectors, such large 'vol orgs' have shown themselves increasingly reluctant to be critical of policy makers to gain contracts, rewards and honours from government. Thus, major charities contracted to deliver welfare reforms have signed agreements with government preventing them from criticising such policies or government representatives (Pring, 2018).

FROM VULNERABLE TO VANGUARD: EMERGING PROGRESSIVE ALLIANCES

This second section, in contrast, highlights the emergence of a newer progressive alliance between user groups. This alliance is characterised by an inclusive self-organising approach that has been codified theoretically in the social model of disability to inform practice via the model of independent living. While historically there have been divisions between user groups, neoliberal attacks have engendered solidarities that have challenged these barriers. Nonetheless, an intersectional lens has been necessary to ensure exclusions are not reproduced within the user movement. The strategies of this new alliance have harnessed more inclusive tools (for example, social media), and sought to further extend inclusive alliances (for example, with women's, BME and trade union movements). This progressive alliance can be seen, in part at least, as a response to the second dominant neoliberal alliance.

The consequence of these developments – the emergence of new regressive alliances and the weakening of traditional supportive ones – has been to leave mental health service users (and indeed disabled people and other marginalised groups generally) more vulnerable to increasingly harsh neoliberal government social policies. Yet even in these current conditions, there are a number of examples of the forging of new campaigns and new forms of political action – especially joint work between different user groups and a newer emphasis on 'remodelling' rather than just resistance.

Thus, what is interesting is the way that such vulnerable groups and their emerging organisations have risen to the challenge and actually come to be at the vanguard of opposition, resistance and challenge to the 'punitive' neoliberal state. It will be helpful to explore this process, whereby some of the most marginalised people in society – mental health service users, people with learning difficulties, people with physical and sensory impairments, people with long-term conditions, older and institutionalised people – have come to play a central and innovative role in reshaping understandings of themselves, as well as in challenging neoliberal policies, politics and philosophy (Beresford, 2012).

The Emergence of Inclusive Self-Organising

Disabled people and service users have a long modern history of collective action, going back as far as the late 1960s. They have sought to develop their own voices and collectivity rather than rely on the support of others. Starting with the disabled people's movement, we have seen the development of movements of mental health service users/survivors, people with learning difficulties, older people and people living with HIV/ AIDS. These have been based on the key principles of valuing people's own first-hand experience and experiential knowledge, and speaking and acting for themselves (Jordan and Lent, 1999). As a result, they have never approached state welfare or the welfare state with rose-tinted spectacles. For many of them, it has meant segregation, stigma, low income and restricted life opportunities. While trades unions have traditionally been concerned with the employment rights of their members, more recently some are seeking to include those who are excluded by or outside the labour market, including older people and other service users. In turn, service user organisations have begun to develop relationships with trades unions and also with professional organisations like the British Association of Social Workers and Social Work Action Network (SWAN) and engaged in joint enterprises with them.

Such relationships and collaborations can be complex fraught and sometimes unequal and unsuccessful. They must always be working to ensure that they support rather than risk replacing the voice of service users and that their relationships with service users and their organisations are equal, inclusive and accessible – which is much easier to say than to achieve (McKeown, Cresswell and Spandler, 2014).

Service users and their organisations have tended to be critical of the market and the charitable sector (Beresford and Harrison, 2018). Often excluded from access to the goods and services of the market, they were held in a paternalistic relationship with traditional charities. Given that disabled people have always been significantly marginalised in the labour market, their movement was as much concerned with gaining control over the ideology affecting them, as over the means of production, from which they were largely excluded. This meant that the disabled people's movement gave priority to developing its own theories and philosophies. Crucial among these have been the social model of disability and the philosophy of independent living.

The social model of disability represents a rejection of the paternalistic medicalised approach on which the old welfare state rested. It distinguishes between people's perceived physical, sensory and intellectual impairments and the negative social reaction to them, which is described as disability. From this flowed the philosophy of independent living and an associated disabled people's movement, which spread rapidly through North America to the UK and Europe (Charlton, 1998). The key principle of independent living is that disabled people and other service users should have the support they need, and access to mainstream opportunities, in order to live their lives on as equal terms as possible to non-disabled people.

This commitment to a social approach to their personal situation and a social understanding of their experience has also largely characterised the survivor movement. However, while there were overlaps, it is also important to be aware that internationally there continue to be distinct mental health service user/survivor and disabled people's movements, with different histories, cultures, objectives and concerns.

Joint Campaigns Across Different Service User Groups

However, in the UK and indeed elsewhere, the neoliberal attacks on health and social care service users seem to have had some significant effects on the nature of such activism and collective action. It has coincided with, if not encouraged changes between and within user movements. First, it has been associated with more cooperation, joint activity and campaigning between different user groups, faced with common attacks on their rights and living standards. It has encouraged different user groups to explore their common rights and exclusions, as well as their specific differences and encouraged greater solidarity and shared understanding, challenging traditional divisions and hierarchies (Beresford, 2015).

Because the attack has been such a broad one and affected such a diverse range of groups affected by cuts in welfare benefits and support services, it has also encouraged more groups to consider their own self-organisation and relation to disability. Thus, groups formerly identified as being on the 'autistic spectrum' have developed their own identity as 'neuro-diverse' (Milton, 2017). Others identified as 'chronically ill' rather than disabled, although their situation could be seen as disabling, have come to see their long-term conditions as 'hidden impairments' and seen this as a basis for closer relationships and alliances with the disabled people's movement (Hale, 2018).

CAMPAIGNING THAT CHALLENGES INSTEAD OF MIRRORING EXCLUSIONS

Not surprisingly, the service user movements including the survivor movement have tended to mirror broader exclusions and discriminations, for example, in relation to gender, ethnicity, sexuality, age, class, culture, disability and so on. Current neoliberal trends in public policy have been to reinforce these divisions and exclusions through the pressure towards increased poverty, inequality and social exclusion. While the post-war UK welfare state increasingly struggled to overcome such inequalities, the tendency of later and current neoliberal policy and politics has instead been to reinforce them, with its modern rhetoric dividing us into 'scroungers' and 'strivers'; employed and unemployed, 'hard working' and 'troubled families', citizens and non-citizens; 'dependent' and 'independent' (O'Hara, 2014; Beresford, 2016).

The mental health service user/survivor and indeed other user movements have increasingly struggled to challenge these inequalities. Increasingly, they have highlighted their internal diversity. They highlight that, even within oppressed and marginalised groups, external hierarchies can operate and they have increasingly evidenced and challenged the way that such exclusions work to mean that some people within such groups face particular discrimination, for example, disabled women and Black disabled people. They analysed these oppressions through the lens of intersectionality, which recognises that different expressions of diversity do not exist separately from each other but are interwoven together, and began to address them, themselves.

Beginning with the disabled people's movement, service users have long highlighted that conventional approaches to participation tend to exclude many groups and individuals. While they have worked hard to make people's involvement more accessible and inclusive, such exclusions continue to operate.

Eurikha, a global project which seeks to privilege the rights and perspectives of people who experience distress, is beginning to highlight both the marginalisation of the Global South in such developments and also the marginalisation of black and minority ethnic communities in the Global North.[1] While the United Nations convention on the rights of persons with disabilities has begun to have an impact on disability legislation, policy and practice globally, the response to it has been qualified in some countries (including the UK) and there have been significant limits to how participatory its implementation has been.

A study by the user-led organisation and network Shaping Our Lives (Beresford, 2013), has evidenced the way in which diverse involvement is restricted. It identified big barriers in the way of four major groups, but also effective strategies to overcome them. Such groups of service users are excluded according to:

1. Equality issues: on the basis of gender, sexuality, ethnicity, class, culture, belief, age, disability and so on
2. Where they live: if they are homeless, travellers, in prison, in welfare institutions, refugees and so on

3. Communicating differently: they do not speak the prevailing language, it is not their first language, they are deaf and used sign language, etc.
4. The nature of their impairments: where these are seen as too complex or severe to mean they could or would want to contribute.

Where they are seen as unwanted voices, they do not necessarily say what authorities wanted to hear, are seen as a problem, disruptive etc. These include neuro-diverse people and people affected by dementia.

The desire of mental health service users/survivors to challenge such exclusions means that they are creating a different kind of fight back, resistance and renewal – a much more inclusive one. The aim is to include people on equal terms, regardless of whether they are restricted to their home, their bed or are in an institution.

From Resistance to Remodelling

Service users themselves have also highlighted the ways in which social media and networking can challenge such barriers (as well as reinforcing them) (Onions *et al.*, 2018). They have foregrounded the importance of and worked for physical, communication and cultural access, challenging conventional barriers and marginalisations that have traditionally operated in mainstream campaigning as well as politics. The development of virtual, online and other electronic networking has helped make this possible. Service users are blogging, vlogging, podcasting, tweeting and communing within their own Facebook groups. More and more, they are both a physical and virtual presence, from flash mobs to pickets and demonstrations. These are not isolated instances but the vanguard of new kinds of activism and collective action. In the UK, for example, check out Black Triangle,[2] Disabled People Against Cuts,[3] Carer Watch, Mental Health Resistance Network,[4] the Broken of Britain,[5] Diary of A Benefits Scrounger[6] or the Hardest Hit Campaign.[7] This is no cosy responding to official consultations, but engagement with the mainstream political process and new forms of direct action.

In the twenty-first century, a new generation of service users' and disabled people's organisations have emerged. They operate at every level, from influencing global principles, to developing their own grassroots ones to enable inclusion (Minkowitz, 2018; National Survivor

User Network, 2017). They have emphasised inclusion and diversity in their ways of working and campaigning. They have also been assertive and sometimes confrontational in their ways of campaigning, linking with progressive labour movements and also returning to earlier days of disabled people's direct action, occupying parliament and state buildings, blocking roads. They have at the same time shown skill and sophistication in the new alliances they have forged, with, for example, the UK House of Lords, grassroots community organisations, trades unions, women's, BME and other new social movement organisations. They have also used parliamentary and judicial processes to challenge government policies and decisions. Campaigners like Mo Stewart and Spartacus have gained research skills to evidence their case. Where they have led, we have sometimes seen government, the House of Commons and the House of Lords follow, drawing on their evidence and reversing hostile decisions. They have also reversed the traditional hierarchy of the progressive powerful making decisions on behalf of the disempowered (Beresford, 2012: 46–57).

While they have fought effectively, sometimes taking the lead in resistance to retrograde cuts and 'reforms', their approach has overwhelmingly been one that has been more than just fighting for existing provision that has been threatened or at risk. The struggle has long been more than a defensive and reactive one. The disabled people's movement, as we have seen, right from its inception in the 1970s has always been more than a protest movement. It has been a civil rights movement committed to a different non-medicalised understanding of disability and disabled people, based on their right to be treated and live as equals in mainstream society, embodied in their philosophy of independent living. Until recently, there has not been a similarly clear-cut philosophy around which mental health service users/survivors have gathered. Nonetheless, there has long been a commitment among them to the depathologisation of distress, their right to speak and act for themselves, their large-scale rejection of compulsion and constraint as legitimate elements of treatment. Thus, just as disabled people redefined 'disability' through the social model to mean the discrimination that they faced as a result of their perceived impairment, so, for example, mental health service users/survivors have coined the term 'sanism', to mean the way in which they are marginalised and discriminated against on the grounds of their perceived 'illness' or 'disorder'. Such remodelling is thus about much more than protest, reaction or defensive response. Instead, it is about developing new ideas, new models, new ways of understanding and supporting people. This is what people are now trying to do with beyond-medicalised responses to madness and distress.

MAD STUDIES – A MODEL FOR THE FUTURE

In this third and final section of the chapter, I want to turn to the emergence of 'Mad Studies', the culmination of survivors' efforts to move beyond isolated, defensive organising, to mobilising in unity with allies for alternative understandings and responses to issues of madness and distress. This user-led development is proposed as a means of offering the survivor movement a site for the theoretical and practical 'remodelling' of core beliefs, values and principles. Despite criticisms from both within and outside the survivor movement, Mad Studies offers a vision that is both user-led and also offers a basis for contributions from professional and academic allies. It is perhaps the most recent and developed example of the 'remodelling' we have been talking about, offering ways forward for building alternatives in the present. It brings together many of the progressive aims and aspirations of mental health service users in relation to their experience, ideas, action, policy, practice and research. It also highlights the possibility of building alliances between different stakeholders to achieve these aims.

Mad Studies is a field of study and action relating to what are more often called 'mental health' policy, services and service users, which has its origins in Canada but has led to international interest and activity. This was particularly triggered by the publication in 2013 of Mad Matters, a report on Mad Studies in Canada, the founding home of the movement (LeFrancois, Menzies and Reaume, 2013). In a relatively short time, it has gained a prominence rare among user-led developments challenging psychiatry (Burstow, LeFrancois and Diamond, 2015; Burstow, 2015; Coles, Keenan and Diamond, 2013; Spandler, Anderson and Sapey, 2015; Russo and Sweeney, 2016). Many mental health service users/survivors seem historically to have been discouraged from aligning themselves with the language and framework of madness because of the demeaning and pejorative ways in which the terminology has been used in dominant media and political discourse (Beresford et al., 2016).

While Mad Studies can be seen as having antecedents in and relationships with earlier movements and developments, like, Anti-Psychiatry, the Mental Patients Union and Mad Pride, it should be recognised as a distinct new social movement in its own right. While it is premised on a rejection of the dominance of the 'psy system', what is special about it is the extent and sophistication of its own philosophy, theorising and praxis – and its commitment to inclusivity. The accent of Mad Studies is very much on developing different survivor-led knowledges, based on a new paradigm and for this to be used first to critique existing arrangements and then to identify, explore and prefigure alternative ones. This offers the possibility of coherent analysis, with a broad-based force to achieve change engaged in sponsoring and developing it.

The widespread interest with which Mad Studies has been met, however, suggests that we may be moving beyond this barrier to reclaiming control over our experience of madness and distress. One of the great strengths of the UK and international disabled people's movement was that it had its own clear philosophy and social-model-based approach. The survivor movement has not had an equivalent and this has seemed to this author, at least, as one of its restricting vulnerabilities. The emergence of Mad Studies offers hopeful signs that it may provide a similar basis for putting distance between survivor action and the pathologising ideas that underpin psychiatry and for which the movement does not always seem to have developed a clear and challenging counter. This is not only likely to offer the survivor movement a stronger unifying approach to self-organisation, but also likely to put its relations with other movements, including the disabled people's movement, on a more equal basis. Ultimately all successful movements have to develop their own core beliefs, values and principles – their own visions of themselves. This has sometimes seemed to be unfinished business in the survivor movement, which can be seen as too close to and dependent on the psychiatric system that has tended to marginalise and co-opt it.

It is perhaps because the Mad Studies movement seems to offer unprecedented hope for a different user-led vision for the future for mental health service users/survivors that it seems in a remarkably short time to have generated some fierce opposition, including among those who might have been expected to be its supporters as service users and allies. Thus, it has come in for attack as being 'elitist', narrowly based in academia and failing adequately to address diversity (Rose, 2018). These are all-important criticisms and Mad Studies needs to address them. Indeed, even though it is a very young movement, it already seems to have been doing just this. That doesn't mean there isn't much more to be done to ensure greater black, minority ethnic and indigenous involvement in the movement both in the Global North and the Global South. That doesn't mean that its advocates shouldn't be alert to and seek to challenge the exclusionary pressures that operate in the present international marketised world of the academy. But ironically, the academy has offered space (sometimes the only free space available) to develop local, national and international discussion about Mad Studies.

Mad Studies also seems to offer the hope of new alliances to combat those currently operating between psychiatry, powerful international pharmaceutical companies and neoliberal ideology. The struggles of mental health service users/survivors have often been lonely ones – fighting on their own with a few allies to forge a different understanding of themselves and what they need. From the publication of *Mad Matters* onwards, we could see the possibility of a renewed force for change. Here a wide range of interests came together with shared objectives and commitments. The book includes many chapters written by people with direct experience on the receiving end of psychiatry but also others written by academics and allies with personal and professional interest in these issues. But the book was written within a framework of madness and emerging Mad Studies which rejected medicalisation and a bio-medical model and its retinue of associated often regressive ideas and ambiguous sentiments, from diagnosis to recovery. We can see the new strength and solidarity possible from rallying round Mad Studies and its ideas. At last, there may be a prospect of resistance and building alternatives that could truly threaten the monolith of psychiatry and not just go the way of anti-psychiatry and other professional as well as service user challenges of the past. And while such resistance and opposition may be broad based, it can be led by service user/survivor experience, ideas and knowledge.

As two of us have set out, drawing on discussions so far, what generally seems to define the key elements of Mad Studies is that:

- First, it is definitely divorcing us and itself from a simplistic bio-medical model, making possible a necessary rupture from it. It allows other understandings and disciplines to come into it challenging the dominance of medical knowledge. It retains space for thinking and discussing ideas emergent from sociology, anthropology, social work, cultural studies, feminist, queer studies, disability studies, history (everything!).

- Second is the value and emphasis it places on first person knowledge – centering on the first person knowledge of everyone, not just those psychiatrised. If you want to talk about yourself, then you have a right to, it is ok to include yourself. It elevates a positioned/situated approach to research. – You can't just be talking from nowhere, as if you had no place in the proceedings.

- And finally of course Mad Studies treats survivors' first hand knowledge with equality and places a core value on it. But Mad Studies values and has a place for *all* our first hand experiential knowledge; that's why such a wide range of roles and standpoints can contribute equally to Mad Studies – if they are happy to sign up to its core principles. It isn't only us as survivors/mental health service users, but it also sees a place for allies, professionals, researchers, loved ones, and so on. It is a venture we can all work for together, in alliance. So it includes the experiential knowledge of service users, the practice knowledge of workers and the knowledge from those offering support, of family carers as important bases for future research and development.

(Beresford and Russo, 2016)

CONCLUSION

Neoliberal reforms to social policy in countries like the United Kingdom have had the effect of transforming 'welfare' from a potential 'equaliser' to a regressive weapon of control with strong similarities to the nineteenth-century industrial poor law. While even under that regime there were prevailing notions of the 'deserving' and 'undeserving' poor, such distinctions seem to have become seriously abbreviated. Groups like mental health service users and disabled people, who would formerly have been included in the former category have come under protracted attack as if they are conceptualised as essentially fraudulent to be included in an undifferentiated larger category. This has not only highlighted overlaps between mental health service users and disabled people, demonstrating potential common causes that may not have seemed so clear before, it also emphasises potential links with others treated under neoliberalism as 'out groups' and 'other'. Traditional supportive alliances have been weakened and new ideological couplings have emerged tied to the values of neoliberalism which have exacerbated the threats faced by mental health service users. Their self-organisation, while constantly under threat and particularly the emergence of user/survivor-led Mad Studies offers the prospect not only of more effective resistance to current threats, but also the development of conceptual and policy alternatives that may have the capacity to threaten dominant psychiatry and psycho-systems. There is much for other areas of resistance to learn from these developments, particularly in relation to building more inclusive, more accessible and more democratic forms of opposition and – perhaps even more important – renewal.

NOTES

1. Eurikha, www.eurikha.org/about/ (accessed 10 September 2018).
2. Black Triangle, http://blacktrianglecampaign.org/ (accessed 13 May 2019).
3. Disabled People Against Cuts, https://dpac.uk.net/ (accessed 13 May 2019).
4. Mental Health Resistance, https://mentalhealthresistance.org/ (accessed 13 May 2019).
5. The Broken of Britain, http://thebrokenofbritain.blogspot.com/ (accessed 13 May 2019).
6. The Diary of a Benefits Scrounger, https://diaryofabenefitscrounger.blogspot.com/ (accessed 13 May 2019).
7. The Hardest Hit, https://thehardesthit.wordpress.com/ (accessed 13 May 2019).

REFERENCES

BBC (2015) Labour Party Divided Over Future Welfare Cuts. 13 July, www.bbc.co.uk/news/uk-politics-33503188.

Beresford, P. (2012) From 'Vulnerable' to Vanguard: Challenging the Coalition. In S. Davison and J. Rutherford (eds), *Welfare Reform: The Dread of Things to Come*. London: Lawrence Wishart, 66–77.

Beresford, P. (2013) *Beyond the Usual Suspects: Towards Inclusive User Involvement – Research Report*. London: Shaping Our Lives.

Beresford, P. (2015) Distress and Disability. Not You, Not Me, But Us? In H. Spandler, J. Anderson and B. Sapey (eds), *Madness, Distress and the Politics of Disablement*. Bristol: Policy Press, 245–59.

Beresford, P. (2016) *All Our Welfare: Towards Participatory Social Policy.* Bristol: Policy Press.

Beresford, P. et al. (2016) *From Mental Illness to a Social Model of Madness and Distress? Exploring What Service Users Say.* London: Shaping and Lives and National Survivor User Network.

Beresford, P. and Harrison, M. (2018) Big Charities in the UK have Lost their Way: Time to Listen and Learn from Service Users! *Labour Briefing,* 27 June, http://labourbriefing.squarespace.com/home/2018/6/27/big-charities-in-the-uk-have-lost-their-way-time-to-listen-and-learn-from-service-users.

Beresford, P. and Russo, J. (2016) Supporting the Sustainability of Mad Studies and Preventing Its Co-Option. *Disability & Society,* 31(2): 270–74.

Brewer, M., Clark, T. and Wakefield, M. (2001) *Social Security Under New Labour: What did the Third Way Mean for Welfare Reform? Summary.* London: Institute for Fiscal Studies.

Burstow, B. (2015) *Psychiatry and the Business of Madness: An Ethical and Epistemological Accounting.* Basingstoke: Palgrave Macmillan.

Burstow, B., LeFrancois, B.A. and Diamond, S. (eds) (2015) *Psychiatry Disrupted. Theorising Resistance and Crafting the (R)evolution.* Montreal: McGill-Queen's University Press.

Charlton, J.I. (1998) *Nothing About Us Without Us. Disability, Oppression and Empowerment.* Berkeley, CA: University of California Press.

Coles, S., Keenan, S. and Diamond, B. (eds) (2013) *Madness Contested: Power and Practice.* Ross-on-Wye: PCCS Books.

Hale, C. (2018) Reclaiming 'Chronic Illness': An Introduction to the Chronic Illness Inclusion Project – a discussion paper from the Centre for Welfare Reform. London: Centre for Welfare Reform.

Harper, D. and Speed, E. (2012) Uncovering Recovery: The Resistible Rise of Recovery and Resilience. *Studies in Social Justice,* 6(1): 9–25.

House of Commons (2018) Work and Pensions Committee, PIP and ESA Assessments: Claimant Experiences, Evidence of Social Worker name withheld PEA0115, 17 January, http://data.parliament.uk/writtenevidence/committeeevidence.svc/evidencedocument/work-and-pensions-committee/pip-and-esa-assessments/written/72187.pdf (accessed 11 September 2018).

Jordan, T. and Lent, A. (eds) (1999) *Storming the Millennium: The New Politics of Change.* London: Lawrence and Wishart.

LeFrancois, B.A., Menzies, R. and Reaume, G. (eds) (2013) *Mad Matters: A Critical Reader in Canadian Mad Studies.* Toronto: Canadian Scholars' Press.

McKeown, M., Cresswell, M. and Spandler, H. (2014) Deeply Engaged Relationships: Alliances Between Mental Health Workers and Psychiatric Survivors in the UK. In B. Burstow, B.A. LeFrancois and S. Diamond (eds), *Psychiatry Disrupted: Theorizing Resistance and Crafting the (R)evolution.* Ithaca, NY: McGill-Queen's University Press, 145–62.

Mills, C. (2018) From 'Invisible Problem' to Global Priority: The Inclusion of Mental Health in the Sustainable Development Goals. *Development and Change*, 49(3): 843–66.

Milton, D.E. (2017) Autistic Expertise: A Critical Reflection on the Production of Knowledge in Autism Studies. *Autism*, 18(7): 794–802.

Minkowitz, T. (2018) Dreams of Justice. In P. Beresford and S. Carr (eds), *Social Policy First Hand: An International Introduction to Participatory Social Welfare*. Bristol: Policy Press, 257–61.

Moncrieff, J. (2008) Neoliberalism and Biopsychiatry: A Marriage of Convenience. In C.I. Cohen and S. Timimi (eds), *Liberatory Psychiatry: Philosophy, Politics and Mental Health*. Cambridge: Cambridge University Press Medical, 235–51.

Mo Stewart Research (2018) www.mostewartresearch.co.uk (accessed 10 September 2018).

National Survivor User Network (2017) *4Pi National Involvement Standards*. London: National Survivor User Network.

O'Hara, M. (2014) *Austerity Bites: A Journey to the Sharp End of Cuts in the UK*. Bristol: Policy Press.

Onions, P. *et al.* (2018) Pat's Petition: The Emerging Role of Social Media and the Internet. In P. Beresford and S. Carr (eds), *Social Policy First Hand: An International Introduction to Participatory Social Welfare*. Bristol: Policy Press, 332–5.

Pellizzoni, L. and Ylönen, M. (eds) (2012) *Neoliberalism and Technoscience: Critical Assessments*. Farnham: Ashgate.

Pring, J. (2018) Charities Fail to Tell MPs About Clauses That 'Prevent Them Attacking McVey and DWP'. *Disability News Service*, 5 July, www.disability newsservice.com/charities-fail-to-tell-mps-about-clauses-that-prevent-them-attacking-mcvey-and-dwp/ (accessed 10 September 2018).

Rose, D. (2018) Renewing Epistemologies: Service User Knowledge. In P. Beresford and S. Carr (eds), *Social Policy First Hand: An International Introduction to Participatory Social Welfare*. Bristol: Policy Press, 132–41.

Russo, J. and Sweeney, A. (eds) (2016) *Searching for a Rose Garden: Challenging Psychiatry, Fostering Mad Studies*. Monmouth: PCCS Books.

Spandler, H., Anderson, J. and Sapey, B. (eds) (2015) *Madness, Distress and the Politics of Disablement*. Bristol: Policy Press.

Stone, J. (2017) DWP's Fit-to-Work Tests 'Cause Permanent Damage to Mental Health', Study Finds. *Independent*, 13 March, www.independent.co.uk/news/uk/politics/fit-to-work-wca-tests-mental-health-dwp-work-capability-assessment-benefits-esa-pip-a7623686.html.

United Nations (2018) Convention on the Rights of People with Disabilities: Concluding Observations on the Initial Report of the United Kingdom of Great Britain and Northern Ireland, Committee on the Rights of People With Disabilities. London: HM Government.

6

Challenging Neoliberal Housing in the Shadow of Grenfell

Glyn Robbins

INTRODUCTION

Grenfell Tower has become a symbol of the punitive – and failing – State (*Independent*, 2017a), raising numerous questions about our increasingly divided society and iniquitous housing system. Among the many reactions was a strong sense that the victims were punished for being poor, many from ethnic minorities, who lived in council housing (Chakrabortty, 2017). Local residents had warned about safety for years, but were ignored by a combination of bureaucratic, political and commercial vested interests. Grenfell represents the culmination of decades-long policies of privatisation of housing in general and the denigration of and disinvestment from council housing in particular.

This structural re-ordering of UK housing is linked to redefining the role of the State (Jessop, 2016), especially by replacing rights with conditionality. Perhaps the starkest evidence of this punitive shift is the requirement that some women declare whether or not they've been raped before receiving benefits (*Guardian*, 2017), but extends to the notorious Bedroom Tax (*Daily Mirror*, 2018a), the disaster that is Universal Credit (*Daily Mirror*, 2018b) and several attempts to withdraw council tenancies from people whose family members have been convicted of crime (*Independent*, 2018).

UK housing policy stands at a crossroads, one route from which leads towards the unvarnished, pro-market brutality of the US model (Robbins, 2017a), but there is also great political uncertainty about which direction to take (Kuensberg, 2018). This is creating an opening for grassroots activism to resist the pro-market orthodoxy and develop alternatives. The first part of this chapter outlines the neoliberal housing project; the second part discusses the campaigns seeking to change it and the challenges they face.

GRENFELL TOWER – A TURNING POINT?

The Grenfell fire elicited a visceral reaction from working-class communities around the UK and beyond – a feeling that their lives are held cheap by a system based on profit, alongside a sense that the horror could have happened anywhere. However, it was the fact that the atrocity occurred in the richest borough in the country (the Royal Borough of Kensington and Chelsea) that heightened the anger which spread quickly from the particular circumstances, to more general questions of housing and social justice. There's been a broad sentiment that Grenfell must be a turning point (Robbins, 2017b). The public inquiry will, we're told, uncover the causes of the fire and why it killed, at least, 72 people. But its narrow scope (BBC News, 2017) is likely to leave out some of the critical issues that make Grenfell such a potent image of our increasingly polarised cities.

The path to Grenfell can be traced back decades. During that time, council housing has passed from mainstream to peripheral. In the early 1980s, approximately 30 per cent of the UK population rented their home from a local authority. It was respectable, stable and aspirational (Boughton, 2018). Today, council housing constitutes 7 per cent of the nation's housing and has been subject to a concerted campaign of negativity and prejudice (Jones, 2011), some of which was evident in the media coverage immediately after the Grenfell fire (MailOnline, 2017). Although there are still 4 million people living in council housing, with significant densities in some areas, what is sometimes referred to as the residualisation of the sector has altered the perceptions and experience of it.

The key feature of this process has been privatisation, which has had multiple adverse consequences, several of which were exposed by Grenfell. The passing of council housing from public to private ownership has taken place in various ways. A watershed moment was the introduction of the Right to Buy in 1980, but it has been followed by large-scale transfers of formerly municipal homes to private housing associations (Pawson and Mullins, 2010). As well as the privatisation of homes, council housing, like public services generally, has been subject to outsourcing of contracts to private companies. This has ranged from the widespread involvement of consultancy firms (often to advise on further privatisation!), to the almost universal use of private subcontractors to carry out building and maintenance works, although in recent years, some councils have been taking such services back 'in-house' (O'Brien, 2018).

The cumulative effect of privatisation has been to weaken what remains of council housing. What was once a financially robust, democratically controlled provider of homes that many people chose to live in for life, has been starved of investment and reduced in social status. Critically, this process has included altering the power relationship between council tenants and their landlords. Council tenants were once described as 'special citizens' (Grayson, 2009). They enjoyed an almost unique degree of control over their homes, both through the ballot box and local tenant associations that exerted real influence on how housing services were delivered. This potential power was also demonstrated by successful resistance to large-scale privatisation of council housing as, for example, in Birmingham (*Guardian*, 2002).

The term 'entitlement' has become pejorative, but it describes a relationship that used to underpin and strengthen council housing, at both an individual and a community-wide level. Council tenants once felt *entitled* to a decent home for life, at a genuinely affordable rent, with a comprehensive repairs service and an accountable (and removable) landlord. This interlinked system of decent housing, community stability and political rights was intrinsic to council housing, but an anathema to neoliberalism.

Grenfell illustrated, in the most appalling way, that council tenants have been re-cast as supplicants. The clear and repeated warnings from residents about the management of their homes, particularly around the fundamental issue of safety, were ignored. Instead, decisions that eventually cost many lives were taken by an autocratic landlord and private businesses. The most disastrous of these was the installation of flammable cladding. It has already been documented that the choice of materials was based on financial, not safety, concerns (*Independent*, 2017b). But there is a deeper significance to the cladding of council tower blocks. As Lucy Masoud from the Fire Brigades Union told an anti-racism conference in October 2017: 'The moment the wealthy people living near Grenfell decided they didn't want to look at an "ugly" building, the residents' fate was sealed.' Whatever the marginal energy-efficiency gains, the real motive for cladding of council housing blocks is the attempt to disguise their true identity. This impulse is based on long-held, often class-based prejudices against the sector and the appearance of its buildings and residents. From Ronan Point to Andy and Lou in *Little Britain*, this stigmatisation has provided the ideological impetus for the systematic dismantling of council housing from its place as part of the post-war settlement.

Another issue the Grenfell inquiry is unlikely to address is how housing policies have fragmented working-class communities, making them softer targets for the punitive State. When I started working on council estates in 1991, approximately 80 per cent of residents were council tenants with permanent secure tenancies, 20 per cent were 'first generation' Right to Buy (RTB) leaseholders. On the relatively small estate where I work today, there are at least half-a-dozen different types of occupancy.[1] This is possibly an underestimate and certainly there are other places where council housing and working-class communities are being further destabilised by short-term letting like Airbnb (*Financial Times*, 2016). I estimate the estate population has an annual turnover of about 30 per cent, predominantly comprising young people in the Private Rented Sector (PRS), who are typically on six-month tenancies and never more than two months away from a mandatory eviction notice. This pattern of transience, which is becoming the norm in urban areas, particularly driven by the exponential rise of the PRS, has multiple – and often unrecognised – consequences.

At a very basic level, this urban churn makes any attempt to build what has long been held as a holy grail of urban policy – 'sustainable communities' – almost impossible. While this aspiration may never have been more than rhetorical for some, it conveys real meaning in terms of resisting the punitive State. Class solidarity and collective action have always been the foundation of successful housing campaigns. Weakening it has been the hidden agenda of UK housing policy for decades. The fragmentation of housing provision almost inevitably leads to atomisation and alienation. People who don't know if they'll be neighbours in six months have very little incentive to get to know each other, nor to get involved in wider community affairs, which could include political activism.

Social Cleansing – 'Clearing the Ground of Poor People'

Perhaps the most vivid expression of the punitive neoliberal State is the threat of demolition. Thousands of council and other social housing tenants in the UK currently face the prospect of their homes and communities being destroyed under the guise of 'regeneration'. Notorious examples are the Heygate estate in Southwark and the West Hendon estate in Barnet, but there are many more, including places outside London (McTigue, 2017). When Jeremy Corbyn described such projects as 'social cleansing' (Merrick, 2017), it found an instant echo.

However, the use of the housing market for the structural re-ordering of working-class communities – what Jay Arena refers to as 'clearing the ground of poor people' (Arena, 2012) – continues as part of a strategic, global, neoliberal onslaught, frequently with the tacit support of local councils, including those controlled by the Labour Party. It was a key feature of the New Labour government's urban policy after 1997. The Blair years amplified the moralistic and conditional narrative around housing provision. In his first major speech as prime minister, significantly made on the Aylesbury council estate in south London (2 June 1997), Blair set out the terms of a new social contract in which '... It is something for something. A society where we play by the rules. You only take out if you put in'.

Had the speech been made in the market square of Royal Tunbridge Wells, it may have conveyed different meanings. On a council estate, the inference that some people were getting 'something' for nothing was clear. The transfer of 1.6 million council homes to private housing associations was the enduring legacy of Labour's 'Third Way' housing and urban policy (Boyle and Rogerson, 2006), but was consistent with the neoliberal agenda before and since. As David Madden and Peter Marcuse correctly observe:

> ... the privatisation of housing since 1989 has probably constituted the largest transfer of property rights in history. The hard-won spaces of partial decommodification developed in the post-war period have been eroded.
>
> (Madden and Marcuse, 2016: 31)

One of the critical paths followed by the punitive State in attempting to unwind the progress won by campaigns for better housing has been imposing conditionality. It was a founding tenet of council housing that it was available to all, without restrictions of time or income. My grandparents lived in their Dagenham council home, as tenants, for over 50 years and they weren't unusual. Since 1985, this right to stay put has been legally protected by secure tenancies. The punitive State has been picking away at secure tenancies as part of a deliberate, concerted effort to redefine UK council housing in similar terms to US 'last resort' public housing. The 2016 Housing and Planning Act sought to phase out permanent tenancies for new council tenants and introduce means testing to the sector for the first time.

Housing Associations (HAs) have played a deliberately pernicious role in undermining the core principles of universal provision of housing services established under the Welfare State. With their origins in a combination of Victorian philanthropy and 1960s hippie entrepreneurialism, HAs were perfectly suited to the government attacks on municipalism instigated by Thatcher and the philosophy of the Third Way that accelerated privatisation during the Blair years. Their charitable origins have also connected with concepts of the deserving and undeserving poor that have underpinned creeping conditionality. HAs (and some local councils) have enthusiastically implemented government policies that have introduced time-limited tenancies, some of them linked to specified types of behaviour such as finding a job or saving for a mortgage. They have become increasingly commercialised, forming group-structures through mergers and getting involved in market-oriented activities that have replaced general needs, social rented homes with income-specific, stratified entitlement backed by de facto means testing.

The Homelessness Crisis

The ultimate victims of the punitive State of housing are the homeless, whose numbers have doubled since 2010, but whose plight is often obfuscated by ignorance, value judgements and the increasingly complex rules around access to housing. These factors are compounded by a perception that the homeless are disconnected from the wider housing crisis – a special interest group supported by charities rather than statutory services. One of the underlying prejudices sometimes visited on the homeless is the perception that they are in some way morally culpable for their situation. This blaming of the victim continues in some quarters, despite the fact that, according to a 2017 report by Shelter, 128,000 children are registered as homeless (Shelter, 2017).

Rights for homeless people have been systematically dismantled since the high-watermark of legislation in 1977. This culminated, after 2011, with the ending of any right for the homeless to be rehoused in secure, non-market rented housing in an area with which they had a local connection. Instead, they were increasingly consigned to the insecurity and exorbitant rents of the minimally regulated private rented sector, often in places far removed from their original home and vital support networks. As an anonymous article by a worker carrying out homelessness assessments for a local authority revealed: 'I work in a service where not helping people is generally seen as doing a good job' (Anon, 2016).

However, it could be argued that those living in sub-standard temporary accommodation are relatively fortunate compared to those without a home of any kind. Such comparisons are invidious. But it is true that even the minimal and reducing statutory housing safety net is not available to all. The complex reasons that can lead people to becoming 'street homeless' reflect a much wider social policy crisis, but as with families living in a bed and breakfast, the root cause is historic under-investment in non-market rented housing in general and council housing in particular. Despite this, street homeless people – most of whom weren't born when the UK turned away from a policy aspiration of universal housing provision – are the targets for vindictive responses designed to further marginalise them from mainstream society.

The punitive State harasses the street homeless in numerous ways. As Victoria Cooper and Daniel McCulloch (2017) have described, the UK has a long history of demonising 'vagrancy', but a new wave of hostility has now made it, in effect, a crime to be homeless. This onslaught has assumed additional impetus with the growing colonisation and privatisation of space, another direct consequence of State-sponsored, market-dominated housing and urban policies. The zones of consumption now found in most UK cities, like Liverpool One, Brindley Place in Birmingham, Gun Wharf in Portsmouth and London's 2012 Olympic Park and Westfield shopping centre, all impose new levels of coercive behaviour control enshrined in by-laws, enforced by private security patrols and surveillance, that give these places the virtual status of mini city-States, where the homeless are not wanted. This socio-spatial exclusion of the homeless has also been physically expressed in the growth of so-called 'defensive architecture' (Andreu, 2015).

Given this State sanctioned 'hostile environment', it is hardly surprising that homeless people are also the targets of abuse and violent attacks by their fellow citizens (Foster, 2016), although it's instructive that in reporting this, the homeless charity Crisis compared attacks on homeless people with those on 'the general public', as though homeless people don't fall within that description.

Other policy measures deliberately limit the housing options for homeless people. In September 2012, the coalition government enacted legislation to criminalise squatting (Blake, 2012), thereby restricting access to empty homes, of which there are an estimated 200,000 in England that have been unoccupied for six months or more. This issue gets to the ideological heart of the punitive State. In the immediate aftermath of the Grenfell disaster, Jeremy Corbyn called for the occupation, compulsory purchase and requisition of empty homes to help the victims. His call provoked an immediate establishment backlash. Prime Minister Theresa May had already made what proved to be the vacuous pledge that all the people who lost their homes because of the Grenfell blaze would be rehoused within three weeks. Six months after the fire, half of the displaced families were still in temporary accommodation. At the time of writing (November 2018), most are still waiting for suitable permanent rehousing. But in answer to Corbyn's demands, May articulated the authentic voice of the ruling class. Her spokesperson said: 'We don't support proposals to seize private property' (Watts, 2017). The extent of the establishment panic to Grenfell and Corbyn's response to it was further demonstrated in a blog on *The Economist* website (16 June 2017), which said: 'Mr Corbyn [called] for the seizure of empty luxury flats for people who are made homeless by the fire ... *British civilisation is based on respect for private property*' (my emphasis). It is the primary function of the punitive State to protect that private property.

There was more evidence that current government policy is turning back the housing clock when the Tory leader of another 'royal borough', Windsor and Maidenhead, called on the police to use the 1824 Vagrancy Act as a way of managing homelessness, particularly in advance of a royal wedding (Sherwood, 2018). Such reactionary political soundbites are not unusual, nor are they restricted to the UK. In November 2017, a senior

Irish civil servant referred to the growing number of homeless people in the country as being guilty of 'years of bad behaviour' (Clarke, 2017). The clearest evidence that UK housing provision has fundamentally shifted is the resurrection of the private landlord. This has been a neoliberal ideological and economic objective for decades and walks hand-in-hand with the attempt to destroy council housing. The Private Rented Sector (PRS) was in decline for most of the twentieth century and settled at less than 10 per cent of all homes. It's now at around 20 per cent and rising. Multiple policy-drivers, including those discussed above, have contributed to this revival, with a host of adverse consequences. But this is also an area where the punitive State becomes a compliant and complicit State, which doesn't just promote the PRS, but uses public money to subsidise it, while turning a blind-eye to its abuses.

Private landlords now receive approximately £10 billion a year in Housing Benefit payments, effectively a public subsidy for excessive rents. In addition, Generation Rent has estimated private landlords receive about £16 billion in various tax-breaks and incentives. As a spokesperson for the organisation said: 'While renters have borne the brunt of austerity, landlords have enjoyed their own little economy the size of Morocco's supported by subsidies from the UK taxpayer that could be better used fixing the housing crisis' (Osborne, 2015).

Within this permissive climate, many private landlords now operate with an impunity to minimal regulations that again evokes an earlier age. Even with short-term contracts that are heavily biased in favour of the landlord, research for Shelter has found that at least 200,000 PRS tenants are victims of 'revenge evictions'. These people lost their home when they complained to the landlord about outstanding repairs, including those that may be a serious safety risk (BBC Newsbeat, 2017). Such punitive actions were made illegal in 2015, but the same Shelter research also found that the law is not being enforced.

In what is essentially an unregulated market, where demand often far outstrips supply, many different types of abuse are possible. Deliberate overcrowding to maximise rental income, 'beds in sheds' and the imposition of unjustifiable fees have all become common features of the PRS. An even more grotesque example of how 'rogue landlords' are exploiting their position is the use of sex for access to housing (Jones, 2018). But attempts to introduce serious controls over the PRS have consistently been blocked by Conservative MPs, many of whom are themselves private landlords (Stone, 2016).

TURNING THE NEOLIBERAL TIDE: BARRIERS AND OPENINGS

A young private renter once said to me 'why aren't there housing riots?' Given the enormous damage caused by a housing system even the government admits is 'broken', that's a reasonable question. Around the UK, many people are fighting to defend their homes, or demanding the right to have one. But there are problems in developing a movement capable of significantly shifting government policy. This section discusses some of those difficulties, before describing some examples that have begun to overcome them.

Moving a Monolith

The housing crisis took decades to develop and will probably take decades to correct, even for a government genuinely committed to radical reform. This, in itself, is a barrier to successful campaigns. There is no quick-fix answer to the problem and most solutions are beyond the horizon of most politicians. Short-termism compounds a pervading sense that housing is out of our control, guided by giant, monolithic forces. This perception can lead to a feeling of impotence and resignation, a vicious circle continued when mainstream politicians appear unable to offer anything but a tokenistic response. For many people, perpetual housing crisis has become hard-wired into our economic and political system and collective consciousness. Meanwhile, there has been a general failure within the labour movement to take up an issue that affects the daily lives of millions of workers, while housing campaigns tend to mirror the labour movement by tending towards being fragmented and sectional.

In some respects, campaigns around Grenfell are a microcosm of the difficulties facing efforts to build a national housing movement. There are several different groups, as there are numerous separate organisations working on housing justice issues around the UK. Although this is understandable in context – and housing campaigns are inherently local – it could also be seen as diluting impact. Like other grassroots campaigns, Grenfell United, in particular, has had to confront the risks of being incorporated by the political establishment in return for money and resources, a potential alternative source of which is the trade union movement. But, in general, unions (not their individual members) have been noticeable by their absence in supporting Grenfell. Similarly, elected politicians (outside the immediate area), have not harnessed the outrage about Grenfell by linking it to local issues. An example is the failure to insist that the government honour its pledge to pay for essential safety works, leaving some councils to borrow money for this purpose (Williams, 2017).

Another stumbling block towards a united, national housing campaign is the role and influence of charities in the sector. This is particularly evident in relation to big organisations like Shelter and Crisis, but there are many others. There is an important debate about the extent to which charity is becoming a threat to and replacement for statutory public services.[2] In the housing field this is further complicated by the nature of housing associations, some of which have charitable origins and/or subsidiaries. The key issue here is that charities are prohibited from involvement in politics, but housing is a political issue. Charities can – and do – divert and canalise housing campaign activity away from direct challenges to the policy status quo, particularly if their funding is at stake. A good example is Shelter's response to Grenfell. It launched a 'Big Conversation' about the future of council and social housing (Shelter, 2018). And 30,000 people responded to this consultation exercise, overseen by a Commission including members of the great and good, with findings to be put to government and politicians. But previous experience suggests this is unlikely to seriously discomfort them.

Building a coordinated, national alliance that cuts across tenure, locality and broader political affiliations faces several wider social issues. Perhaps the first is trying to rebuild the type of organic solidarity that was so inspiring and powerful in the aftermath of Grenfell. While the authorities floundered in negligence and ignorance, people from the community rallied to provide practical and emotional support in the best tradition of working-class communities. However, to borrow Aneurin Bevan's phrase, the 'living fabric'[3] of such communities has been severely worn by the neoliberal onslaught. Tellingly, the UN's Special Rapporteur on poverty used a similar phrase in relation to the impact of public service cuts during a highly critical visit to the UK in November 2018 (Booth and Butler, 2018). Privatisation then, plays out in different ways. As well as enabling a massive transfer of wealth from public to private sectors, the ideology of individualism infects attitudes around the housing question. The sense that housing is a personal, rather than social responsibility has been successfully inculcated by the establishment, underpinned by a moral judgementalism that is deliberately divisive.

To have real impact, the critical question is the extent to which different housing campaigns can link and unite their efforts. For this to happen, there will need to be some mutual understanding of different tactical approaches and organisational cultures. Defend Council Housing (DCH), for example, has tended to orientate itself towards the labour movement and could be characterised as 'middle aged, working class', while emerging PRS groups tend to be younger and (perhaps as a result) sceptical of traditional political formations. For all housing campaigns, involving more black and Asian people is essential, particularly given the endemic racism within housing policies and the way the far-right repeatedly scapegoats minorities for the housing crisis.

No issue more graphically illustrates the democratic deficit than housing. The disconnect between the concerns of millions of citizens and the impotence of their political representatives to address them is vivid. Ireland faces a similar situation; which campaigners say has 'gone beyond crisis'. Diarmaid Ó Cadhla from Cork expresses a sentiment that would be shared in many other places:

> It seems in government that there is no sense of emergency, there is no sense of urgency in solving an acute problem which has actually seen people die on the streets, which has seen families with young kids become homeless.
>
> (English, 2015)

However, in Ireland, a painstaking process has led to the successful creation of a national coalition comprising housing and anti-austerity campaigners, opposition politicians, unions and church leaders which is putting the government under serious pressure (Bray, 2018). There's not yet an equivalent in the UK. It's doubtful that many people could even name the UK housing minister – unsurprising given there have been four in the past three years.

This revolving door confirms the seriousness with which the situation is treated by the political establishment, but responsibility for this chronic failure should be shared by the labour movement. UK trade unions, with significant resources and thousands of members who are suffering because of their housing predicament, have not led a sustained, coordinated campaign to demand change, as has happened in Ireland. Neither the Labour Party nor Momentum and other elements of the left have given the issue sufficient attention. This failure to address a day-to-day quality of life issue for millions of working-class people is letting the government off the hook and bolstering support for reactionary forces.

Breakthrough Moments

Despite the barriers, housing campaigns are growing. Grenfell heightened fears, but also anger, about the deadly consequences of market-driven policies. In the immediate aftermath, establishment politicians were compelled to make statements which often proved hollow and exposed how detached they'd become from the lives of working-class communities. The task of fighting for truth and justice has therefore fallen to local campaigners. It was the Grenfell Action Group[4] that originally warned about safety risks and has continued to demand answers. Grenfell United[5] has become the 'official' group representing survivors and bereaved families, including through discussions with government and other statutory agencies. Justice for Grenfell[6] plays a more overtly political role, for example, by organising the brilliant 'three billboards' stunt (Mumford, 2018) and there have been numerous other examples of community solidarity, particularly the commemorative Silent Walks held on the 14th of every month, attracting thousands of people from within and beyond the local community.

Among the active supporters of Grenfell has been Defend Council Housing (DCH).[7] The campaign was formed in 1997 to oppose the privatisation of council homes through New Labour's 'stock transfer' programme (Ginsburg, 2005) and has been the leading grassroots advocacy group for council housing ever since. DCH is non-party political,[8] combining local activism with local and national lobbying and the regular production of campaign materials. This has contributed towards some important victories (as well as Birmingham, many other areas have rejected privatisation of their council housing). Like other housing campaigns, DCH has sometimes struggled to reach beyond its single-issue identity, but has maintained a consistent message, which is now on the cusp of a significant breakthrough. On 3 October 2018, the then Prime Minister, Theresa May, announced the intention to lift the 'borrowing cap' that has hamstrung councils from building new homes (Merrick, 2018). This has been a long-held demand of DCH, as an essential part of restoring council housing to the mainstream, something that is now a distinct possibility.

Announcing the end of council housing may be premature (Harris, 2016), but there's no question that attacks on the sector have directly contributed to the exponential rise of private renting, as they were intended to do. The unpredictability and transience of the PRS militates against successful organising, but again, this could be changing. At least three campaigns are beginning to give a voice to tenants who had hitherto suffered in silence. Acorn,[9] originally a US-based organisation influenced by the theories of Saul Alinsky, is organising PRS tenants at a grassroots level and is making some headway in particular cities like Brighton, Sheffield and Bristol. The London Renters Union[10] is following a similar approach in the capital. Both groups are developing through painstaking door-knocking, casework and protests targeting rogue landlords, estate agents and other corporate property interests. By contrast, Generation Rent[11] adopts a more strategic, lobbying role, campaigning on specific issues such as ending no-fault, 'section 21', evictions.

Housing Association (HA) tenants don't have the same tradition of organised resistance as other tenants, but that's changing too. There's been active opposition to HA mergers (Weaver, 2018) and successful campaigns against proposed estate demolitions, for example, the Foxhill estate in Bath (Barker, 2018). Tenants of One Housing HA in east London threatened a rent strike which compelled their landlord to withdraw a 40 per cent rent hike (Socialist Party, 2017). HA tenants have also found common cause with HA workers in the Unite union, many of whom have seen their pay and conditions attacked within the increasingly ruthless HA corporate culture. A particularly imaginative and pertinent example is the Alternative Housing Awards,[12] demonstrations outside the glitzy hotels where HA bosses in evening dress come to celebrate their 'success', but are met by tenants and workers presenting cardboard cups for 'Worst HA Landlord' and 'Worst HA Employer'.

Some local activists have succeeded in getting national attention by taking direct action. In 2008, Newham Council, one of the poorest in the UK and an out-rider for New Labour policy under former mayor Robin Wales, declared that it 'had enough social housing' (Robbins, 2012). This misplaced conclusion was exemplified at the Carpenters Estate where the council deliberately left several hundred of its homes empty, pending a possible redevelopment deal with University College London, who were interested in the commercial potential of acquiring a site adjacent to the 2012 Olympic Park. When the deal collapsed in May 2013, it led to one of the most high-profile housing campaigns of recent years, Focus E15 (Kwei, 2015). In what was almost a parable of the housing crisis and its punitive effects, a group of women who had been housed in a hostel for single parents, but forced out because of the changing commercial focus of the housing association that ran it, began to demand permanent rehousing in their borough. They staged protests at the council's housing offices and organised regular street stalls that secured wide support in and beyond the local area. In autumn 2014, they occupied a block of the moth-balled Carpenters Estate, an action that generated significant media attention. Although the occupation only lasted a couple of weeks, by making the obvious, but irrefutable argument 'These homes need people – these people need homes', Focus E15 succeeded in raising a fundamental issue about the failure and iniquity of current housing policy. Newham Council eventually had to apologise to the Focus E15 mums and offer some concessions on rehousing and using the Carpenters Estate for temporary housing.[13]

Another very significant grassroots campaign has developed in Haringey, north London, where there's been concerted and successful (BBC News, 2018) opposition to the local council's plans for the wholesale transfer of publicly owned homes, facilities and land to a multinational developer.[14] The Stop HDV campaign has also catalysed a shift to the left in the local Labour Party (Barnes, 2018). Estate demolition projects have also been stopped or stalled in Bath, Waltham Forest and Southend. The London-based Demolition Watch[15] campaign demands binding ballots of residents living on threatened estates and helped coordinate a 'No demolition without permission' protest of 300 people outside City Hall on 3 November 2018. This basic democratic principle has been conceded (albeit with caveats) by the Mayor of London and is included in the Labour Party's green paper on housing (Labour, 2018).

A broad alliance, including tenants of all tenures, trade unions, opposition politicians and faith groups came together to oppose the potentially ruinous Housing and Planning Act. Initially called 'Kill the Bill' and subsequently (after the Bill became law in May 2016), 'Axe the Act',[16] the highlight of the campaign was a demonstration in central London on 13 March 2016 that attracted approximately 10,000 people, the largest housing related protest since the campaign against the Housing Finance Act in the early 1970s. Sustained pressure inside and outside parliament has led to the Act being substantially watered down, with key elements of it effectively dropped. However, the underlying ideology remains a threat.

With the Irish example in mind, UK housing campaigners are continuing efforts to establish a national alliance to demand real government action to reverse the neoliberal onslaught. The Radical Housing Network[17] has brought together a wide range of groups, particularly from private renter, squatting and student oriented activists. The forces that came together to successfully confront the Housing and Planning Act has pivoted towards a wider focus under the heading 'Homes for All'. None of these formations are the finished article. But while recognising the potential difficulties discussed above, it's clear that to win lasting change, housing activists must remember the difference between four fingers – and a fist!

CONCLUSION

Housing has become the new front line of class war. The damage caused by current policy failure is incalculable. Changing it should be considered alongside health and education as setting the foundation of the kind of society we want to live in. There is a latent consensus that these vital services cannot be left to the market. The task before us is translating the pent-up demand for a more equitable, sustainable and humane housing system into concrete, unifying demands. Restoring council housing to the mainstream is a necessary, if not sufficient, part of this, based on a recognition that it now represents the only genuinely affordable, secure form of rented housing with the capacity to promote more collective social attitudes, while also reinvigorating moribund local political engagement. Council housing for the twenty-first century has numerous potential multiplier benefits, including apprenticeship and job creation, improving domestic energy efficiency and reducing the enormous public expenditure resulting from poor housing. Above all, council housing is the antithesis of housing for private profit.

A new generation of council housing must be linked to other demands. Action to improve private renting is essential, including rent control, secure tenancies and enforcement of repair conditions. Unless Housing Associations rediscover their original social purpose and become more democratic, they should not receive public money. After Grenfell, with hundreds of homes, including private blocks (as well as schools and hospitals) still covered with flammable material (Booth, 2018), there is a wider, but potentially unifying, campaign issue around fire safety. But these are only transitional demands towards a fundamental rethink of housing in our society. The decades-long neoliberal economic onslaught has been heavily reliant upon the financialisation of housing through global networks of speculative investment. The 2007–08 crash illustrated the inherent volatility of the belief-system that sees a home as a private commodity, instead of a public asset and a human right.

These arguments have been won in the past and can be again, but time is running out.

NOTES

1. Council tenants with secure tenancies, council tenants with probationary tenancies, a homeless family living (scandalously) in temporary accommodation within the council's own stock, resident RTB leaseholders, absentee RTB leaseholders and private renters.
2. House of Lords Library Note, Debate on 5 October: The Charitable Sector and Civil Society, 1 October 2010.
3. Hansard, Vol. 414, 17 October 1945.
4. Grenfell Action Group, https://grenfellactiongroup.wordpress.com/ (accessed 20 May 2019).
5. Grenfell United, www.grenfellunited.org/ (accessed 20 May 2019).
6. Justice4Grenfell, https://justice4grenfell.org/ (accessed 20 May 2019).
7. Defend Council Housing, www.defendcouncilhousing.org.uk/dch/ (accessed 20 May 2019). NB. The author has been an active supporter of DCH since its inception.
8. Another issue DCH has repeatedly had to confront is the suggestion that it's a 'front' organisation for the Socialist Workers Party, which it is not.
9. Acorn the Union, https://acorntheunion.org.uk/ (accessed 20 May 2019).
10. London Renters Union, https://londonrentersunion.org/ (accessed 20 May 2019).
11. Generation Rent, www.generationrent.org/ (accessed 20 May 2019).
12. The Alternative Housing Awards, www.housingworkers.org.uk/sub-page/ 158/the-alternative-housing-awards.html (accessed 20 May 2019).

13. At the time of writing (November 2018), the long-term future of the estate is unknown.
14. LendLease, the same company that profited from the redevelopment of the Heygate estate.
15. Demolition Watch London, www.demolitionwatchlondon.com/ (accessed 20 May 2019).
16. Homes for All, *Axe the Act*, www.axethehousingact.org.uk/ (accessed 20 May 2019).
17. Radical Housing Network, https://radicalhousingnetwork.org/ (accessed 20 May 2019).

REFERENCES

Andreu, A. (2015) Anti-Homeless Spikes: 'Sleeping Rough Opened My Eyes to the City's Barbed Cruelty'. *Guardian*, 18 February.

Anon (2016) I Work in a Service Where Not Helping People is Generally Seen as Doing a Good Job. *Guardian*, 11 June.

Arena, J. (2012) *Driven from New Orleans: How Non-Profits Betray Public Housing and Promote Privatisation*. Minneapolis, MN: University of Minnesota Press.

Barker, N. (2018) Curo Abandons Foxhill Regeneration Plans Following Resident Legal Action. *Inside Housing*, 28 February.

Barnes, D. (2018) Relief as Labour Confirms Scrapping of Controversial HDV Housing Project. *Guardian*, 26 July.

BBC News (2017) Grenfell Tower Fire: Judge 'Doubt' Over Inquiry Scope. 29 June.

BBC News (2018) Haringey Council Row: Authority Scraps £2bn Housing Project. 19 July.

BBC Newsbeat (2017) Revenge Eviction Law 'Not Working'. 9 February.

Blake, J. (2012) Criminalising Squatting Hurts the Poor and Benefits the Rich. *Guardian*, 31 August.

Booth, R. (2018) Grenfell Tower-Style Cladding Identified in 470 High-Rise Blocks. *Guardian*, 28 June.

Booth, R. and Butler, P. (2018) UK Austerity has Inflicted 'Great Misery' on Citizens, UN says. *Guardian*, 16 November.

Boughton, J. (2018) *Municipal Dreams: The Rise and Fall of Council Housing*. London: Verso.

Boyle, M. and Rogerson, R. (2006) 'Third Way' Urban Policy and the New Moral Politics of Community: Conflicts over the Virtuous Community in Ballymun in Dublin and the Gorbals in Glasgow. *Urban Geography*, 27(3): 201–27.

Bray, J. (2018) Confidence Threat Vote to Eoghan Murphy on Housing. *The Sunday Times*, 29 August.

Chakrabortty, A. (2017), Over 170 Years after Engels, Britain is still a Country that Murders its Poor. *Guardian*, 20 June.

Clarke, V. (2017) Campaigners 'Appalled' and 'Furious' at Homeless Comments. *The Irish Times*, 15 November.

Cooper, V. and McCulloch, D. (2017) Britain's Dark History of Criminalising Homeless People in Public Spaces. *The Conversation*, 10 March.

Daily Mirror (2018a) Despairing Foster Mum 'Took Her Own Life' After Building up Bedroom Tax Debt While Waiting for Next Child. 12 March.

Daily Mirror (2018b) Council House Tenants on Universal Credit Owe Almost Three Times as Much Rent as Those on Old Benefits. 12 November.

English, E. (2015) This Homeless Situation is Gone Beyond Crisis. *Irish Examiner*, 9 October.

Financial Times (2016) Airbnb Backlash Spells Trouble for Landlords. 9 December.

Foster, D. (2016) Crisis Report Reveals Shocking Dangers of Being Homeless. *Guardian*, 23 December.

Ginsburg, N. (2005) The Privatisation of Council Housing. *Critical Social Policy*, 25(1): 115–35.

Grayson, J. (2009) *Looking at Tenant History: Different Histories, Different Politics*. Leeds: Leeds Tenants Federation.

Guardian (2002) Blow to Council Housing Transfer Campaign. 9 April.

Guardian (2017) Government Under Fire Over New Child Tax Credit Form for Rape Victims. 6 April.

Harris, J. (2016) The End of Council Housing. *Guardian*, 4 January.

Independent (2017a) Editorial: Grenfell Tower – A Monument to a Broken Society. 14 June.

Independent (2017b) Grenfell Tower's Fireproof Cladding was 'Downgraded to Save £293,000', Show Leaked Documents. 30 June.

Independent (2018) Take Council Homes Away From Families of Gang Members, Tory Minister Says. 23 June.

Jessop, B. (2016) *The State: Past, Present, Future*. Cambridge: Polity Press.

Jones, H. (2018) Sex for Rent: The Rogue Landlords who Offer Free Rooms in Return for 'Favours'. *Guardian*, 2 April.

Jones, O. (2011) *Chavs: The Demonization of the Working Class*. London: Verso.

Kuensberg, L. (2018) Tories Struggle to Agree a Way Ahead on Housing. *BBC News*, 23 June.

Kwei, S. (2015) Focus E15 Mums have Fought for the Right to a Home: This is Only the Start. *Guardian*, 5 October.

Labour (2018) *Housing for the Many: A Labour Party Green Paper*. London.

McTigue, A. (2017) Social Rent Housing Estate may be Demolished to Make Way for New Homes in Southend. *Southend Echo*, 3 October.

MailOnline (2017) The Man Whose Faulty Fridge Started Tower Inferno. 15 June.

Madden, D. and Marcuse, P. (2016) *In Defence of Housing: The Politics of Crisis*. London: Verso.

Merrick, R. (2017) Jeremy Corbyn Pledges to Stop 'Social Cleansing' in Regeneration Schemes after Grenfell Tower Tragedy. *Independent*, 27 September.

Merrick, R. (2018) Theresa May Lifts Borrowing Cap on Local Councils to Help 'Solve Housing Crisis'. *Independent*, 3 October.

Mumford, G. (2018) Grenfell Activists Use Three Billboards Protest to Highlight Lack of Progress. *Guardian*, 15 February.

O'Brien, T. (2018) *Tackling the Housing Crisis: With Publicly Owned Construction Direct Labour Organisations*. Self-published.

Osborne, H. (2015) Private Landlords Gain £26.7 Billion from UK Taxpayer, Says Campaign Group. *Guardian*, 9 February.

Pawson, H. and Mullins, D. (2010) *After Council Housing: Britain's New Social Landlords*. Basingstoke: Palgrave Macmillan.

Robbins, G. (2012) Send Newham Families to Stoke? It Reflects a Broken Housing Policy. *Guardian*, 25 April.

Robbins, G. (2017a) *There's No Place: The American Housing Crisis and What it Means for the UK*. London: Red Roof.

Robbins, G. (2017b) Grenfell must be a Turning Point in Housing – for Staff and Residents. *Guardian*, 7 August.

Shelter (2017) 'We've got no Home': The Experiences of Homeless Children in Emergency Accommodation. London: Shelter.

Shelter (2018) *Building for our Future: A Vision for Social Housing*. London: Shelter.

Sherwood, H. (2018) Windsor Council Leader Calls for Removal of Homeless Before Royal Wedding. *Guardian*, 3 January.

Socialist Party (2017) One Housing's Rent Hikes are met with Tenants Resistance. 28 March.

Stone, J. (2016) The Tories Vote Down Law Requiring Landlords Make their Homes Fit for Human Habitation. *Independent*, 13 January.

Watts, J. (2017) Grenfell Tower Fire: Theresa May Snubs Jeremy Corbyn's Call to Seize Private Properties to House High-Rise Victims. *Independent*, 19 June.

Weaver, M. (2018) Housing Association Merger will Lead to Social Cleansing, Warn Tenants'. *Guardian*, 11 January.

Williams, J. (2017) Salford Council to Borrow £25m to Make Cladding Safe in Wake of Grenfell Tower Tragedy. *Manchester Evening News*, 16 August 2017.

7

The Disabled People's Movement in the Age of Austerity

Rights, Resistance and Reclamation

Bob Williams-Findlay

INTRODUCTION

This chapter provides an account of the last four decades of activism by the disabled people's movement.[1] It will be argued that the recent erosion of the rights of disabled people under austerity has deeper roots than austerity-related policy shifts since 2010. The roots will be traced back to the accommodation by some sections of the disability charity sector, and others, to a legalistic conception of enhanced individual rights which culminated in the Disability Discrimination Act 1995. This heralded the ascendancy, from the late 1990s to 2010, of an unholy alliance between traditional disability charities and market facing disabled people's organisations (DPOs). This alliance promoted a limited and individualised disability rights agenda, easily incorporated within a wider neoliberal restructuring of social care. However, towards the end of the New Labour period, elements within the radical wing of the disabled people's movement began to regroup in the face of increasingly punitive social policies. This culminated in the formation of Disabled People Against Cuts (DPAC), when the Coalition government came to power in 2010. This grassroots network was led by disabled people and articulated a clear break from what I refer to as 'Janus politics'. DPAC's focus went beyond an exclusive orientation to individual legal rights and advocated campaigning on wider material issues impacting disabled people. This approach has had some notable successes and has placed disabled activists at the heart of the anti-austerity movement in the UK. However, the chapter will conclude by arguing for the need for continued work to reclaim and further develop a radical historical materialist social model of disability to inform more fundamentally transformative political interventions to challenge the neoliberal market agenda.

HISTORICAL ROOTS OF THE EROSION OF DISABLED PEOPLE'S RIGHTS

The current situation for disabled people in the United Kingdom is without doubt one of the most oppressive in living memory. Many disabled people are experiencing cuts to services and social security benefits which they rely upon to live independent lives, while others fear that reductions in services will ultimately lead to them being forced back into residential care. The root cause of many disabled people's negative experiences over the last decade has been the government's punitive reform agenda – the dismantling of the welfare state (in terms of both benefits and services) and the promotion of self-reliance. This framework was initially developed by the Blair Labour government, then built upon by the Conservative-Liberal Democrat coalition and subsequent Cameron and May governments during the 'age of austerity' (Grover and Soldatic, 2012). This attack is however not essentially about reducing the welfare bill. Its primary focus is on making disabled people 'disappear' and therefore no longer a concern for the state. This is achieved by redefining the categories imposed upon people with chronic ill health or permanent impairments to constrain the numbers falling within these. Consequently, while we have witnessed a decrease in the extent to which disabled people are presented as 'dependent', 'deserving' or 'vulnerable', we have also seen a growing number of disabled people denied access to a raft of welfare services including social care and independent living because of changing and more circumscribed criteria. In particular, this more restricted 'disability category' is related to the neoliberal policy focus on labour market engagement and welfare-to-work (Grover and Soldatic, 2012: 226).

The Movement for Disability Rights and Anti-Discrimination Legislation (1970s to mid-1990s)

However, any discussion of the erosion of the rights of disabled people requires historical context. A central argument of this chapter is that there has been a narrowing of interpretations of 'the rights agenda', which has distorted how both disability politics and 'disability rights' have come to be understood.

Since the 1970s, disabled people have challenged the way social and welfare policies have maintained their inequality, with demands for full human and civil rights articulated in a number of ways. In the 1980s, disabled activists, through Disabled People's International, began to press the United Nations for a Convention on the Rights of Disabled People. The aim of the Convention was not to grant disabled people new rights but instead offer a framework, based upon the social model of disability, which would enable governments to apply human rights in meaningful ways for disabled people. By the social model, we mean the barriers imposed on top of people's impairments by the organisation of society through which they are disadvantaged and excluded. By the 1990s, the achievement of anti-discrimination legislation (ADL) had become the primary focus for the disabled people's movement in the UK.

In order to promote the development of ADL, the British Council of Disabled People (BCODP), the leading umbrella organisation at that time, commissioned research into discrimination against disabled people. The outcome was a comprehensive and authoritative study, *Disabled People in Britain and Discrimination* by disabled researcher Colin Barnes, which became a useful campaigning tool as well as a symbol for empowerment and inspiration (Barnes, 1991; Evans, 1996). The case made in the report did not focus primarily on individual but rather on institutional forms of discrimination (Barnes, 1991: 2). Speaking of the research he undertook for the book, Barnes explained: 'It shows that the negative attitudes and discriminatory practices, which effectively deny basic human rights to disabled people, are ingrained in the core institutions of our society' (Barnes, 1991).

In line with this analysis, the disabled people's movement championed the Civil Rights (Disabled Persons) Bill introduced by Roger Berry MP in 1993. The Bill sought to make unjustified discrimination against disabled people illegal. Alongside BCODP's campaign, a 'liberationist' wing of the disabled people's movement, which included groups such as Disability Action Network (DAN), who had a campaigning and direct action-based strategic orientation, also emerged at this time. Evans captures the political atmosphere prevailing between 1992 and 1994 when he writes:

Direct action no doubt heightened the profile for the need for civil rights legislation in the eyes of the general public and did a lot to shake up the politicians' complacency on the issue, but it could never be enough by itself. Without the lobbying of parliament and meetings with politicians putting forward constructive arguments based on available evidence of discrimination and seeking their support the cause would have been lost. ... At the same time, disabled experts and lawyers have to work alongside other lawyers and politicians in writing up the Bill. This work was co-ordinated by a group called Rights Now ... which was a coalition of about 50 disability organisations and charities who were formed to work together to help bring about ADL.

(Evans, 1996)

However, while the combination of both lobbying and direct action generated significant momentum for ADL, the movement was ultimately to be disappointed. The legislation that was subsequently passed, the Disability Discrimination Act (DDA) 1995, failed in both its design and enactment to address wider civil rights issues and the institutionalised oppression of disabled people. Moreover, divergent political perspectives within the various strands of this disability coalition began to become more visible at this point, with differences between the charity and liberationist elements of the disability lobby becoming increasingly marked. At the very moment that inadequate legal rights were being established for disabled people, the liberationist wing of the movement was outflanked by the big disability charities and then marginalised by the Conservative government (and later by subsequent New Labour administrations).

Following the defeat of the Civil Rights Bill and the introduction of the DDA 1995, internal division engulfed the disabled people's movement. Senior disabled activists accused BCODP of 'putting all its eggs in one basket' by having legislation as its prime focus and failing to cultivate grassroots structures and organisations. Furthermore, any hope of repealing and replacing the DDA with the Civil Rights Bill when New Labour came to power in 1997 were quickly dashed. Membership of the Task Force established by Labour to review the DDA was hand-picked with the more radical elements of the disabled people's movement excluded. As a result of these developments, the disabled people's movement went into decline after 1995.

The Birth of Janus Politics (mid-1990s to 2010)

Having noted the decline of radical sections of the disabled people's movement, in this section I will describe the ascendancy of neoliberal market-facing developments in the disability field from the mid-1990s until 2010. The nature of 'Janus politics' will be outlined, in particular the promotion of an individualised rights agenda and the dilution of more radical policy demands as they were accommodated within a neoliberal service provider framework.

In the period after the DDA became law, some elements within the disabled people's movement began to move away from, or reinterpret, liberatory politics. As activists such as Finkelstein, Oliver and Barnes noted, wider liberatory political alliances between disabled people and other groups such as LGBT movements failed to emerge, while other social divisions continued to widen (Oliver and Barnes, 2006). One outcome of this was a process of dilution and marginalisation of more radical demands as they were incorporated into the political mainstream (Williams-Findlay, 2015a). From the mid-1990s, there was a growing tendency among charities, public and voluntary sector bodies to adopt the language and concepts of the disabled people's movement. For example, many local authorities and charities committed to supporting the social model or implementing forms of 'independent living'. At this time, some disabled people's organisations (DPOs) and individuals moved away from radical interpretations of social oppression and began to open a dialogue with traditional disability charities such as Scope and Leonard Cheshire, of which the movement had previously been highly critical. Leading figures associated with the disabled people's movement such as Tom Shakespeare argued these charities and bodies had changed and were now 'using the right language' (sic). However, critics continued to point to the double standards employed by such organisations – speaking about 'disability rights' one minute and promoting 'disability as a personal tragedy' the next or implementing ideas such as the social model in superficial ways, emptied of their original meaning. These differing positions were early indicators of a fundamental split emerging within the disabled people's movement between the liberationist wing who stood for radical political action to promote wider social change and a revisionist tendency focused on a much narrower conception of protecting and extending 'disability rights'.

However, although it was relatively straightforward to demarcate the two strategies, differentiating the social forces making up these two camps was not always as simple. The background to the depoliticisation of the disability field and 'disability rights' approach was an increasing role for the market in social care and welfare policy under Conservative and then New Labour governments. In this new marketised environment, the mainstream disability charities and some market-facing DPOs adopted a Janus-faced approach in which the legacy, terminology and meanings of earlier struggles, and the social model itself, were transformed in order to align with the requirements of a service provider model and corporate business approach to disability within a broadly capitalist framework.

As I argued earlier: it is necessary to question the extent to which direct payments, independent living and now personalisation have employed the dynamic meaning of disability as understood by Finkelstein and UPIAS (Union of the Physical Impaired Against Segregation).[2] What we have seen is a set of accommodating 'interpretations' employed by more liberal and reformist disabled activists and sections of the disabled community, which in turn has allowed service providers and the state to exploit this situation (Williams-Findlay, 2015a: 83).

Consequently, the struggle for 'disability rights' has been reduced to little more than a question of consumer rights – a business opportunity for the delivery of social inclusion within the social care marketplace – with key concepts from the Disabled People's Movement shorn of their original radical intent and transformed into status quo policy mechanisms (Williams-Findlay, 2015a).

The Radical Materialist Social Model and Critique of Rights

How then should the legacy of this campaign for 'rights' be appraised? The logic of the individual legal 'rights' approach described above is that by modifying existing societal structures and dismantling barriers to increase equality of opportunity disabled people will be 'freed' (Hasler, 2003). This is based on the belief that entitlements to formal rights within the existing competitive market society would automatically confer 'social acceptance' or lead to an end to social oppression. However, Russell and Malhotra explain the problem with this mode of thinking: 'Liberal anti-discrimination laws cannot end systemic unemployment and individual rights cannot override the economic structure. Neither the market nor civil rights laws can end the exclusion of disabled people from the labour force' (Russell and Malhotra, 2002).

This individualised market-oriented approach has spawned the idealistic notion of a 'barrier free' society, which has been used to undermine the original social model (Shakespeare, 2006; Williams-Findlay, 2015b). Consequently, this 'approach diverts attention from the mode of production and the concrete social relations that produce the disabling barriers, exclusion and inequalities facing disabled persons' (Russell and Malhotra, 2002: 212).

A more satisfactory theoretical alternative is the radical materialist social approach developed by Finkelstein (2001: 4). In this framework, the social oppression experienced by disabled people is seen as an integral part of the way society is organised, structured into the very fabric of capitalism. For the radical social model, therefore, it is only by overthrowing and transforming current social arrangements that people with impairments will be able to realize liberation along with humanity as a whole (Finkelstein, 2001).

The emergence of the tensions described above in the disabled people's movement is to some degree underpinned by these differing theoretical assumptions about the nature of oppression. Moreover, people with impairments come from a diverse array of socio-economic and political backgrounds. As a consequence of these differentiated class locations, disability activists may have divergent interpretations of disability and social oppression resulting in conflicting views regarding what campaigns for 'rights' could achieve. Rather than seeing disabled people as automatically having a 'shared agenda', these distinct perspectives can be linked to the different social strata from which activists are drawn. The perspectives of the leadership of the corporate 'disability lobby' indeed seem to have been shaped by their economic interests within the structures of the social care marketplace.

RESISTANCE IN THE AGE OF AUSTERITY

In this section, however, it will be argued that Disabled People Against Cuts (DPAC) articulated a clear break from the 'Janus politics' introduced during the New Labour era, and instead sought to build a diverse and broad-based social movement from below involving alliances with other groups such as psychiatric survivors and the labour and trade union movement. This section describes DPAC's grassroots self-organisation approach, repertoires of protest and alliances with wider social movements.

While the New Labour era can be characterised mainly by the shift towards an individualised and market-friendly approach to social inclusion, a turn towards greater conditionality in the welfare system became visible in its latter stages. However, the economic downturn and financial crisis of 2008 was soon followed by the election of the Coalition government in 2010, which hastened the transition to a more draconian relationship between the State and its citizens, which swept away the last vestiges of post-war Social Democratic welfarist policy (Williams-Findlay, 2011: 773–4). The savage nature of the Coalition's austerity measures left large sections of the community of disabled people in a state of shock, living in fear of losing their services and homes. Welfare 'reform' has become emblematic of the punitive nature of the State's policies towards disabled people since the Coalition government. Disabled people have described the process of applying for benefits as increasingly difficult and distressing with fear of being plunged into poverty and there have been numerous reports of deaths and suicides linked to unsuccessful assessments. Meanwhile, disabled women and survivors of sexual violence and abuse are being failed by benefits system processes which re-ignite trauma through the additional requirements placed on rape survivors to access tax credits, or a failure to recognise the extra barriers faced by disabled women subjected to domestic abuse (Thewliss, 2017; Ryan, 2012). And this is all amplified by a political and media rhetoric about skivers and scroungers that has left disabled people feeling stigmatised, vulnerable and isolated (Inclusion Scotland, 2015).

The Birth of DPAC and the Return to Grassroots Self-Organisation

Against this backdrop, a small group of disabled activists came together to organise the 'Disabled People Protest', part of a wider demonstration outside the Conservative Party's annual conference in October 2010. At the time of this protest, it was clear that the Disabled People's Movement had been in decline for a decade and it was a radical core group of disabled activists who had the insight to use this opportunity to pick up the pieces. Using the march as a catalyst, these activists founded DPAC.

From the outset, DPAC presented a radical framework for establishing a new resistance movement. As I argued at the time:

> The co-founders of DPAC believe disabled people are currently disabled by systems, structures and services which either fail to meet or inadequately meet our needs, but the reduction in public expenditure at national and local levels, the removal of services, the destruction of jobs and communities will only result in greater hardship and social exclusion. We oppose all cuts because they impact upon disabled and nondisabled people's ability to bring about a just and inclusive society.
>
> (Williams-Findlay, 2011: 777)

This position statement signalled a political dynamic that was without precedent in the traditional disabled people's movement; a disabled people's network not simply wishing to raise disability politics within the mainstream, but with a clear agenda to work alongside and within wider progressive campaigns, such as UK Uncut, to influence and shape the mainstream resistance agenda. This orientation recognised the life or death nature of the struggle faced by disabled people and the necessity to force disability issues onto the public agenda through collective political engagement. This utilised new social media to good effect while also challenging the disabling barriers that currently exist in traditional trade union and labour politics. Ultimately, for DPAC, the social model of disability was viewed as a cornerstone in the creation of a new and more diverse anti-capitalist movement (Williams-Findlay, 2011: 778).

However, in the first half of the decade, the charity-led campaigns such as the Disability Benefits Consortium's '*Hardest Hit*' continued to pander to traditional frameworks characterising benefit claimants and service users as 'vulnerable'. Organisations such Disability Rights UK, United Kingdom Disabled People's Council, Scope, and Leonard Cheshire Disability – all key players in fostering 'Janus politics' – failed to challenge the patronising notion of 'those in most need', and thereby colluded with the old reworked 'deserving and undeserving' agenda being peddled by the mass media and the State (Jolly, 2012). In sharp contrast to these 'protect the vulnerable' charity-driven narratives, DPAC and its Scottish sister organisation, the Black Triangle, developed an alternative narrative based on the premise that the 'new ways society is being organised further disables those of us with impairments'. DPAC saw a clear division between those engaged in 'Janus politics' through compromising with the oppressive State and the emerging resistance movement of disabled people and their allies. This demarcation underpinned the strategy for building a new resistance movement.[3]

Because of these concerns, and alongside the focus on anti-capitalist movement building, DPAC recognised the need to retain the idea of self-organisation of disabled activists at its core. To this end, it sought to attract disabled activists who supported the earlier Direct Action Network (DAN)[4] as well as disabled people involved in labour and trade union activity, including those who had not had much previous engagement with the disabled people's movement. Another important step in the rebuilding of grassroots networks was a conference in autumn 2012 arising from Jenny Morris's Joseph Rowntree Foundation (JRF) paper 'Rethinking Disability Policy', which explored the lessons for the disabled people's movement in the current period (Morris, 2011). The conference inspired the formation of the *Reclaiming Our Futures Alliance* (ROFA), which aimed to keep the activist spirit of the disabled people's movement alive. ROFA argued for prioritising the development of an effective grassroots UK-wide network of DPOs to create a united voice against the onslaught on disabled people's rights by the coalition Government. This was considered especially important in light of the lack of any functioning national DPO and the close collaboration between disability charities, some traditional disabled people's organisations and the government.[5]

DPAC's Organisational Form

DPAC has grown from a small group of activists into a network of groups and individuals that are overseen by a national steering group. It is estimated that there are over 30 local groups with a reported formal membership of 1,500, with 2,500 members of the Facebook page and 4,500 followers on Twitter.[6] While the steering group has overall responsibility for the national direction of the network, local groups are autonomous provided they follow a common constitution.

Since DPAC's formation a number of campaigns have been organised centrally, for instance national days of action targeting specific issues such as the introduction of Universal Credit. DPAC also organises a 'week of action' each year involving national, regional and local events.

Geographically based DPAC groups can also plan and lead their own local activities and initiatives.

DPAC's Repertoires of Action and Protest

During this period, DPAC's resistance has largely centred around highlighting the detrimental impact of national and local government's policies on disabled people's lives and providing evidence to show how these have undermined rights of this group according to the United Nations Convention on the Rights of Disabled People. These interventions have had three main dimensions:

a. Providing disabled people and the wider public with information about disability rights and the impact of government cuts;

b. Campaigning with other communities which are also affected by cuts such as trade unions and other grassroots groups so as to pool resources for solidarity while maintaining a distinct voice for disabled people; and

c. Working within all sections of the disabled community to advocate self-determination, establish a collective voice and promote user-led services and participation in decision-making processes: 'nothing about us, without us'.

From its inception, DPAC has developed a broad repertoire of forms of political action. These include:

- Organising campaigns,
- Engaging in protests,
- Mounting legal challenges,
- Attempting to influence the mass media,
- Making full use of social media as a campaigning tool, and
- Employing research and academic platforms to both oppose and promote policy changes.

DPAC's reputation for organising forms of direct action involving high-profile civil disobedience has earned it a great deal of admiration. The first to capture the public's attention and imagination was in January

2012, when DPAC along with UK Uncut, blockaded Regent Street in London to protest against welfare cuts (Walker, 2012). This was followed three months later by a further blockade of Trafalgar Square (Taylor and Van Steenbergen, 2012). In April 2013, there was a novel and widely reported shift in these civil disobedience tactics, with DPAC staging the 'mock eviction' of the then Work and Pensions Secretary of State Iain Duncan Smith from his home to draw attention to the homelessness and displacement caused by so-called 'bedroom tax' cuts.[7]

Duncan Smith's Department had long been a focal point for protestors' ire because of its draconian welfare reform programme, leading to many protests at assessment centres run by private sector multinational outsourcing firms such as Atos, Maximus and Capita, to whom DWP assessments are contracted.[8] However, in September 2016, DPAC's attention turned to Westminster itself with protesters closing down Westminster Bridge for several hours to bring attention to deaths arising from welfare 'reforms'. Ten months later, they returned to occupy the Lobby of Parliament, blocking the main entrance to the Commons Chamber with protestors chanting, 'no justice, no peace'. This was not DPAC's first political action within the Houses of Parliament. On 24 June 2015, activists, angered by the ending of The Independent Living Fund for disabled people, had to be prevented from accessing the House of Commons Chamber during Prime Minister's Questions. This action was repeated in 2017 and received national television coverage (Kentish and Cowburn, 2017).

DPAC actively built solidarity and links with other parts of the labour, trade union and anti-austerity movement, but it was also willing to challenge disabled people's marginalisation by this movement's leadership when necessary. Throughout this period, disabled people's organisations have been critical of how both the labour and trade union movements have responded to their access needs and efforts to be included in political events. Indeed, a very different type of street blockade in October 2012 marked a watershed moment when DPAC became increasingly frustrated with the patronising attitude and uncooperative response from the Trade Union Congress (TUC), organisers of the main anti-austerity protest march that year. Consequently, on the day of the march, DPAC held an impromptu protest to make it known that disabled people were not prepared to be pushed around or ignored.[9] Similarly, DPAC and many disabled people's organisations were openly critical of the People's Assembly umbrella anti-austerity campaign by whom they felt both marginalised and left responsible for getting disability politics on its agenda.[10]

Many of DPAC's actions are inventive, moving beyond traditional activist repertoires. For instance, 2016 saw DPAC activists invade the Tate Modern in London and produce an unscheduled 'pop up gallery' of artworks by disabled people. The art highlighted the experiences of disabled people dealing with the welfare system.[11] Another outlet for this activist creativity is the annual 'week of action' noted above. For instance, in the London Olympics year of 2012, DPAC hosted a week-long 'Atos Games', which highlighted the hypocrisy of the sponsorship of the Paralympic Games by Atos, one of the companies employed to carry out the highly controversial Work Capability Assessments for the DWP. Events included a spoof 'Paralympic award ceremony', and the delivery of a coffin to Atos offices. On the closing day of the Paralympic Games, a demonstration took place outside Atos's head office before moving to the DWP offices at Caxton Hall, where protestors chained themselves to the main entrance prompting significant police violence.[12]

Another crucial area of work in the resistance struggle has been the production of research to highlight the harm to disabled people caused by recent policy agendas. From the beginning, DPAC has placed a high value on both academic and non-academic research, drawing upon work by disabled researchers such as Mo Stewart among many others (Stewart, 2016). DPAC's own research and reports include four papers and ten reports on a variety of subjects, including a substantial focus on DPAC's evidence to the United Nations (UN) Committee of Inquiry into the application of Convention on the Rights of Persons with Disabilities (CRPD).[13] The value of this became apparent when, in August 2017, the UN Committee publicly declared that UK government was guilty of 'grave or systematic violations of the rights of persons with disabilities' and that UK Government austerity cuts have led to a 'human catastrophe' (Pring, 2017).

DPAC and Alliances with Wider Social Movements

Rather than campaigning on behalf of disabled people in isolation from other groups, DPAC situates the struggles of disabled people within the mainstream of political and social activism. I have already noted above how DPAC has fought for recognition of its important role as part of the wider anti-austerity movement. DPAC has also campaigned alongside and in solidarity with other groups affected by issues such as welfare reform, for instance with mental health survivor activists, including Mad Pride and Mental Health Resistance Network.[14] Similarly, in April 2018, DPAC joined with Single Mothers' Self-Defence and disabled women's activist group WinVisible to call upon the government to #StopAnd-Scrap the rollout of new benefit Universal Credit.

Furthermore, DPAC has also built links with the labour and trade union movement. For instance, DPAC West Midlands coordinated a series of 'No More "Cinderella" Role – We Will Go To The Ball!' themed actions in 2016 to protest against the Conservative Party Conference in Birmingham. A key demand of the protest was to support action by rail workers in the National Union of Rail, Maritime and Transport Workers (RMT) to keep guards on trains in the face of cuts to this role that would reduce the accessibility of train travel for disabled passengers.[15]

A third area of alliance building has been with green movements. In August 2013, for example, DPAC members took part in the 'Reclaim the Power' anti-fracking protest camp at Balcombe, West Sussex. The reasoning behind this was to engage with training in non-violent Direct action, and to emphasise the needs of disabled people for clean, affordable and sustainable energy.

DPAC's civil disobedience actions are original, creative, colourful, eye-catching and considered inspirational to both disabled and non-disabled people alike, making disabled people's issues within the anti-austerity movement highly visible and hard to ignore. Moreover, DPAC has collated, contributed to and supported user-led as well as more traditional research to provide evidence to underpin its political campaigning. In summary, DPAC has built alliances with a range of social and trade union activists as part of building a broad-based movement for social justice.

THE STRUGGLE TO RECLAIM OUR POLITICS AND OUR LIVES

In this section, I will argue there have been two stages in the development of DPAC's strategic orientation. It was noted above that, from 2010 to 2013, DPAC's main focus was challenging austerity politics. However, since the Reclaiming Our Futures Manifesto of 2013, I will contend that alongside anti-austerity work there has been an additional focus on 'reclaiming disability pride' in the face of the government's denigrating scrounger rhetoric.

In 2013, DPAC marched on parliament to launch the *UK Disabled People's Manifesto: Reclaiming Our Futures*. The Manifesto, which was developed by UK disabled people and their organisations, set out to strengthen campaigning and lobbying by disabled people and their allies by mapping the central principles, demands and commitments necessary for a rebirth of the movement. This marked a watershed moment because this alliance of disabled people's organisations represented an embryonic relaunch of a social movement combining *both* anti-austerity resistance *and* core elements of the earlier disabled people's movement championing disability politics and rights. In particular, the manifesto called on the Westminster and devolved governments to recognise and act on their responsibilities to fully and effectively implement the United Nations Convention on the Rights of Persons with Disabilities (UNCRPD) across the UK (Equal Lives, 2013).

It could be argued this brought together two 'paths'. One was the continuation of an established trajectory of protest against the harmful impacts of austerity measures on disabled people. The other path related to the desire of disabled activists to struggle to reclaim our politics and our lives, including celebration of the value, pride and self-determination of disabled people. Both disability culture and disability pride seek to challenge 'the mistaken assumption that there are naturally negative social consequences of having an impairment and make clear the civilising vision for all citizens that we are creating in our disability culture' (Finkelstein, 1996). Thus, 'disability pride' combines a challenge to the way disabled people are subjected to negative societal appraisals and treatment and the promotion of lifestyles and cultural production controlled by disabled people.

One of the symbols of this re-alignment with 'disability pride' was the organising of a 'Disability, Art and Protest' exhibition at this time focusing on art by disabled people in a cultural and political context. The background to this desire and necessity to restate and strengthen disability pride was the 'scrounger rhetoric' that has emanated from and dominated mainstream media and political discourse in recent years. Consequently, part of that year's 'week of action' was also a protest outside the BBC to highlight the biased representation of disabled people. This was further strengthened by campaigning alongside and in solidarity with other groups affected by these processes such as mental health survivor activists, including Mad Pride and Mental Health Resistance Network.[16]

Alongside this renewed emphasis on pride was a return to a focus on issues synonymous with earlier phases of the disabled people's movement such as accessible transport. An example of this was the Torch Relay protest organised by Transport for All in 2013 to highlight a lack of accessibility on the new Crossrail trainline currently under construction in London – this marked a lack of progress one year on from the London Paralympics (BBC News, 2013).

Reclaiming a Radical Social Materialist Model in the Twenty-First Century

DPAC has made a valuable contribution to challenging the Janus service provider politics that have dominated since the 1990s. DPAC's eclectic approach has the strength of bringing together the old and new disabled people's movement but more work is necessary to reclaim and further develop a radical historical materialist social model to inform these political interventions and challenge the neoliberal market agenda.

The chapter has argued that, with the collusion of market-facing DPOs and charity elements of the disability lobby, the neoliberal 'transformation of meaning' of key concepts such as: 'the social model', 'disability rights' and 'independent living' serves to further embed a market agenda into the policies and practices of state and disability service providers. In effect, the language and concepts of the disabled people's movement have been reworked to sell neoliberal concepts like co-production and personalisation to disabled people rather than strengthen philosophies and principles such as independent living that have been developed through disabled people's self-organisation. In opposition to this agenda, I argue that a renewed historical materialist approach is long overdue (Williams-Findlay, 2015a). The more radical aims of the original social model, as Oliver and Barnes note, were: to be 'consciously engaged in critical evaluation of capitalist society and in the creation of alternative models of social organisation ... as well as trying to reconstruct the world ideologically and to create alternative forms of service provision' (Oliver and Barnes, 2012: 173).

The disabled activists schooled within the British historical materialist social approach believed there was a need to combine fighting for improvements within existing structures while at the same time seeking ways to transform them beyond serving the interests of capital. From this perspective, 'disability rights' means 'self-determination'; the right not to be subjected to discriminatory practice or social exclusion, the right not to be dependent upon charity and the right not to be de-humanised. While the fight for improved legislation may play a role in realizing these rights, ultimately achieving genuine disability rights requires social change and greater respect for the whole of humanity and for the planet we inhabit.

As Finkelstein has noted, it is the competitive market system of capitalism under which we live that ultimately disables us, creating a social prison for disabled people. While campaigning for enhanced rights that create a more humane environment is laudable, in order to realize genuine emancipation, the ultimate aim must be to dismantle the prison itself. This prison exists due to the exploitative economic structure of capitalist society: one which created (and continues to oppress) those categorised as 'disabled'. In this sense, disability emerges from some of the key features of capitalist society such as the emphasis on competition and the distribution of status and wealth where participation in the labour market is a crucial feature. A reclaimed radical social model should constitute a guide to the kind of collective class-based struggles necessary to fundamentally transcend this disabling and competitive system and condition (Finkelstein, 2001).

In summary, reversing the attacks on disabled people and educating our communities around the radical potentials of the disabled people's movement is difficult because of the latter's decline until recently, the lack of resources and the poverty of knowledge of disability politics within disabled people's networks. Small steps have been taken nonetheless. A National Disabled People's Summit was held in November 2017 to bring together Deaf and disabled people from the trade union movement, Deaf and DPOs and grassroots campaigns to explore how we can more effectively coordinate our resistance and organise joint campaigning in identified areas (Graby, 2017). The depth and breadth of the savage attacks by the punitive State has taken its toll on disabled people's morale and capabilities but, as acts of resistance such as the DPAC Day of Action in April 2018 against Universal Credit show, the fight goes on.

CONCLUSION

This chapter has provided an examination of the contemporary sites of struggle for the disabled people's movement, through a lens of historically changing political dynamics. The chapter identified three significant stages in this process. The first was the struggle for civil rights by disabled people up until the 1990s. This was followed, from the 1990s onwards, by the accommodation of sections of the disability lobby to the service sector. This process was underpinned by shifts in the wider political context with the decline during the 1990s of the radical 'liberationist' wing of the disabled people's movement and the rise to prominence of an unholy alliance between charities and some mainstream disabled activists. However, I have argued that the erosion of disabled people's rights under austerity has seen a return to grassroots self-organisation since 2010, best symbolised by DPAC. The chapter has noted the enormous contribution of DPAC to the struggle for the liberation of disabled people. However, it has concluded that 'the social model' and 'disability rights' have been hijacked and transformed by neoliberal social policies. Instead, it will be necessary to reclaim and develop, at a political and ideological level, a more radical social model of disability that can assist the political struggle for fundamental societal transformation to end disabling capitalism.

This chapter is dedicated to the memory of our sister, Debbie Jolly.

NOTES

1. This chapter builds on an analysis first articulated in 2013 by this author and Debbie Jolly (both founding members of Disabled People Against Cuts).
2. UPIAS is the founding organisation of the British disabled people's movement.
3. DPAC was highly critical of the Hardest Hit campaign and refused to participate. This brought some criticism, however, DPAC sought to justify its position. See Disabled People Against the Cuts, Too little, Too Late – The Hardest Hit campaign's Christmas card to Cameron and Clegg, https://dpac.uk.net/2011/12/too-little-too-late-the-hardest-hit-campaigns-christmas-card-to-cameron-and-clegg/ (accessed 20 May 2019).
4. Direct Action Network (DAN) – a UK-wide network of disabled activists, who use non-violent civil disobedience as direct action to fight for equal treatment and full civil and human rights. They are part of the disabled people's movement: campaigning for equality.

5. Reclaiming Our Futures Alliance, www.rofa.org.uk/reclaiming-our-futures-alliance-rofa-terms-of-reference/ (accessed 20 May 2019).
6. Wikipedia, Disabled People Against Cuts, https://en.wikipedia.org/wiki/Disabled_People_Against_Cuts (accessed 20 May 2019).
7. 'Benefits Protests Outside Ian Duncan Smith's Home', ITV News, 13 April 2013.
8. Disabled People Against the Cuts, 28 August 2012, Newcastle Atos Protest, https://dpac.uk.net/tag/atos-protest/.
9. Disability News Services, TUC Protest: Disabled People Play Part in Rally, www.disabilitynewsservice.com/tuc-protest-disabled-people-play-part-in-march-and-rally/ (accessed 1 February 2019).
10. A campaign called Operation Invisible was launched on Facebook: www.facebook.com/groups/906875132730084/about/.
11. Disability News Services, TUC Protest: Disabled People Play Part in Rally.
12. 'Police Scuffles with Disabled Protestors'. ITV News, 31 August 2012.
13. Disabled People Against the Cuts, Research, https://dpac.uk.net/research/ (accessed 20 May 2019).
14. Mad Pride is a global mass movement of the users of mental health services, and their allies, that began in Toronto. As the Mental Health Resistance Network (MHRN) website states:

> MHRN was set up by people who live with mental distress in order to defend ourselves from the assault on us by a cruel government whose only constituents are the super rich and who value everyone else according to how much they serve the interests of this selfish minority,

see Mental Health Resistance Network, http://mentalhealthresistance.org/ (accessed 20 May 2019).
15. Disabled People Against Cuts, DPAC WM Day of Action 2 and 3 October 2016, https://dpac.uk.net/2016/09/protest-at-tory-party-conference-birmingham-2nd-3rd-october/ (accessed 20 May 2019).
16. Mental Health Resistance Network, http://mentalhealthresistance.org/ (accessed 20 May 2019).

REFERENCES

Barnes, C. (1991) *Disabled People in Britain and Discrimination: A Case for Anti-Discrimination Legislation*. London: BCODP/Hurst & Company.
BBC News (2013) Disability Campaigners Torch Relay Protest. 29 August.
Evans, J. (1996) The U.K. Civil Rights Campaign and The Disability Discrimination Act. Speech by ENIL Chairperson, Vienna, 1 and 2 November. Available from: https://disability-studies.leeds.ac.uk/wp-content/uploads/sites/40/library/evans-ADLWIEN.pdf.

Equal Lives (2013) UK Disabled People's Manifesto: Reclaiming Our Futures, 12 September. https://equallives.org.uk/uk-disabled-peoples-reclaiming-futures-manifesto/.

Finkelstein, V. (1996) We Want to Re-Model the World. *DAIL Magazine*, 4 October. https://disability-studies.leeds.ac.uk/wp-content/uploads/sites/40/library/finkelstein-Remodel-the-world.pdf.

Finkelstein, V. (2001) The Social Model of Disability Repossessed. Paper presented at the Manchester Coalition of Disabled People, 1 December.

Graby, S. (2017) Steve Graby: Disability Researcher, National Disabled People's Summit: My Report, 8 November. https://sgraby.wordpress.com/2017/11/08/national-disabled-peoples-summit-my-report/.

Grover, C. and Soldatic, K. (2012) Neoliberal Restructuring, Disabled People and Social (In)Security in Australia and Britain. *Scandinavian Journal of Disability Research*, 15(3): 216–32.

Hasler, F. (2003) Philosophy of Independent Living. www.independentliving.org/docs6/hasler2003.html (accessed 20 May 2019).

Inclusion Scotland (2015) Welfare Reform Impacts on Disabled People – The Facts, 9 July. http://inclusionscotland.org/welfare-reform-impacts-on-disabled-people-the-facts/#.

Jolly, D. (2012) Disabled People Against the Cuts, A Tale of Two Models: Disabled People vs Unum, Atos, Government and Disability Charities. www.dpac.uk.net/2012/04/a-tale-of-two-models-disabled-people-vs-unum-atos-government-and-disability-charities-debbie-jolly/ (accessed 20 May 2019).

Kentish, B. and Cowburn, A. (2017) Demonstrators in Wheelchairs Blockade House of Commons in Protest at Disability Cuts. *Independent*, 19 July.

Morris, J. (2011) *Rethinking Disability Policy Viewpoint*. York: Joseph Rowntree Foundation.

Oliver, M. and Barnes, C. (2006) Disability Politics and the Disability Movement in Britain: Where Did It All Go Wrong?. June. https://disability-studies.leeds.ac.uk/wp-content/uploads/sites/40/library/Barnes-Coalition-disability-politics-paper.pdf (accessed 20 May 2019).

Oliver, M. and Barnes, C. (2012) *The New Politics of Disablement*. London: Palgrave Macmillan.

Pring, J. (2017) 'UK Faces UN Examination'. *Disability News Service*, 24 August, www.disabilitynewsservice.com/uk-faces-un-examination-government-cuts-caused-human-catastrophe/.

Russell, M. and Malhotra, R. (2002) Capitalism and Disability. *Socialist Register*, 38: 211–18.

Ryan, F. (2012) Domestic Violence and Disabled Women: An Abuse of Power. *Guardian*, 19 November.

Shakespeare, T. (2006) *Disability Rights and Wrongs*. Oxford: Routledge.

Stewart, M. (2016) *Cash Not Care: The Planned Demolition of the UK Welfare State*. London: New Generation Publishing.

Taylor, M. and Van Steenbergen, M. (2012) Disability Rights Protesters Bring Trafalgar Square Traffic to a Standstill. *Guardian*, 18 April.

Thewliss, A. (2017) No Woman Should Have to Prove They Were Raped to Claim Child Benefit. What is This Madness? *Telegraph*, 6 April.

Walker, P. (2012) Disability Campaigners Stage Central London Protest Against Welfare Reforms. *Guardian*, 28 January.

Williams-Findlay, R. (2011) Lifting the Lid on Disabled People Against Cuts. *Disability & Society*, 26(6): 773–8.

Williams-Findlay, B. (2015a) Personalisation and Self-Determination: The Same Difference? *Critical and Radical Social Work*, 3(1): 67–87.

Williams-Findlay, B. (2015b) UK Disability History Month, The Falsification of History: The Twenty Year Burial of the Civil Rights Bill. 8 November.

8

The 'Hostile Environment' for Immigrants: The Windrush Scandal and Resistance

Ken Olende

INTRODUCTION

This chapter will open with a brief historical account of British immigration policy and its adaptation in the context of austerity over the past decade. In particular, it will examine the emergence of the 'hostile environment' policy during this period and the Windrush scandal that arose from it. The chapter will then provide an overview of resistance to this agenda, beginning with wider coalitions such as Stand Up To Racism before turning to activism in the healthcare sector by campaigns such as Docs Not Cops. Campaigning interventions such as these have led to a government retreat on Windrush and indicate the possibilities for such challenges to derail the wider 'hostile environment' project. The chapter will conclude with observations on the potential for greater trade union involvement in challenging this agenda to strengthen, deepen and generalise the resistance visible in these campaigns.

CAPITALISM, MIGRATION AND RACISM

Migration is a natural phenomenon driven by the universal human need to seek and secure better conditions of life. However, the development of capitalism led to greater shifts in a shorter period of time than any previous system of social organisation. The need of this new system for labour led to the creation of a class of people who had nothing to sell but their labour power. As Britain developed into the first industrial nation, its factories tended to employ workers expropriated from agricultural land within a local area and forced to migrate to urban centres in search of work. People drawn from further afield, largely Ireland, supplemented this supply. This flow reached a peak as Irish refugees fled famine in the 1850s. Furthermore, the wealth that paid for the development of British industry and the raw cotton that fed the early mills came from the forced migration of millions of Africans through the Atlantic slave trade (Blackburn, 1997). Accompanying these differentiated processes of migration at the birth and early stages of capitalism was the emergence of the ideology of racism. This set of ideas sought to square a funda-mental contradiction between the ideas of greater equality developed by Enlightenment thinkers of the time and the iniquities of the Atlantic slave trade that generated the massive profits that would kick start indus-trial capitalism. However, ideas of racial superiority did not remain static and were modified first as slavery was abolished to fit with a colonial ideology of empire and national identity, and then again as the needs of an expanding nineteenth-century capitalism for workers led to the mass migration of Europeans to the USA and Irish labour to Victorian Britain. At this stage, the creation and maintenance of racial divisions between workers functioned to weaken an internally diverse working class and buttress the power of capitalists (for more details, see Olende, 2013).

Unrestricted immigration was the norm in nineteenth-century Europe and America. However, the state combined reliance on migrant workers with 'divide and rule' that set immigrants against more established workers in order to distract from problems inherent within the system such as recession. Such scapegoating indelibly associated immigration with race and was linked with a growth in the use of borders to control migration in times of crisis. For instance, the first legislation limiting access to Britain was the Aliens Act of 1905, which aimed to prevent access by Jewish refugees from Eastern Europe. This legal intervention both drew upon and exacerbated the widespread anti-Semitism of the time. More comprehensive legislation – and passports – were introduced at the time of the First World War in 1914. During the Great Depression, the idea of free trade was minimised and in its place the importance of imperial economic blocks emphasised. With this shift, the idea of people of the Empire being subjects of one Commonwealth gained currency (Holmes, 1988: 94). This was made explicit in the British Nationality Act 1948, which stated that British Empire subjects could live anywhere across the Empire. After the Second World War, the British economy was desperately short of labour and the act helped encourage immigration from British colonies including those in the Caribbean.

The Windrush Generation and Post-War Immigration Policy

The first arrivals from Jamaica came on the former troop ship *Empire Windrush* that brought 417 migrants in 1948 (Panayi, 2010: 60). Just weeks after the Windrush arrived, Labour prime minister Clement Attlee replied to a group of Labour MPs, who opposed non-white immigration saying, 'It is traditional that British subjects ... should be freely admissible to the United Kingdom. That tradition is not ... to be lightly discarded, particularly at a time when we are importing foreign labour in large numbers' (Gupta, 2002: 204). Both Labour and Conservative governments maintained a consensus that immigration was in the 'national interest' throughout the boom years of the 1950s, and actively encouraged such migration.

However, by the 1960s, this notion of shared 'national' interests between the state, British workers and subjects of Empire came under severe strain. One by one, the countries that made up the British Empire gained independence. These new countries issued their own passports and their residents became Commonwealth citizens rather than British subjects. Though by the end of the 1950s people in Britain, on average, had never had it so good economically, the country was experiencing severe relative economic decline. The Conservative government started listening to those on its right wing, who now claimed post-imperial Britain was 'a small island'. These MPs encouraged people to see immigrants rather than government policy as undercutting wages and responsible for substandard housing. In 1962, the government introduced the Commonwealth Immigrants Act, the first controls to be imposed on people from the Commonwealth – in this case, work permits. Labour leader Hugh Gaitskell opposed this, describing it as 'cruel and brutal anti-colour legislation' Sharma, 2016: 9).

However, when it came to office in 1964, Labour did not repeal the legislation, and it was a Labour government that introduced further restrictions after the panic over the arrival of British passport-holding Asians from Kenya in a way bluntly based on race (Holmes, 1988: 267). This subsequent reform, the Commonwealth Immigrants Act 1968, signalled a new political consensus based on the notion that, while immigration might be of economic benefit, it was to be regarded as a social problem. This policy direction crystallised in the Immigration Act 1971, which finally removed the right of Commonwealth citizens to settle in Britain and introduced a comprehensive framework of immigration control for all nationalities. This legislation would later cause specific problems for many individuals of the 'Windrush Generation'. Anyone settled before January 1973, when the new act came into force, whether adult or child who had travelled on their parent's passport had full residency rights, and needed no documentation to prove them (Holmes, 1988: 267). However, once the new legislation was in place, it was possible for officials to suggest that such people had in fact arrived after the law changed. When the 'hostile environment' was introduced in 2012, it institutionalised such suspicion and had catastrophic consequences, a point to which I will return later.

IMMIGRATION POLICY AND AUSTERITY

Britain's preparations to join the European Economic Community, the European Union (EU)'s predecessor, in 1973 had been an important factor in the decision to restrict Commonwealth immigration. However, the introduction of free movement within the EU led to a significant increase in net migration in the early years of the twenty-first century – with most people coming from countries that acceded in 2004. Consequently, the Conservative-led Coalition government elected in 2010 signalled a renewed assault on the rights of migrants. Then prime minister David Cameron had come to the leadership of the Conservative Party as a moderniser, who complained in his victory speech that too many party MPs were 'white men' and promised, 'no more grumbling about modern Britain' (Cameron, 2006). However, he changed his position with the onset of the recession that followed the Financial Crisis of 2007–2008. As his government's austerity measures began to cut into the standard of living of the majority of the population, Cameron shifted to a much more critical stance on immigration and multiculturalism, stating in a 2011 speech: 'Frankly, we need a lot less of the passive tolerance of recent years and a much more active, muscular liberalism' (Cameron, 2006).

This repositioning reflected wider attempts to construct a new anti-immigration consensus. By 2014, shifts in what was acceptable in the establishment discussion of immigration appeared in a number of contexts. BBC political editor Nick Robinson produced a programme, *The Truth About Immigration*, which presented large-scale immigration as a cause of social problems. Two books, *Britain's Dream: Successes and Failures of Post-War Immigration* by David Goodhart (2013) and *Exodus: How Migration Is Changing Our World* by Paul Collier (2013) staked out similar territory. These interventions were, in Italian Marxist Antonio Gramsci's terms, attempts to rework an establishment 'common sense' by modifying the previous view that managed immigration had created a 'multicultural' melting pot which been enormously successful for Britain. Before the election of Jeremy Corbyn as party leader in 2015, this project to create a new consensus also received a degree of support from the 'Blue Labour' group within the Labour Party, which has articulated concern for the so-called 'white working class'.[1]

A genuine sense of grievance among workers in Britain at deteriorating services and conditions is visible in the context of swingeing austerity cuts. Strains on public services such as schools and the NHS have affected popular attitudes to immigration. For example, in 2010, the three English councils with the highest rates of immigration – Peterborough, Slough and Boston – complained that they could not cope with the strain on resources. Many papers treated this story as a problem caused by immigration. However, as the *Financial Times* noted: 'All three councils were at pains to point out that they welcomed immigration, which had boosted local economies ... But they said it was essential that their grants from central government reflected their true population' (Boxell, 2010). The key issue was a failure by central government to properly adjust funding to these councils to reflect their changing population demographic rather than immigration per se.

A HOSTILE ENVIRONMENT FOR IMMIGRANTS

Against this background of austerity, the Coalition government launched its new policy on immigration. As elsewhere in Europe, the fear of refugees, tinged with Islamophobia, remained dominant. However, this new policy agenda had a particular focus on illegal immigration. This had the political advantage for the government of raising the spectre of immigration without directly attacking the vast majority of migrants from the EU, who were legally working in Britain. The genesis of this policy was a 2010 Conservative manifesto target to reduce net migration from hundreds to tens of thousands per annum. The main architect of the policy was Theresa May, at that time Home Secretary. She explained in a 2012 interview that, 'the aim is to create here in Britain a really hostile environment for illegal migration' (Kirkup and Winnett, 2012). This initiative directly linked the twin agendas of criminalising migrants and the detention of 'failed' asylum seekers. This became a flagship policy for the government and the campaign was launched soon after in 2013 with the deployment of the notorious 'Go home or face arrest' billboard vans to various parts of London (BBC, 2013).

The 'hostile environment' was then more formally implemented via the Immigration Acts of 2014 and 2016. These new legal frameworks were intended to broaden the remit of immigration control and draw a far wider section of society into the role of de facto border guards, with 'measures seeking to restrict illegal immigrants from renting property in the UK, driving, having bank accounts and accessing benefits and free healthcare' (House of Lords, 2018: 1). Polly Mackenzie, at the time Director of Policy to the Liberal Democrat Deputy Prime Minister Nick Clegg, explained that: 'Theresa May's mission was to make it systematically difficult to get by without papers. At no point was evidence presented on the scale or importance of abuse in order to justify this agenda' (Mackenzie, 2018). The policy had several aims including a widening of the social control of illegal migrants, increasing the public and media focus on immigration and also heightening the pressure on and disciplining of legal immigrants. The latter was evidenced by May's comment in 2013 that this legislation will, 'ensure that legal immigrants make a proper contribution to our key public services' (Home Office, 2013: 2).

The Windrush Scandal

The Windrush scandal emerged as a direct result of these 'hostile environment' policies. The scandal first came to light in 2014 when it emerged that thousands of British residents, mainly of Caribbean origin, who had legally come to the UK before 1973, were being treated as illegal immigrants and losing their jobs or being deemed ineligible for benefits or health care. At least 164 of these people were wrongly detained or even removed from the UK. Campaigners raised concerns with the Home Office but were met with denial (Webber and Edmond-Pettitt, 2018). They turned to the media for support and in a series of articles from late

2017 Amelia Gentleman of the *Guardian* publically revealed what had been happening. Typical were cases such as that of Paulette Wilson who:

> [H]ad been in Britain for 50 years when she received a letter informing her that she was an illegal immigrant and was going to be removed and sent back to Jamaica, the country she left when she was 10 and has never visited since … It was only a last-minute intervention from her MP and a local charity that prevented a forced removal.
>
> (Gentleman, 2017)

As noted above, many of the Windrush generation had initially travelled to the UK on their parents' passports. Until 1962, there had been no control on the immigration of Commonwealth citizens, 'at entry such persons were given a cursory examination and their passports were not stamped, and there were no restrictions on the time they could remain in the UK or on their employment' (Mennell, 2018: 1). The current crisis results from later changes in legislation, in particular the removal from the 2014 Act of a key clause from the 1999 Immigration and Asylum Act, which had ensured that long-term resident Commonwealth citizens would not be deported. Further, 'the government did not announce the removal of this clause, nor did it consult on the potential ramifications' (Taylor, 2018).

The treatment meted out to Windrush victims was a direct result of these formal legal provisions and informal state practices implemented as part of the 'hostile environment' agenda. The latter included the decision to restrict the use of Home Office records to establish the legal status of those affected, or in some cases to actively dispose of such information, while at the same time placing the onus on the individual to access and supply their own evidence. An example of this was the controversial Home Office decision in 2010 to destroy its archive of landing cards from the 1950s and 1960s. These recorded the names of migrants, dates of arrival and in some cases the name of the ship. This information later became vital for people who were now expected to prove when they had arrived in the UK. A former Home Office employee disclosed that when 'hostile environment' policies led to increasing numbers of people requesting this information, the reply would be a standard letter stating, 'we have searched our records, we can find no trace of you in our files' (Gentleman, 2018c). Furthermore, as a BBC investigation explained,

'[The Home Office] has not been using central tax and pension records, which could prove someone has been working, to support people's applications' (BBC, 2018). It relies on people having their own documentation, including payslips and bank statements. Few people retain such information over an extended period. But even when all the required information had been kept, the Home Office did not necessarily accept it. So Windrush scandal victims such as Renford McIntyre gathered together paperwork showing 35 years of national insurance contributions but this was still considered insufficient (Gentleman, 2018a). The fundamental disregard for the rights of this group of citizens, the unrealistic expectations to provide evidence and the way it targeted elderly people, make it appear what it is, an unusually vindictive policy. However, the logic of this agenda needs to be understood through the lens of the colonial and post-colonial legacy of institutional racism, violence and exclusion of migrants by the British state.

The underlying intention of the 'hostile environment' policy was both to isolate migrants and also to deflect blame and anger at the pressures on health or education provision onto them and away from ongoing austerity measures. However, this strategy backfired causing damage to the government when the policy became associated with the unfolding Windrush scandal. The experiences of Windrush victims exposed the hypocrisy and contradictions of immigration policy based on the notion that 'good' immigrants who integrate are treated fairly. A significant proportion of the British public was shocked by the treatment of the Windrush victims who they saw as law-abiding citizens who had been unfairly victimised. As a result, the policy came under severe scrutiny and faced opposition from pro-migrant groups and anti-racist campaigners. This resistance will be examined further below.

EVERYDAY BORDERS

I noted earlier the way in which the Immigration Acts 2014 and 2016 require workers in a variety of roles to take on extra responsibilities as *de facto* border guards required to check immigration status in order to establish entitlements. The effects of these 'everyday borders' (Yuval-Davis, Wemyss and Cassidy, 2017) are already visible in areas of service provision such as housing and health care, and these will be outlined further below, but I will begin with consideration of their implications and harmful impacts on migrant workers' access to employment. The 'hostile environment' has had a variety of impacts within the labour market setting. The first is an increasing tendency to incorrectly reject job applicants with legal rights to live and work in Britain. One recent study highlighted a shop owner who turned away jobseekers who had the correct papers – in one case an Italian identity card – because he was unaware that it was one of a range of acceptable documents (Yuval-Davis *et al.*, 2017: 10). Another related issue is the deterrent effect on businesses that are likely to employ migrants, often those run by people from minority backgrounds, who may be concerned about the effect on their trade of immigration raids. Consequently, the effect of these policies has been 'to sensitize people to who carries a British passport and who does not. In this way citizenship status became a salient feature of ascribed identity' (Yuval-Davis *et al.*, 2017: 15). Another effect has been to increase the extent and burden of documentary proof demanded of job applicants by employers who, because 'they are untrained ... choose the easy route of demanding official papers which are not required' (Yuval-Davis *et al.*, 2017: 12). A further concern relates to the additional burdens and surveillance to which migrant employees are increasingly subjected. In an example from higher education, 'Sussex University warned international staff that the institution was due to be audited by UK Borders and Immigration and they needed to report times when they were absent from their offices between 9am and 5pm, Monday to Friday' (Swain, 2018). These examples highlight the escalating discrimination, monitoring and victimisation experienced by migrant workers.

The draconian effects of 'everyday borders' are also visible in service sectors such as housing. Recent government figures show that:

> 42 percent of landlords were now less likely to rent to someone without a British passport [which includes 17 per cent of British nationals]; 49 percent of landlords were less likely to rent to someone with limited leave to remain; [and] 44 percent of landlords would only rent to those with documents familiar to them.
>
> (Bolt, 2018: 45)

In each of these cases, life becomes harder for people seeking to access housing, even when they are eligible or in possession of the correct documents, because of apparent or potential presumptions by the untrained people who are managing their access.

Another policy area in which the government's 'hostile environment' reforms have been particularly damaging is health care. While the NHS has rightly been celebrated for providing free health care to all, migrants are now charged for many NHS services. The 2014 Immigration Act introduced an NHS surcharge of £200 a year – £150 for students – for many categories of people visiting the UK for more than six months (Glennerster and Hodson, 2018). This was enforced from 2015 and the amount was doubled in January 2019.[2] Under these rules, even people who are living in Britain with 'indefinite leave to remain' can be charged for secondary care, which is not 'urgent'. Many migrants are charged for treatment at 150 per cent of the cost to the NHS (Department of Health and Social Care, 2018: 112). As a result of these charges, health workers now face escalating pressures to check patient entitlements, and this is exacerbated by legislation that deems the NHS Trusts liable for any such costs owed by a patient but not recovered (Department of Health and Social Care, 2018: 9). Moreover, the application of incredibly complex immigration law within the health service is likely to result in reduced patient access at a time when NHS staff have less time to engage with and advocate on behalf of patients (Pluto Press Podcast, 2019).

In line with these reforms, the NHS has begun to introduce compulsory identity verification at some hospitals before patients are able to access treatment, in spite of a history in Britain of popular rejection of internal identity checks (Porter and Kirkup, 2010). For those found by these checks to be ineligible for free care, upfront charging has been introduced with non-urgent treatment withheld until payment is received (Forster, 2017). For people subject to immigration control, an outstanding NHS debt of £500 or more is now regarded as a basis for the refusal of a right to remain, which could potentially lead to removal from the UK (Hiam, Steele and McKee, 2018). A related development is the data-sharing agreement between the Home Office and NHS Digital and the Department of Health for address and contact details from patients' medical records. This has led to a vast increase in the amount of information being collected and passed to the Home Office, with patients and health workers frequently unaware of this use of personal data at the point it is collected (Liberty, 2018). As a result of this practice, 'the Home Office made 8,127 requests for patient details in the first eleven months of 2016, which led to 5,854 people being traced by immigration enforcement' (Travis, 2017). Everyday borders are also increasingly visible to patients when they register for health care. In 2015, the government introduced a 'Migrant and Visitor NHS Cost Recovery Programme'. As part of this, people registering as new patients at GP practices are asked to provide proof of identity. Concerns have been raised that:

> this is slightly misleading because, although a practice may ask to see identification, the inability to present identification is not, contrary to NHS CFS [Counter Fraud Services]'s implication, reasonable grounds for a practice to deny registration. The law does not currently preclude anyone in England from free access to primary healthcare.
>
> (Glennerster and Hodson, 2018)

The article notes that despite this many GP practice websites say that documents, sometimes including a passport are necessary. Such demands for proof of identity do not only affect immigrants or people who look like they might be immigrants even though such people are likely to be hardest hit. They will also affect anyone who does not have a passport, driving licence or proof of address.

Finally, these reforms also have the effect of reinforcing gender inequality. For instance, as Catherine Pellegrino of Maternity Action has argued, 'current regulations mean the NHS Trust must report women's unpaid debts for maternity care to the Home Office after only two months of non-payment. Since 2017, NHS Trusts must also flag the patient records of those who are chargeable' (Pellegrino, 2018). This leads to high levels of stress and anxiety for affected women who may be worried about being reported to the Home Office or having future immigration applications refused. This has implications for their own health and the outcomes of the pregnancy, while also increasing risks for those women who find themselves in particularly insecure or abusive situations (Pellegrino, 2018).

RESISTANCE

As the discussions above have highlighted, the development of immigration law and policy have always been entangled with wider economic and social interests. However, it is also important to recognise the extent to which immigration policy agendas are simultaneously shaped by levels of resistance to the scapegoating of migrants. This final section of the chapter will consider some of the different kinds of resistance that have emerged to challenge the UK government's 'hostile environment' approach and assess their effectiveness at various levels.

The initial focus of campaigners responding to the 'hostile environment' and Windrush scandal was on casework, lobbying and awareness-raising. With large volumes of legislation passed each year, the impact of which is not always immediately clear beyond specialist communities, approaches that enable understanding and awareness of policy consequences can be an important starting point. In the case of the Windrush scandal, the government eventually retreated because growing public awareness of what the policy actually entailed made it increasingly unpopular. The public's understanding grew out of casework by charities and MPs, which was later publicised by the *Guardian* newspaper. Following the newspaper exposés, a wider range of charities, NGOs, trade unions and other activist organisations began to raise their voices against the policy. Many trade union branches passed policy to protect their members and challenge dismissals resulting from 'hostile environment' policies (Camden Unison, 2018). Nonetheless, at this point, resistance was largely focused on mobilising organisations such as charities and trade unions as well as MPs to support and lobby the Home Office around individual cases.[3]

The casework approach is vital, but does not necessarily lead to a widening of resistance to the policy or political clarity on the philosophy underpinning it. The latter aspects were strengthened through the interventions from the campaign group Stand Up To Racism (SUTR), a united front of trade unionists, Labour Party members and other socialists formed in 2013 to oppose racism against migrants. SUTR put the issues in a wider political context, arguing that the Windrush scandal was closely linked to the refugee crisis and other examples of institutionalised racism.[4] Furthermore, it called for broader resistance to this policy agenda. In April 2018, SUTR organised a demonstration in Brixton, south London, an area still identified with the Windrush generation. On the day of the protest, Labour's Shadow Home Secretary, Diane Abbott, addressed a packed and angry rally on Windrush Square. Abbott argued that then Home Secretary, 'Amber Rudd and [her predecessor] Theresa May shouldn't be apologising. You know why? Because you only apologise when you make a mistake – they knew what they were doing' (Bowden and Wearmouth, 2018). The SUTR protest and related activities began to shift the predominant strategy beyond an individual casework approach, showing that Windrush was an issue on which the government could be forced to retreat. In early May, SUTR called a further protest in Whitehall, central London, demanding the end of the 'hostile environment' deportation policy. The demonstrations built links and solidarity between, among others, Windrush generation campaigners and women who had spent months detained in Yarl's Wood immigration removal centre (Slawson, 2018). Similar demonstrations were held in Birmingham and Coventry. These protests were part of a process that changed public perception of the issue from one largely concerned with the treatment of a particular group of immigrants to a critique of immigration policy itself.

In April 2018, escalating protests over the Windrush scandal by anti-racist campaigners and victims forced Conservative Home Secretary Amber Rudd to resign. In an apology, she said, 'I am concerned that the Home Office has become too concerned with policy and strategy and sometimes loses sight of the individual' (Gentleman, 2018b). This gives the impression that these events were an unfortunate accident, when in fact they were an entirely predictable consequence of the racist design of the 'hostile environment' agenda. By July 2018, her replacement, Sajid Javid, had announced government plans to halt the policy for anyone over 30 to prevent more people being 'wrongly and erroneously impacted' by [these] measures, and it was rebranded as the 'compliant environment' (Bulman, 2018). This demonstrated how vulnerable this policy agenda is to concerted campaigning, and represented an important victory for campaigners. However, in practice, most legal aspects of this policy remained in place. Consequently, the necessity to build a wider political response and a broad-based movement to challenge this agenda continued.

#PatientsNotPassports

One arena in which resistance to the 'hostile environment' has grown is the NHS. The campaign group Docs Not Cops (DNC) offers a good case study of practical activism to challenge this agenda, in particular, the #PatientsNotPassports campaign. DNC is composed of NHS professionals who are opposed to the imposition of immigration enforcement roles on NHS services and staff by the Home Office under the 'hostile environment' agenda (Kmietowicz, 2018). DNC instead promotes the principle that health should be a right and not a privilege, arguing that, 'as NHS staff, we are trained to care for all who need it, not turn people away. We are campaigning to restore the values that built our NHS of universal care and compassion.'[5] In this way, DNC and other similar activist networks of healthcare workers have utilised, 'the potential spaces and ambiguities between moral standards – such as those that underpin human rights laws or professional codes of conduct … and government policies and legislation' as the basis for building resistance to the 'hostile environment' within the NHS (Potter, 2018).

DNC combines online and social media work, for instance, disseminating information to counter the government's 'hostile environment' narrative on immigration as well as its wider hospital reform programme, with lobbying and protests. A recent article by a nurse and DNC activist illustrates the campaign's counter-narrative. The article challenges the contention that health tourism is a major issue for the NHS by utilising the government's own figures to demonstrate that it:

accounts for only 0.3 percent of the NHS budget, a figure that pales in comparison to the £2 billion [about 2 per cent] a year spent servicing PFI debt … [I]ndependent research found that of 8,900 patients asked to show ID [for immigration purposes] only 50 were found to be chargeable.

(Skinner, 2018)

DNC has organised a number of demonstrations involving NHS doctors and nurses to highlight their rejection of immigration enforcement roles. These include a protest outside St Thomas' hospital in September 2017, at the Department of Health in April 2018, and a lobby of Westminster in May 2018 that utilised a van parodying the government's 'go home or face arrest' mobile billboards. DNC have also linked up with and organised alongside patient and migrant activist groups (Kmietowicz, 2018; Montemayor, 2017).

The struggle against 'hostile environment' ID checks and upfront charging in hospitals has since been taken up by a wider range of health campaigners. In September 2018, a protest was called by NELSON, an umbrella group coordinating NHS anti-cuts and anti-privatisation campaigns (such as Keep Our NHS Public) across east London. The lobby took place at Barts Health Trust's Annual General Meeting (AGM) at Mile End Hospital. The Barts Trust runs five hospitals in east London and is the largest NHS Trust in England. As part of a government pilot scheme the Trust required patients to complete pre-attendance forms, which included passport, employer contact, visa and travel insurance details, to test their entitlement to free treatment. Barts was making about 100 enquiries a week to the Home Office in relation to these forms to establish patients' immigration status. A Freedom of Information request from the campaign revealed that the Trust had not been monitoring the ethnicity of those asked to fill out forms and had no equalities statistics for the new policy (Richardson, 2018). The protest at Barts AGM was attended by dozens of health workers, with campaigners setting up mock immigration checkpoints outside the meeting. One campaigner noted, 'the hospital keeps saying that no one is refused treatment. But the point is that it's not free treatment – patients are whacked with a massive bill at the end' (Tengely-Evans, 2018). This highlights that anti-privatisation campaigners' objections to these new procedures are both due to their specific discriminatory impacts but also because the reforms undermine the NHS as a free and universal service. The Barts protest was successful in forcing the Trust to remove threatening posters that were generating intimidation and fear and discouraging people from seeking health care, to halt a pilot project which required women seeking maternity care in Newham to show their passports, and to review the non-health-related information patients were asked by the Trust to provide (Day, 2018).

Another issue of concern for health workers and campaigners has been the practice of significantly increased data sharing (of demographic information such as last known address) between the NHS and Home Office under the 'hostile environment'. In response, a number of organisations including Doctors of the World and Migrants Rights Network have lobbied the government highlighting the risks of migrants being deterred from accessing health care due to the threat of deportation. This joint campaign was successful and the government eventually acceded to demands to limit data sharing to instances of conviction for serious crime (Potter, 2018).

I have described the contribution of a casework and lobbying approach to challenge the 'hostile environment', and highlighted the leading role played by NGOs and grassroots campaigns in organising protest and making important ideological interventions to reframe the debate, in the process achieving some small but significant victories. However, while celebrating these, I will conclude by making the case for the need for greater trade union involvement in resisting this policy agenda. Trade unions have an essential role in working-class organisation in spite of the limits often imposed on rank-and-file struggles by trade union bureaucracies and this remains true even as the labour market in Britain has shifted from largely manual into white-collar employment. Moreover, the trade union movement played an important role in anti-racist struggles during the 1970s, leading to the increasing involvement of minority ethnic groups through the 1980s and 1990s. Consequently, as Virdee notes, a 'durable current of anti-racism ... [has become] institutionalised in key sectors of the organised labour movement and the public sector' (2014: 161). This has been visible in the national motions to oppose the 'hostile environment' passed by trade unions such as Unite, as well as local casework in support of members affected (Unite, 2013: 12). However, by limiting their intervention to a casework approach, trade unions have not utilised their potential to draw on the kind of inspiring and dynamic resistance seen in campaigns such as Docs Not Cops and to generalise this to much wider layers of workers in the NHS and beyond. Indeed, many activists within Docs Not Cops are active trade unionists who were involved in the junior doctors strike of 2016 (Lewis, 2016). This highlights the possibilities for broadening and deepening the struggle against the 'hostile environment' that combining the militancy of campaigners with the institutional power of trade unions might offer. The successful campaigns against the outsourcing of cleaners in a number of London universities provide an example of how such coalitions might look. At the School of Oriental and African Studies (SOAS), an 11-year campaign to end outsourcing built links and solidarity between the largely migrant cleaners with lecturers, support staff and students. As the branch secretary of the Unison trade union at SOAS argued,

> if anyone is unsure what low paid, largely migrant workers can achieve when their union supports them, look no further than our inspirational fight at SOAS ... As has been the case throughout the history of the British labour movement, migrant workers can lead and inspire our class.

> (Nicoll, 2017)

CONCLUSION

In this chapter, I have briefly described the historic link between immigration policy and racism, before going on to describe its contemporary manifestation in the 'hostile environment' initiative that was first announced in 2012. I then indicated the role of this policy in creating the Windrush scandal that devastated the lives of the many thousands of people of Caribbean heritage, who became caught up in its punitive and discriminatory web. I have contended, from a Marxist perspective that locates racism and immigration policy within the historical development of capitalism and class relations, that this scandal and the contradictory attitude to migrants are not aberrations but illustrate key aspects of the long-term treatment of migrant workers by successive British governments. I then noted the emergence of campaigns such as SUTR and Docs Not Cops to resist this agenda and their successes in challenging a number of elements of the 'hostile environment' agenda. Nonetheless, I have concluded with the argument that, were the trade union movement to move beyond a casework approach and take a leading and militant role in this campaign, this could potentially extend and escalate the struggle in ways that would provide a deeper and more systematic challenge to this policy and at the same time contribute to strengthening and rebuilding the movement itself.

NOTES

1. In 2011, Blue Labour argued, 'Increased flexibility across borders has brought huge benefits to urban, liberal middle classes … But for those who are less educated … it has often meant an erosion of jobs, wages and autonomy' Davis (2011: 25). This is a return to the fallacy identified initially by Marx. There are no separate black, white or Chinese working classes – the working class contains them all and is weakened if it is divided.
2. NHS Employers, 8 January 2019, Immigration health surcharge increased to £400 per year.
3. GMB North West, 1 May 2018, Peter Watson, long-term GMB member, tells us about his experience after he was caught up in the Windrush Scandal, https://tinyurl.com/y9knyhf6.
4. I declare an interest here. I am a supporter of Stand Up To Racism and edited *Unity*, the magazine it produces jointly with Unite Against Fascism, through 2016.
5. About Docs Not Cops, www.docsnotcops.co.uk/about (accessed 20 May 2019).

REFERENCES

BBC (2013) Eleven Immigrants Left UK After Seeing 'Go Home' Van Adverts. 31 October.

BBC (2018) Windrush: How do You Prove You've Been Living in the UK? 18 April.

Blackburn, R. (1997) *The Making of New World Slavery*. London: Verso.

Bolt, D. (2018) An Inspection of the 'Right to Rent' Scheme. Independent Chief Inspector of Borders and Immigration, March.

Bowden, G. and Wearmouth, R. (2018) Windrush Campaigners Vow to Get Justice as May Backs 'Appropriate' Compensation. *Huffington Post*, 20 April.

Boxell, J. (2010) Immigration Pushes Councils to Limit. *Financial Times*, 15 February.

Bulman, M. (2018) Government Halts 'Hostile Environment' Immigration Policy After Windrush Scandal. *Independent*, 17 July.

Camden Unison (2018) The Windrush Generation and a Hostile Environment. 24 April. https://tinyurl.com/ycd5flm3.

Cameron, D. (2006) David Cameron's Victory Speech: Full Text. *Guardian*, 6 December.

Collier, P. (2013) *Exodus: How Migration Is Changing Our World*. Oxford: Oxford University Press.

Davis, R. (2011) *Tangled Up in Blue*. London: Short.

Day, T. (2018) Hospitals Should not be Hostile. *Waltham Forest Echo*, 14 October.

Department of Health and Social Care (2018) Guidance on Implementing the Overseas Visitor Charging Regulations. Department of Health and Social Care. London: Crown.

Forster, K. (2017) Patients at 20 NHS Hospitals Forced to Show Passports and ID in 'Health Tourism' Crackdown. *Independent*, 17 January.

Gentleman, A. (2017) 'I Can't Eat or Sleep': The Woman Threatened with Deportation After 50 Years in Britain. *Guardian*, 28 November.

Gentleman, A. (2018a) The Children of Windrush: 'I'm Here Legally, But They're Asking Me to Prove I'm British'. *Guardian*, 15 April.

Gentleman, A. (2018b) Amber Rudd 'Sorry' for Appalling Treatment of Windrush-Era Citizens. *Guardian*, 16 April.

Gentleman, A. (2018c) Home Office Destroyed Windrush Landing Cards, Says Ex-Staffer. *Guardian*, 17 April.

Glennerster, R. and Hodson, N. (2018) Access to Primary Care in a 'Hostile Environment'. *Journal of Medical Ethics Blog*, 11 September.

Goodhart, D. (2013) *Britain's Dream: Successes and Failures of Post-War Immigration*. London: Atlantic Books.

Gupta, P.S. (2002) *Power, Politics and the People*. Bath: Anthem.

Hiam, L., Steele, S. and McKee, M. (2018) Creating a 'Hostile Environment for Migrants': The British Government's Use of Health Service Data to restrict

Immigration is a Very Bad Idea. *Health Economics, Policy and Law*, 13(2): 107–17.

Holmes, C. (1988). *John Bull's Island: Immigration and British Society 1871–1971*. London: Macmillan.

Home Office (2013) Tackling Illegal Immigration in Privately Rented Accommodation: The Government's Response to the Consultation. 10 October.

House of Lords (2018) Impact of 'Hostile Environment' Policy. House of Lords Library Briefing, 11 June.

Kirkup, J. and Winnett, R. (2012) Theresa May Interview: 'We're Going to Give Illegal Migrants a Really Hostile Reception'. *Telegraph*, 25 May.

Kmietowicz, Z. (2018) Doctors Protest Against 'Hostile Environment' Immigration Policy Spreading to NHS. *BMJ*, 361: k1953.

Lewis, S. (2016) 'Docs Not Cops' Migrant Solidarity at the Heart of Healthcare Fightback. *Uneven Earth*, 17 March. http://unevenearth.org/2016/03/docs-not-cops/.

Liberty (2018) *A Guide to The Hostile Environment*. London: Liberty.

Mackenzie, P. (2018) @pollymackenzie Twitter, 17 April.

Mennell, B. (2018) UK Immigration Law Affecting Commonwealth Citizens who Migrated to the United Kingdom Before 1973. *Passportia*, 19 April. https://tinyurl.com/ycbw8zes (accessed 20 May 2019).

Montemayor, C. (2017) Patients Not Passports Action. Migrants Organise, 5 April. www.migrantsorganise.org/?p=26424 (accessed 20 May 2019).

Nicoll, S. (2017) Low Paid University Workers Provide a Lesson for the Whole Labour Movement. *Socialist Worker*, 9 August.

Olende, K. (2013) The Roots of Racism. In B. Richardson (ed.), *Say it Loud!: Marxism and the Fight Against Racism*. London: Bookmarks, 30–73.

Panayi, P. (2010) *An Immigration History of Britain*. Abingdon: Routledge.

Pellegrino, C. (2018) 'NHS Workers Aren't Border Guards – So Why are They Forced to Act Like Them?' *TUC blogs*, 18 September. https://tinyurl.com/yyyyxv9m.

Pluto Press Podcast (2019), Healthcare and the Hostile Environment. Pluto Press: Radicals in Conversation, 25 January, www.plutobooks.com/blog/podcast-healthcare-hostile-environment/.

Porter, A. and Kirkup, J. (2010) ID Card Scheme will be Scrapped with No Refund to Holders. *Telegraph*, 24 May.

Potter, J.L. (2018) Patients Not Passports – No Borders in the NHS! *Justice, Power and Resistance*, 2(2): 417–29.

Richardson, A. (2018) Campaigners Challenge Hospitals Acting as 'Immigration Checkpoints'. *East London and West Sussex Guardian*, 13 September.

Sharma, S. (2016) *Postcolonial Minorities in Britain and France*. Oxford: Oxford University Press.

Skinner, J. (2018) As a Nurse, I'm Not Surprised the Government Warped Facts About NHS Migrant Fraud. *Huffington Post*, 27 November.

Slawson, N. (2018) Diane Abbott Joins Windrush Protest March on Whitehall. *Guardian*, 5 May.

Swain, H. (2018) Hostile Environment: How Risk-Averse Universities Penalise Migrants. *Guardian*, 5 June.

Taylor, D. (2018) UK Removed Legal Protection for Windrush Immigrants in 2014. *Guardian*, 16 April.

Tengely-Evans, T. (2018) East London Health Trust Drops Racist ID Checks After Protest. *Socialist Worker*, 13 September.

Travis, A. (2017) NHS Hands Over Patient Records to Home Office for Immigration Crackdown. *Guardian*, 24 January.

Unite (2013) *Unite Strategy for Equality 2014–2017*. London: Unite.

Virdee, S. (2014) *Racism, Class and the Racialized Outsider*. Basingstoke: Palgrave Macmillan.

Webber, F. and Edmond-Pettitt, A. (2018) *The Embedding of State Hostility: A Background Paper on the Windrush Scandal*. London: Institute of Race Relations.

Yuval-Davis, N., Wemyss, G. and Cassidy, K. (2017) Everyday Bordering, Belonging and the Reorientation of British Immigration Legislation. *Sociology*, 52(2): 228–44.

PART III

SUBVERSIVE KNOWLEDGE AND RESISTANCE:
RECONCEPTUALISING CRIMINALISATION,
PENALITY AND VIOLENCE

9

Resisting the Surveillance State

Deviant Knowledge and Undercover Policing

Raphael Schlembach

INTRODUCTION

In summer 2016, police in Hamburg, Germany, went to remarkable lengths in an effort to 'clean up' two large fly posters (Trautwein, 2017). At five o'clock in the morning, some 30 officers wearing fire-resistant clothing and protective helmets loaded extendable ladders and pots of black paint from their vans. Securing the area around a large, run-down building covered from top to bottom in colourful graffiti, they began painting over the fly-posters. Minutes later, with their mission complete, they left. The offending items had been posted onto the façade of the left-wing cultural and political centre 'Rote Flora' in the lively Schanzen district of the city. The large lettering of the word 'FOUND' resembled that of a police officer recruitment campaign. Above it, the perpetrator had glued four portrait images showing the faces of undercover police officers, together with their names. The four had been outed as police infiltrators in the activist groups that met and socialised in the building.

It is true that invisibility is rarely maintained in such dramatic night-time deployments. More typically, it consists of legal, administrative and intellectual strategies of neutralisation that implicates public authorities in denial and white wash. But the Hamburg example illustrates the lengths to which secrecy is central to the tradecraft of police infiltrators. While the public scrutiny of policing has undoubtedly led to new ways of accountability and democratic oversight, it has also been met with new ways of institutional reputation management. And, as I shall argue in this chapter, criminological knowledge encounters real problems of its own if it aims to increase the visibility of some policing practices.

Even though the title for this chapter is obviously a riff on the 'blue code of silence', which in policing studies jargon describes a homogenous and inward-looking organisational culture, it is not so much a contribution to policing scholarship as expressing an interest in the contentious politics of social movements. But to understand a riff, one has to appreciate the chorus to which it offers a variation. 'Policing by deception' (in this case, the infiltration and manipulation of social movements) is of course a variation on the notion of 'policing by consent', a foundation myth that continues to be the guiding principle of policing in (mainland) Britain. Policing by consent proposes that the relationship between police and the public is one of cooperation and that, in turn, police are accountable to the communities they serve. Yet, accountability and transparency have always been partial at best, and perhaps necessarily so. Intelligence work, specifically when carried out by covert means, is by definition a form of statecraft based on secrecy and deceit.

Using the example of undercover policing, this chapter argues that even though there have been carefully managed moves towards opening up this culture of secrecy, this has happened not so much through increased transparency but rather accelerated co-optation. This is because criminological knowledge, specifically, is tied up in uncomfortable ways with the institutions that control access to the desired data and information. My entry point for this argument is a research project into the political use of undercover policing in England and Wales, which I have been working on since 2015.

Most of the information available about police infiltration has been a closely guarded secret by the British state, but, in 2011, activists and investigative journalists began probing these secrets in a systematic manner. They exposed a number of (former) undercover police officers who had targeted a range of campaign groups for long-term infiltration. We now know that since 1968, specialist policing units were tasked with placing more than 100 infiltrators in political campaigns to gather intelligence and allegedly also to subvert their activism. Beginning with groups who campaigned against the Vietnam War, the police have sent undercover officers into peace, anti-apartheid, socialist, anti-racist, anti-globalisation, environmental, animal rights and far-right organisations. Many of them were small, grassroots campaigns. I refer to it here as the #spycops scandal, after the hashtag that is used for social media discussions of the cases it concerns.

DEVIANT KNOWLEDGE

What strategies are available to expand the sociological or criminological understanding of such policing practices? Picking up some recent discussions of 'activist' or 'alternative' criminology (Belknapp, 2015; Carlen and Ayres França, 2017), the chapter revisits Reece Walters' outline of a 'sociology of criminological knowledge', which casts a critical eye on the production of pragmatic knowledge. Walters' 2003 book *Deviant Knowledge* sets out to examine the politics of criminological research and how the production of knowledge in universities increasingly yields to the pressures of regulation and market governance. The effect has been a silencing of critical perspectives and an overly accommodating relationship between researchers and the institutions that set research priorities. I have a specific interest in the way that research, which exposes uncomfortable truths, can be seen as deviant knowledge. The political policing of social movements is underpinned by secrecy surrounding policies and practices that often evade accountability as cases rarely make it to court. In what follows, I outline how deviant knowledge can play a role in rendering transparent some of those state secrets and what this means for the research relationships between (former) police officers and (independent) researchers.

The crucial issue here is the very understandable desire to produce knowledge that is useful, relevant, practical and instrumental. For some, such a desire results directly from institutional pressures on university-based researchers, a theme that is central to Reece Walters' work on 'deviant knowledge'. Walters describes criminology, specifically, as a field of inquiry dominated by market demands and policy-relevance, unable to elevate critical and 'deviant knowledge' to the same level of importance as the utilitarian pragmatism of public authorities and civil servants.

Famously, Michel Foucault also included criminological texts in his critique of disciplining knowledge:

Have you ever read any criminological texts? They are staggering. And I say this out of astonishment, not aggressiveness, because I fail to comprehend how the discourse of criminology has been able to go on at this level. One has the impression that it is of such utility, is needed so urgently and rendered so vital for the working of the system, that it does not even seek a theoretical justification for itself, or even simply a coherent framework. It is entirely utilitarian.

(Foucault, 1975/1980, cited in Carrabine *et al.*, 2014: 112)

Walters argues for 'knowledges of resistance' as a mode of critique that challenges power and maintains intellectual distance from governmental and market-led knowledge industries. As a starting point, for Walters, this means that 'academics should refuse to participate in contract research where the methods, questions, content and conclusions of the research are framed, determined and even altered by government' (Walters, 2003: 166–7).

While such a position broadly informs my argument, I recognise that these matters are a bit more complicated than that. Academic knowledge does not become deviant or non-instrumental as soon as it becomes independent from state or market influence. In the light of the under-cover policing scandal, what would such knowledges of resistance that Walters speaks of look like? Is it not, in fact, the surveillance state that is engaging in resistance, including resisting against research by outsiders? In this context, deviant knowledge can mean recognising the limitations in accessing official accounts of undercover policing, and of treating with scepticism, if not outright suspicion, the narratives offered by those embedded within covert policing practices themselves.

PUBLIC ORDER POLICING AND POLITICAL PROTEST

Anti-capitalist opposition and police violence have provided a common backdrop to major international summits from Seattle's WTO confer-ence to Hamburg's G20 meeting. This has renewed academic interest in the issue of protest policing in Western democracies. Much of this research is empirical, with observations of police and protester interac-tions in public order situations a favoured method of data collection. There are indications in the literature that the ideals and values of liberal democracies find (flawed and contested) recognition in the styles of protest policing. As Donatella Della Porta and Herbert Reiter wrote in the late 1990s: 'A general trend emerges regarding protest policing styles, which [...] can be defined as "soft", tolerant, selective, legal, preventive, consensual, flexible, and professional' (Della Porta and Reiter, 1998: 6). This general trend is affirmed by much of the research on protest policing in Britain, although it rarely takes into account deceptive and undercover tactics. Take for example the 1994 work by P.A.J. Waddington, *Liberty and Order*, which details his in-depth observation of the Metropolitan Police's Public Order Unit, or riot squad, in the early 1990s. The book length-study is often seen as a leading example of research into protest policing and has given us a memorable lingua franca from the lexicon of a former serving officer, for example, 'dying in a ditch' (Waddington, 1994: 42). The book's publication in 1994 followed the miner's strike in 1984 and the introduction of the 1986 Public Order Act. The Act was seen by critics as an assault on civil liberties and the right to protest, granting the police powers to restrict and ban political assemblies which they deemed to be at risk of violent disorder. Waddington's book sought to assuage such fears. He argued that rather than representing a drift towards an authoritarian state, the new legislation had little impact on police strategy when dealing with protest in the capital. In any case, the practice of public order policing was more influenced by operational and pragmatic concerns, such as wanting to avoid 'on the job' and 'in the job' trouble. Waddington's work is not easily categorised as 'the police's view' – in fact, much of his exposition shows how police discretion and knowledge extend police power far beyond its legal constraints. But his account of protest policing by the Metropolitan Police, even though it extends into the control rooms and back-room negotiations, remains locked into a world of surface relations between protesters (and organisers) and officers (and police commanders).

The possible presence of undercover actors rarely features in such academic observations of protest policing, either empirically or conceptually. Where it is discussed, it often leads to a departure from the idea of policing as a political project and reduces it to crime fighting. As P.A.J. Waddington writes elsewhere about infiltration, it is the policeman's burden to tussle with the moral ambiguity of his profession and to 'perform dreadful deeds for the higher good'; and 'moral ambiguity does not extend only to the use of force for police officers also lie, deceive and cheat for the greater good' (Waddington, 1994: 113). When Waddington describes aspects of policing that are deceptive or manipulative, he considers them to be 'dirty work', a view that is also reflected in Gary

Marx's account of undercover policing as a 'necessary evil' (1988). While Marx's starting point is the infiltration of the protest group he was involved with as a student, Waddington remains unperturbed by the threats to democracy in the wake of the #spycops scandal. In fact, it is the 'dirty work' analysis that prevails even here in a blog post written in 2016 after new guidance on undercover policing was issued by the College of Policing:

> Activist groups present a particularly seductive milieu for promoting identification. They are composed of 'true believers', eager to convince others of the truth that has been revealed to them. Often they feel beleaguered, a sense of threat that binds them closely together. Of course, they fear infiltration, and so any newcomer will need to establish the strength of their commitment, but an undercover agent will need to work especially hard at doing so. In order to accomplish this they must necessarily empathise with activists. They must laugh at the same jokes, regret the same setbacks, and celebrate the same 'victories.' Most of all, they must share the same beliefs. As they do so they might find that the activists 'have a point' and that stereotypes are misleading. It is easy to imagine how, under these circumstances, an undercover officer might form a bond with an attractive member of the group that matures into a sexual relationship. Certainly, rules, procedures and structures could not hope to prevent it.
>
> (Waddington, 2016)

The author of *Liberty and Order* here finds little danger to liberty, only to the operational success of the infiltration and the psychological impact on the undercover officers.

UNDERCOVER POLICING AND POLITICAL PROTEST

By contrast, my argument focuses on the societal impact of intrusive undercover policing, or policing by deception. There is an ongoing and much delayed public inquiry into undercover policing in England and Wales and since it started I have carried out several observations of its preliminary hearings and conducted some 20 interviews with activists who discovered that they had been subject to long-term infiltration by undercover police. Despite having racked up millions in public funding and lasting for years, it is clear that the official inquiry suffers from a number of shortcomings; for example, the restriction of the inquiry's remit to England and Wales only (Schlembach, 2016). Another key issue is that the chairing judge, Lord Mitting, has resolved to grant anonymity to a large majority of former undercover officers. Unless targeted activists are told at least the cover names used in undercover deployments, they have little opportunity to provide evidence to the inquiry, and it is now likely that the scale and extent of political undercover policing will remain unknown.

There are some things that we do know. From the first records in 1968 until 2011, the police have admitted that over 1,000 political campaign groups were monitored by an estimated 170 officers working in the National Public Order Intelligence Unit and its predecessor the Special Demonstration Squad. What marks these units out from others is that they were not tasked with helping convict serious criminals but with providing intelligence for the purpose of public order policing – or we could call it political policing. Police infiltrators were placed in a range of mostly progressive and non-violent campaign groups, whether they were anti-war, Trotskyist, anti-racist, animal rights or environmental. Over the years, the spectre of 'subversives', was gradually replaced by the language of 'domestic extremism' (Schlembach, 2018).

Beyond a few exceptions, the political deployment of undercover officers is an area that policing scholarship has frequently shied away from. This is understandable, as it is a field of inquiry cloaked in secrecy, denial and conspiracy theories. The obstacles for academics are all too obvious: much criminological research into policing is reliant on police–academic research partnerships, or at least on police willingness to offer access to academic researchers. Where the object of analysis is the surveillance state or 'secret' state practices, reliance on such Insider knowledge is necessarily limited. While most academic research has an interest in rendering police practices 'visible' and transparent, the secret state maintains an interest in 'invisibility' and confidentiality.

To illustrate this point further, let me quote a lengthy passage written by Rob Reiner, from his Foreword to a recent edited book titled *Introduction to Policing Research: Taking Lessons from Practice*:

Professor Jennifer Brown, a pioneer of cooperation between police and academic researchers, has usefully distinguished between four possible roles in accessing policing for research. She contrasted the difficulties, ethical or other dilemmas, and opportunities facing what she called: inside insiders, outside insiders, inside outsiders and outside outsiders. Inside insiders were police officers themselves conducting research on policing; outside insiders were former officers who had become academics; inside outsiders were academics employed within police organisations for research; and outside outsiders were academics with no formal connection with the police seeking to research policing.

When I began research on a police force for my PhD nearly half a century ago, the few academics who ventured into this territory were all outside outsiders. In the heyday of students protest and counter-culture deviance there was more than a little mutual hostility and suspicion between the cops and the campuses. [...]

This fascinating and invaluable collection of essays is testimony to the sea change since then. [The authors] all illustrate the intellectual and practical policy payoff of the cooperative and mutually beneficial relationship now established between the police and academe.

(Reiner, 2016: xiii)

Reiner's description may well be a useful narrative of how policing studies has evolved, in Britain, over the past 50 years. But my intention is to complicate the picture a bit more and, in fact, to advocate for a return to the more cautious atmosphere between cops and campus that Reiner describes – if there ever had been one.

This raises methodological and political issues, especially if we consider the voices of Outside Insiders in policing research. One such Outside-Inside voice is that of Robert Lambert, a retired undercover and counter-terrorism officer in London's Metropolitan Police. In recent years, he resigned from academic positions in terrorism studies at the University of St Andrews and criminology at the John Grieve Centre for Policing & Community Safety at London Metropolitan University. His career profile as a police officer and researcher, meticulously pieced together by the Undercover Research Group (http://powerbase.info/index.php/Bob_Lambert), is of particular interest here, not least because Lambert remains one of the most controversial figures at the centre of political undercover policing.

The precise circumstances of the nature of Lambert's role is yet to be revealed. At the time of writing, the Undercover Policing Inquiry website simply provides the cover name 'Bob Robinson', the cipher HN10, and lists his groups of deployment as 'London Greenpeace/Animal Liberal Front' between 1984 and 1989. But activist accounts, information in the public domain and reports seen by investigative journalists suggest a degree of involvement beyond what is implied by these bare facts.

According to the Undercover Research Group, Lambert joined the Metropolitan Police in 1977 and was soon deployed by a unit within Special Branch, the Special Demonstration Squad. In his role as a covert operative, he adopted the identity of Bob Robinson as part of a controversial tactic to assume the names of dead children. The 'real' Bob Robinson had died aged seven of a heart condition.

Lambert was deployed to inform on animal rights activism. His covert role was underpinned by a relationship he struck up with an activist known as 'Jacqui', who was 22 years old – ten years younger than Lambert. Jacqui was unaware that Lambert was a police officer, or the fact that he was married with children, when she became pregnant. Like other officers who targeted political campaigners, Lambert eventually disappeared from Jacqui's life and left her to support their son by herself. Jacqui only found out about Lambert's true identity when she discovered a grainy photograph of him alongside a newspaper article naming him as an undercover officer.

According to other activists involved in the animal rights group, Lambert encouraged the use of direct action, which would ultimately bring them to the attention of the police. They also claim that he co-wrote a leaflet titled 'What is Wrong with McDonalds?', infamous for sparking a libel suit by McDonalds, which resulted in the longest libel trial in English legal history.

In 1993, Lambert became a manager of Special Demonstration Squad operations, apparently ordering intelligence gathering on a number of family justice campaigns and their supporters. Lambert was in charge of undercover officer (and now whistle-blower) Peter Francis, who says that he was tasked with smearing the Stephen Lawrence justice campaign. Lambert eventually retired from the Metropolitan Police in 2006 and was awarded an MBE for his services to policing in 2008.

This is just a rough sketch of Lambert's deployment and his managerial responsibilities. Much of the detail remains hidden from public view, with activists taking responsibility for piecing together a fuller profile. Lubbers (2019) describes how the painstaking work of investigating and profiling former undercover deployments in social movements is crucial for activists whose lives were infiltrated. Working together with the activists concerned, journalists and researchers within and outside of the university have been able to expose a range of 'distasteful police practices', including 'stealing the identities of dead children, and tricking targets into intimate and even sexual relationships with agents – in some cases leading to the birth of children who were subsequently abandoned' (Lubbers, 2019: 225).

Most of what we know about undercover agents placed into political campaigns by the British police has been brought to light by the persistence of activist investigations – perhaps a prime example of deviant knowledge. They helped reveal that the Bob Lambert deployment was just one of many, and while some of it stands out as particularly manipulative and harmful, it is also indicative of the wider policing strategies used to target and disrupt activist groups. Very little information has come from former police officers themselves, even when, as in the case of Lambert, their academic and police work are directly related.

CRITICAL STUDIES IN (COUNTER-)TERRORISM

'Moral ambiguity', as described by P.A.J. Waddington, hardly characterises Robert Lambert's role in Special Branch. In an unprecedented apology and out of court settlement with a number of women who were deceived into long-term manipulative relationships with undercover officers, the Metropolitan Police admitted to human rights violations and abuse of police powers (see Evans, 2015). But what about Lambert's role as an academic? What about the research partnerships he was involved in? Here we have a different 'seductive milieu' (Waddington's words again), in which the former policeman encounters a critical and deliberative environment, in which his knowledge is actively sought out and where he finds recognition for his 'expertise'.

Lambert made his name as a left-leaning academic on the periphery of the Critical Terrorism Studies project. Critical Terrorism Studies was launched as a series of conversations and publications to offer a counter-narrative to the dominant, mainstream understanding of terrorism. At the core of this project is the argument that:

... real partnerships between researchers and counterterrorism police officers are possible, and arguably vital in the name of scholarly endeavour and the deconstruction of problematic hegemonies, *but only when adequate safeguards are placed around any research relationships or that the relationships are alive to the inadequacies of [the] same.*

(Spalek and O'Rawe, 2014)

In an article published in the project's journal, *Critical Studies on Terrorism, after* the stories surrounding the political undercover units had come to light, Basia Spalek and Mary O'Rawe offer their perspective on the undercover operations that involved the infiltration of social justice and environmental activist communities.

Spalek and O'Rawe make two important disclaimers: first, that there is no accepted definition of terrorism, and therefore counter-terrorism; and second, that the policing field is steeped in the unique difficulty of research access with senior police managers acting as gatekeepers. It is, in their words, a field of research 'geared to keeping outsiders guessing and firmly out of the inside track' (Spalek and O'Rawe, 2014: 152). Keeping these disclaimers in mind, it is highly surprising then that they insist on referring to the deployments of Special Branch undercover officers in a range of political groups as 'counter-terrorism work', or that they would come to the conclusion that the 'missing voices' in existing research are those of (former) undercover officers themselves.

Certainly, knowledge of undercover protest policing is hindered by a number of 'strategies of denial' and cultural practices aimed at maintaining invisibility within undercover units. Or as Spalek and O'Rawe put it: '... it is important for researchers to understand that working within the counterterrorism field involves degrees and shades of risk in the service of trust-building, sensitivity and the empowerment of communities' (2014: 150).

The possible gains from applying the lens of *Critical Terrorism Studies* to the infiltration of protest groups in recent times is therefore appealing. As police work continues to confuse political campaigning with domestic extremism and conflates civil disobedience with terrorism gathers apace, we may also see further efforts to approach police infiltration of protest groups through the lens of terrorism prevention. However, I fundamentally reject its framing as belonging to the field of counter-terrorism – critical or not. Instead, I find that in its efforts to learn from policing failures and to improve current practice, analysts risk conflating the non-violent direct action repertoires of political protest groups with terrorism.

This is true even where police operations are treated with critical scepticism. For example, Spalek and O'Rawe do not question the fact that counter-terrorist activity involves the infiltration of protest groups, although they concede that 'having sexual relationships, and indeed, on occasion, children, with women while undercover and of potentially working to entrap vulnerable individuals into planning terrorist acts', raises issues of 'trust, credibility [and] legitimacy' (2014: 151).

Spalek and O'Rawe cherish the possibility that academic researchers can benefit from working relationships with former counter-terror and undercover police officers. It is clear that the perspectives of former undercover officers can contribute to understanding of 'police knowledge', that is, the perceptions by police of the protest groups they are deployed to infiltrate, often revealing the persistence of stereotypes and exaggeration. But I contend that the evidence of undercover police hiding their true identity from British courts and juries, their refusal to answer questions regarding sexual infiltration practices, and the Metropolitan Police's stance of 'neither confirming, nor denying' the existence of undercover police severely questions and possibly invalidates the information gathered from closer working relationships, and that the research community's insistence on bringing former police officers into research projects is of detriment to critical knowledge.

This is not to suggest that the information received from activists is not also selective, incomplete or misleading. However, considering the narratives told by activists gives us an angle from which to consider the actual harm caused by infiltration. Groups that have sprung up following the #spycops scandal, such as the Undercover Research Group, Police Spies Out of Lives, or the Campaign against Police Surveillance, are examples of collaborations between the affected political activists and there have been arguments that bottom-up, activist-led research should be fundamental in complementing or (in the absence of any progress of official inquiries) upstaging top-down attempts at fact-finding (Lubbers, 2015). Together, they offer an important corrective to much of the protest policing literature that too rarely considers the views of protesters.

The reason for this conflation of terrorism and protest may lie in the nature of the relationship between the criminological profession and active and former police officers. Spalek and O'Rawe's intervention in the debate around undercover policing throws up important questions facing academic researchers, specifically those working within policy-facing disciplines. Key issues that arise include the possible impact of research on policy and police practice, the levels of trust that can be achieved vis-à-vis communities subjected to surveillance, the legitimacy and reliability of information provided by the police, and obvious and operationally necessary lack of transparency regarding surveillance operations.

Spalek and O'Rawe argue that it is indeed possible, and crucial, for working relationships between counter-terror police officers and academic researchers to be established (apparently also where counter-terror police are actively engaged in counter-protest activity). It is an opening gladly accepted (as in their earlier collaboration, see Spalek and Lambert 2008) by Bob Lambert (2014), who finds in it the justification for his Outside Insider status as a former police officer within the academic research community. After all, his academic roles are due to 'his counter-terrorism experience', not mentioning of course that this included his 15 years within the Special Demonstration Squad. Lambert, of course, does little (so far) to answer the allegations against him other than to point to ongoing criminal investigations.

Then consider the scepticism that Spalek and O'Rawe rightly display:

> Researchers can grow to like and trust the counterterrorism police officers that they engage and do research with, but ultimately, there is no rational conclusion that can be reached as to whether or not researchers also are being manipulated ...
>
> (Spalek and O'Rawe, 2014: 159)

Viewing the issues raised by the infiltration of campaign groups as an aspect of counter-terrorism or domestic extremism serves to accord a special status to former police infiltrators, some of whom have made the transition into academic careers themselves. It is hoped that academic research can benefit from 'police knowledge' and that 'any research relationships that are developed between researchers and counterterrorism police officers serve as critical vehicles through which to hold officers to account' (Spalek and O'Rawe, 2014: 159). I can see no evidence of this.

THE NEW VISIBILITY

The argument for research cooperation hinges on the plausibility that researcher–police relationships can make the invisible visible. But this view runs into similar trouble as those arguments made for a new accountability in overt public order policing. There have been frequent suggestions in academic publications and public commentary, already way before the rise of social media, that police use of force, especially during political demonstrations, is now a lot less likely because it is held accountable in new ways – basically because of hand-held recording devices and their use for some form of 'citizen journalism'. Mobile and smart phones are the obvious examples here, and it is true that there have been high-profile incidents where footage recorded by protesters has exposed police brutality.

Often, Ian Tomlinson's death in 2009 at the G20 demonstration in London is used as an example of this (Greer and McLaughlin, 2011). A couple of articles in the *British Journal of Criminology*, for example, have argued that 'citizen journalism' now has a profound impact on protest policing, undermining the police's version of events that led to Tomlinson's death. One, by Andrew Goldsmith, argued that the police's new visibility 'diminishes their power, making the surveillance of others less possible at times and exposing them to disciplinary and legal liability' (Goldsmith, 2010).

There is an assumption made in such accounts that 'sousveillance', meaning the everyday surveillance capacities in the hands of 'ordinary citizens', increases the visibility of policing not just quantitatively but qualitatively. However, phone footage only captures isolated incidents, devoid of context or a larger operational picture. For communication theorists, this is the double-edged sword of the new visibility: new media render transparent previously opaque processes and hierarchies, but this does not necessarily increase democratic participation. Rather, it leads to new ways of cynical distortion of reality through PR, spin and communication consultants (Thompson, 2005). Arguably, this is the case in the #spycops scandal. The invisibility of some forms of policing remains untouched by citizens' new sousveillance powers.

CONCLUSION

As a researcher Robert Lambert was an Outside-Insider – a former undercover cop who had become an academic criminologist. While his autonomy to conduct research from his perspective and with his background is not in question, his failure and unwillingness to outline this perspective and to account for his past in a transparent manner, makes the working partnerships between him and Outside-Outsiders manipulative.

In the case of political undercover policing, it is very questionable that academic research can benefit from a close and cosy relationship with retired and practising police officers, who refuse to answer questions relating to their own involvement in political policing, who may be bound by the Official Secrets Act or by potential criminal proceedings against them, who are protected by the Regulation of Investigatory Powers Act, and who are taken out of the firing line by the police's Neither Confirm Nor Deny strategy and the public inquiry's granting of anonymity for all undercovers still in the field. There may be exceptions. But, in summary, as a police institution that has shown so much interest in maintaining secrecy about its own practices and policies, Special Branch simply does not make for a good research participant.

I started this chapter citing Robert Reiner's assessment that the research relationships between the police institution and universities can be mutually beneficial. But when it comes to political policing, this is highly doubtful. The secrecy and techniques of neutralisation that confronts those who research undercover policing methods, especially where the targets for infiltration are political campaigners, further strengthens the need for 'deviant knowledge'.

REFERENCES

Belknapp, J. (2015) Activist Criminology. *Criminology*, 53(1): 1–22.

Carlen, P. and Ayres França, L. (2017) (eds) *Alternative Criminologies*. London: Routledge.

Carrabine, E. *et al.* (2014) *Criminology: A Sociological Introduction*, 3rd edn, Abingdon: Routledge.

Della Porta, D. and Reiter, H. (1998) Introduction. In D. Della Porta and H. Reiter (eds), *Policing Protest: The Control of Mass Demonstrations in Western Democracies*. Minneapolis, MN: University of Minnesota Press.

Evans, R. (2015) Police Apologise to Women who had Relationships with Undercover Officers. *Guardian*, 20 November. www.theguardian.com/uk-news/2015/nov/20/met-police-apologise-women-had-relationships-with-undercover-officers.

Goldsmith, A. (2010) Policing's New Visibility. *British Journal of Criminology*, 50(5): 914–34.

Greer, C. and McLaughlin, E. (2011) 'This is Not Justice': Ian Tomlinson, Institutional Failure and the Press Politics of Outrage. *British Journal of Criminology*, 52(2): 272–93.

Lambert, R. (2014) Researching Counter-Terrorism: A Personal Perspective from a Former Undercover Police Officer. *Critical Studies on Terrorism*, 7(1): 165–81.

Lubbers, E. (2015) Undercover Research: Corporate and Police Spying on Activists: An Introduction to Activist Intelligence as a New Field of Study. *Surveillance & Society*, 13(3/4): 338–53.

Lubbers, E. (2019) Undercover Research: Academics, Activists and Others Investigate Political Policing. In A. Choudry (ed.), *Activists and the Surveillance State*. London: Pluto.

Marx, G. (1988) *Undercover: Police Surveillance in America*. Berkeley, CA: University of California Press.

Reiner, R. (2016) Foreword. In M. Brunger, S. Tong and D. Martin (eds), *Introduction to Policing Research: Taking Lessons from Practice*. London: Routledge.

Schlembach, R. (2016) The Pitchford Inquiry into Undercover Policing: Some Lessons from the Preliminary Hearings. Papers from the British Criminology Conference, Vol. 16. www.britsoccrim.org/wp-content/uploads/2016/12/pbcc_2016_Schlembach.pdf.

Schlembach, R. (2018) Undercover Policing and the Spectre of 'Domestic Extremism': The Covert Surveillance of Environmental Activism in Britain. *Social Movement Studies*, 17 (5): 491–506.

Spalek, B. and Lambert, R. (2008) 2008) Muslim Communities, Counter-Terrorism and Counter-Radicalisation: A Critically Reflective Approach to Engagement. *International Journal of Law, Crime and Justice*, 36 (4): 257–70.

Spalek, B. and O'Rawe, M. (2014) Researching Counter-Terrorism: A Critical Perspective from the Field in Light of Allegations and Findings of Covert Activities by Undercover Police Officers. *Critical Studies on Terrorism*, 7(1): 150–64.

Thompson, J.B. (2005) The New Visibility. *Theory, Culture & Society*, 22(6): 31–51.

Trautwein, A. (2017) Seit 28 Jahren ist die Flora infiltriert. *Zeit Online*, 21 June. www.zeit.de/hamburg/2017-06/rote-flora-verdeckte-ermittler-prozess-interview.

Waddington, P.A.J. (1994) *Liberty and Order: Public Order Policing in a Capital City*. London: UCL Press.

Waddington, P.A.J. (2016) Is Undercover Policing Worth the Risk? *Oxford University Press Blog*. https://blog.oup.com/2016/08/undercover-policing-risk-law/.

Walters, R. (2003) *Deviant Knowledge: Criminology, Politics and Policy*. Cullompton: Willan Publishing.

10

Ordinary Rebels, Everyone

Abolitionist Activist-Scholars and the Mega Prisons

David Scott

INTRODUCTION

In the United Kingdom today, we appear to have developed a fetish for punitiveness. What I mean by this is that we currently have an excessive and unhealthy commitment to punishment. Over the last couple of decades, collectively our society has come to think that punishment is somehow invested with magical powers that can not only solve our deep-rooted social problems and ease our anxieties but also provide a secure platform for a better future. In fact, it can do none of these things. Talk of punishments' magical powers are just a clever illusion, masking the fact that our excessive commitment to punishment actually exacerbates existing social problems, anxieties and insecurities (Scott, 2018). One of the most pressing pieces of evidence of this *punishment fetish* – and more broadly the development of an increasingly punitive state – are the current government plans to build six new 'mega prisons' in England and Wales.

The locations of the new 'mega prisons' were announced between November 2016 and March 2017. They were Wellingborough, Northampton; Glen Parva, Leicester; Full Sutton, Yorkshire; Rochester, Kent; Port Talbot, South Wales; and Hindley, Greater Manchester) (Travis, 2017). Four of the mega prisons are also planned to be built on sites of existing prisons (HMP Wellingborough, HMP Glen Parva, HMP Full Sutton and HMP Hindley). I want to focus in this chapter only on the encounters with ordinary people in the campaign revolving around the rebuilding of HMP Hindley, in Bickershaw, which is a small village in the borough of Wigan, Greater Manchester from March to November 2017. Although full details of the proposed redevelopment at HMP Hindley have not been made public (and indeed plans appear to have stalled entirely at the time of writing in January 2018), the building of the new 'mega prison', if it does go ahead in 2022, would have capacity to hold at least 1,300 prisoners.[1]

For penal abolitionists the prison – whatever the size – will always be an inhumane and immoral institution, and therefore prisons should be closed down and alternative life affirming alternatives promoted in their place (Scott, 2018). Abolitionism is about raising political consciousness and the realization of humanity for all. Thus, a key goal is to render visible broader issues around social and economic inequities and the commitment to social transformation. The abolitionist struggle then is ultimately one of liberation, freedom and social justice. Abolitionists aim to awaken our cultural consciousness and to alter the direction of the punitive wind by changing the way people see both the punitive state and the role of the prison within our society. For the abolitionist, though, the prison is not the protector, but *the enemy of ordinary people.*

The punitive state and its punishment fetish presents a clear danger to democracy. The aim for abolitionists is not just about dismantling the prison but also about generating a philosophy of hope, building communities and fostering a widespread commitment to acknowledging the common humanity of all. Abolitionism aims to strengthen democracy by building stronger bonds and networks of association in the community, developing community-based models of resistance and organising political activities that can work towards improving the safety and well-being of neighbourhoods. There are clear advantages for abolitionists to engage in political activism – *being part of the community and networking with like-minded people can renew energy as well as mutually affirming the abolitionist position.* So while aiming to produce politically useful analysis, abolitionism at the same time recognises the importance of key political agendas being defined by community members themselves. Underscoring this is the strong belief that democratic grassroots activism can be an effective way to challenge the punitive state. Of great importance for abolitionists is to stretch out their hand to activists (who are not abolitionists) and to other members of the community, who are neither abolitionists nor activists. Abolitionists recognise that what we require collectively, and indeed should aspire to be individually, are to be *ordinary rebels* fighting for a truly democratic and socially just society.

The discussion below starts with a brief outline of the rules of engagement for penal abolitionists when attempting to build alliances among activists, academics and members of the public. These rules of engagement are specifically directed at the 'activist-scholar' (Sudbury, 2008) to ensure that activists, scholars and members of the general public all work equally together for radically progressive transformations as 'ordinary rebels'. This focus on the ethics and politics of abolitionist activist-scholars is shaped by the experiences, skills and motivations of the author, who is both an academic working in higher education and also someone who has engaged directly in struggles against the punitive state. The first part of the discussion is therefore reflexive and based from the standpoint of an 'activist-scholar'. It acknowledges that while academics can bring certain skills and knowledge and can perform an important role in building the capacity of other members of the community, at the same time, they are only a very small part of the struggle against the punitive state, whose overall success is dependent upon mutual cooperation and support and everyone working together collectively. Hence, ordinary rebels, everyone. The chapter then moves on to discuss the importance of stepping outside of 'safer spaces' to engage in a critical encounter with ordinary people in local communities near to the proposed Mega Prison site in Bickershaw, Wigan during the height of the local campaign and engagement with the local community from March to November 2017. The chapter concludes with a consideration of how we can all work together, as *ordinary rebels everyone*, towards building an abolitionist future grounded in emancipatory politics and praxis.

SEVEN RULES OF ENGAGEMENT FOR ACTIVIST-SCHOLARS

For the great Italian philosopher Antonio Gramsci, everyone in society can be considered as an intellectual but not everyone in society has the function of intellectuals (i.e. are employed as an academic scholar) (1971: 9). By simply using our mental capacities, we think and *intellectualise*. A person who engages in writing, organising and devising political strategies is using their intellectual capabilities. For some activists, the term 'intellectual' (and especially the shorthand term 'academic') has become a pejorative term and is used today with disdain. Yet the very people who are most likely to be critical of intellectuals are, following the definition of Gramsci, intellectuals themselves. We then have the paradox of *anti-intellectual intellectual* (Collini, 2002). There is tendency to construct the 'intellectual' as extraordinary – they are either put on a pedestal, romanticised and glamorised or dismissed, treated with contempt and demonised. What gets lost is that intellectuals are neither. They are just *ordinary people*. The most striking aspect of most people employed as 'intellectuals' (i.e. academics) is their everyday mundaneness. They undertake ordinary tasks and largely live ordinary lives. Some academics are apolitical or attempt to distance themselves from politics, but there are also academics who are rebels – 'ordinary rebels'. The ordinary people (like myself) rebelling against the punitive state who work in the academy are referred to in this chapter as 'activist-scholars'. They work and campaign alongside other ordinary rebels from the community and non-academic professions, but I use this term to refer to academics engaged in rebellious activism.

The challenge today is to unite as one movement and collectively send the abolitionist message to ordinary people (the general public). The activist-scholar should not play the elitist academic game but rather collaboratively work with others for a more just world. The people with whom the activist-scholar speaks should include public audiences rather than just other paid intellectuals, and this shapes their intellectual outputs and contributions. The role of the activist-scholar is therefore the production of knowledge and active engagement in struggles in the service of progressive social movements fighting for social justice. This focus on the production of useful knowledge for activists is the focus of the second part of this chapter. While it would be correct to argue that any one of us as ordinary rebels can produce knowledge, activist-scholars have had privileged training and education through the university system. My focus then is on the ethical and political responsibility to utilise these skills and knowledge in ways that can best support ongoing struggles against the punitive state. Other ordinary rebels may not have had such support. We may well all be equal in certain ways, but, at the same time, different life experiences (harmful or beneficent) mean we also all remain different. The point of this chapter is to identify how the different skills of the activist-scholar can best serve other ordinary rebels. Hence, the inequitable power relations invested in paid intellectuals means that there must be 'rules of engagement' for this. Below are detailed seven central ethical principles underscoring the political actions of the abolitionist activist-scholar.

1. Challenging privilege: The thorny question of privilege and education should be confronted head on. Privilege is embodied and lived in the everyday (Sudbury, 2008). Privilege reflects life course and access to resources and the privileged university context may be alienating or disconnecting from ordinary people. We may have to just accept that the flattening of privilege is impossible, but it should be part of the daily struggle to live in a genuine democracy. Activist-scholars should recognise that their tenure, salaries (sometimes with research grants) and technical support from their university give them significant advantages, but it is not impossible for academic 'activist' scholars to support radical social movements and to use their privilege in ethically principled ways. What it does involve though is moving towards ideas that have no connection to university priorities but do have direct relevance to activist concerns and can foster locally based intellectual solidarities. Education is profoundly elitist and can be based on promoting exclusionary and technicist knowledge. There should be no exploitation of community members by those in a privileged position to serve either individual career priorities or the demands of the university research assessments. Activists (and activist-scholars) are right to be sceptical and raise serious questions about the motives of academics in becoming involved in social movements. While it can be difficult to 'fit' rebellious and radical activism within the criteria many universities use to impact (hence reducing the attractiveness of such activism to unscrupulous academics), there is always a danger that more is gained by the academic from the community than vice versa. Hence, the importance of reflexivity on the part of the activist-scholar – we all must always guard against exploitation and opportunism – and the adoption of an approach of service to others and utilising any privilege possessed (whether that be access, knowledge, skills, networks) to the benefit of all involved in the struggles against the punitive state.

2. The relational dimension: The activist-scholar exemplifies good character and excels in what it means to be honourable, comradely and supportive activists. Activist-scholars should give their time generously and be guided by the principles of kindness, care, compassion, love, friendship and the spirit of solidarity. It is essential that horizontal and democratically accountable relationships are fostered. An anti-hierarchical ethos and the sharing of resources, knowledge and information should be key priorities. There should be loyalty and transparency in all that is done. Recognition of the value of others is key – being involved in local campaigns means being involved in life-affirming, life-changing activities and this should underscore all relationships. Community solidarity, shared values and common beliefs in socialist politics and values should form the basis for reconstituting a collective radical agenda as a way of helping *communities to challenge state violence and coercion.* The important value of dialogue and conversation in developing a new consciousness of daily life are an important part of being of service to the local community. Activist-scholars should have a commitment to becoming a responsible and 'virtuous hearer' (Fricker, 2007: 5), that is, someone prepared to listen carefully, empathetically, sensitively and without prejudice to not only what is said but also listening out for what is not said and thus identifying structural denials of voice.

3. *Accountability to the community*: Activist-scholars must be prepared to unlearn their sense of privilege and instead recognise their accountability to local communities, grassroots activism and struggles for social justice. This entails working towards collective knowledge and the building of trust. It is essential that the abolitionist is prepared to listen and learn from the community. This is exceptionally important in terms of decision-making processes. This means *not being in control* and allowing others to have their voice, enabling them to shape and direct the movement. Local struggles are locally based movements that require local knowledge and locally embedded activist-scholars. Alongside this the role of the abolitionist may be, at times, to provide a platform for the voice of others, for example, those whose voice is not normally heard, such as prisoners and ex-prisoners. The activist-scholar should draw upon their expertise and *ensure* that their work is accessible to the general public.

4. *Levelling up and capacity building*: The activist-scholar should aim to improve ordinary people's capacity to function democratically to develop a critical kind of mindfulness and awareness of the socialist vision of justice. Abolitionists should aim to fulfil the potential of people around them and thus provide the intellectual milieu for socially transformative social movements. This means building potential and raising consciousness as a means of creating rebels from ordinary people in the community. Rather than silencing – there must never be levelling down

– activist-scholars should aim to level up by sharing knowledge, strategies and key ideas in capacity-building workshops. In order to promote a transformative political programme, we need to build a radical historical and cultural narrative, uniting abolitionist movement solidarity and providing inspiration for the agents of change for tomorrow – the ordinary rebel.

5. *Consciousness raising among the populace*: Activist-scholars must be prepared to challenge dominant myths and official accounts of the prison place, as well as going directly against the received wisdom and common sense understandings to promote penological literacy. The activist-scholar must then cut against the grain, questioning received ideas and treating the critical encounter with ordinary people in the local community through 'dialogical transformation' (i.e. critical and challenging conversations) through promoting anti-punishment education and contribution to the spreading of democratic norms (Friere, 1973). The abolitionist activist-scholar should not be a soloist playing their own tune, but perform a central role in creating a new abolitionist orchestra. Liberation is of paramount importance in the concept of raising abolitionist consciousness and the activist-scholar should attempt to infuse the local community with confidence, renewed belief, pride and dignity.

6. *Building new alliances and power bloc based on difference*: To build a new world together we must work towards a solidarity through difference. Activist-scholars should promote the importance of building solidarity and recognition of commonality across differences of interests of all in a new coalition of progressive forces. This means building relationships and addressing multiple crises – so when thinking about the 'punitive state', it means creating solidarities with communities who are experiencing the violence of austerity (Cooper and Whyte, 2017) racialised capitalism and other forms of oppression. We need to cooperate in sustainable ways that can give expression to a collective vision. This means greater collaboration and cooperation and thus breaking down the silos between academics and activists framed by activist consciousness and activist concerns (such as those highlighted above that academics will be exploitative and focused on personal or professional gain rather than rebelling against social injustice and the punitive state) and abolishing the punishment fetish mentality.

7. *Community spaces and the agora*: There is currently an absence of an appropriate public arena in which to hold detailed and deliberative dialogues on prisons and punishment. The mainstream media currently hold the monopoly on this, but what we urgently need is an 'agora' (public space for rational debate), where ordinary people can raise discussion of the problems that concern them the most. The activist-scholar somehow needs to create a public democratic space where ordinary people can both question and dream – a space where they can develop and use their imagination to find a new way of doing politics and to awaken and educate new desires for a better world. What is urgently required is a public seminar that is open to all and guided by the rules of rationale discourse. This agora would be a space where informed debate could help convince sceptics that another type of world is possible – a world without prisons, with an authentic democracy promoting the interest of all.

THE ENCOUNTER: ABOLITIONISM BEYOND SAFE[R] SPACES

Emancipatory politics and praxis, like all forms of knowledge genera-tion and practical ethico-political engagement, are dependent upon and shaped by an actual encounter with someone else. The encounter, by which I mean a face-to-face relationship, is inevitable. We will always have encounters with other people and sometimes those encounters will be with people that we find difficult to understand, or find their embodied privilege problematic for us. They may have done something hurtful to others or may simply hold views that we find incomprehensible or morally reprehensible. Yet if we want to create a new and better world grounded in social justice, we need to generate support from ordinary people who may not think like we do, share our values and principles or have the same interpretation of the world. An inclusionary vision of a socially just and truly democratic society must be grounded in reaching out to those who on many issues are on the 'other side' and somehow generating solidarities of difference predicated upon successful engage-ment with others. Indeed, it is the only way which activist-scholars can help facilitate a movement constituting ordinary rebels.

We need then to ensure that a given community is heard, even when words are not spoken, or they are spoken but in anger or misunder-standing. We have to try and look at the world through the eyes of the ordinary person, adopting or translating their language, meanings and understandings and trying to read unexpected forms of communication. But for Dussel (2013), we need to do even more than this – we need show solidarity to sufferers by taking responsibility for facilitating (communal) storytelling that can *rebuild lives and world collectively* alongside the political commitment to attempt to *transform existing asymmetrical power relations* (Haiven and Khasnabish, 2014). As a bottom line, inclusionary visions of social reality acknowledge difference and diversity while at the same time recognising what we share: a common humanity. The only way we can challenge the punitive state and build a more progressive and humane future is by reaching out to local communities as they are currently constituted today. But it is also important to recognise that the encounter with other people in itself is a central feature of all of our experiences and not something special. We have encounters with ordinary people every day: sometimes they will be in the context of emancipatory politics and praxis.

Effective activism requires the activist-scholars to reach out to the wider community. No struggle against the mega prisons will be taken seriously by local and national politicians unless it is deeply embedded in local communities. The activist-scholar must then be prepared to perform a balancing act between listening and learning from the local community and challenging problematic categories and interpretive frameworks. As highlighted above, the activist-scholar must recognise and take into account their own privileged position and be prepared to negotiate how they present their political analysis in light of the diverse (and potentially hostile environment), where the community-based activism takes place. There must also be recognition of the oppressive structure that the everyday lived experiences of the community and how the community itself is socially constructed, potentially in problematic ways. Moving beyond 'safe[r] spaces' is inevitable. Safe space policies, for Wang, not only fail to effectively address privilege and power but in practice means that: 'it becomes impossible to develop a revolutionary political programme' (2018: 285). Safe spaces cannot remove structural violence – they can only make it less visible and create a little distance from its presence. To bring about the world we desire requires direct encounters, perhaps involving some kind of confrontation, in public and undoubtedly less safe spaces. The following discussion details the engagement with local people in Wigan Borough, Greater Manchester by activist-scholars and some of the challenges this presents. The account below is written from the perspective of this author and is based on extensive field notes undertaken during the campaign from March to November 2017.[2] It follows the emergence of the pressure group *Pies Not Prisons*; the direct encounters with local people in Wigan and Bickershaw; and engagement with the local politicians and media. This 'warts and all' account is in chronological order and is followed by a consideration of how well it connected to the seven rules of engagement for abolitionist activist-scholars and it is hoped will provide useful insights for future emancipatory politics and praxis.

Pies Not Prisons

Almost as soon as the plans for the mega prisons were announced in March 2017 (Travis, 2017, March), a strategy was put in place by a number of local activists for a local meeting to be set up. The government plan was to demolish HMP Hindley, the existing prison in the area, and to rebuild a much larger prison on this land. Knowledge of the local prison area – Wigan Borough – was greatly aided by previous connections to local socialist activists who'd been involved in establishing the *Diggers Festival*[3] in Wigan. Of these connections, the most crucial proved to be with Tony Broxson,[4] a hugely influential local activist who was well-regarded by people in the local community and especially by the local left-wing socialist community. Tony Broxson immediately arranged a venue and potential speakers for a Wigan meeting to start the debate on resisting the mega prison. Speakers included activist-scholars (Emily Luise Hart and this author), a former prisoner and also a leading member of the Momentum wing of the Labour Party, who acted as chair. At this first meeting on 3 April 2017, people came from around the local area, including activists from *Manchester No Prison*[5] and activist abolitionists who were based in Liverpool as well as a number of people from the local community. The meeting was attended by 60 people, some of whom were local councillors. The meeting was then followed up almost immediately with further discussion at a local NHS crisis meeting event in Wigan town centre a few days later. Here, once again, concerns about the mega prison were expressed and information was given to members of the Socialist and left-wing constituency of Wigan borough.

These meetings, with the aid of local activist Tony Broxson, helped to generate considerable interest in the prison-building programme, and notably the transformation of HMP Hindley into a new 1,300 capacity prison. There were following meetings with members of the *Momentum*[6] group in Wigan in May 2017, which once again included both long-term socialist activists and left-leaning councillors. The end result of these interventions was the creation of a Wigan borough based pressure group. This new group was given the rather quirky title of *Pies Not Prisons,* a title which reflected the tradition of pie making in Wigan borough. Underscoring this of course was also a rather simple message: that rather than locking people up, we should feed them. In a town with a number of food banks and high rate of social inequality, this message clearly resonated (Scott, 2018).

The Encounter – Bickershaw Social Club

Although the meetings in Wigan town centre had proved to be hugely successful both in terms of getting the key message across (Scott, 2018) and also generating some 'momentum' towards providing a sustained critique of the proposed mega prison, it was felt essential that *Pies Not Prisons* should engage directly with the community that was most affected – that is, the local community in the area surrounding the existing prison (HMP Hindley) in Bickershaw, a small village just on the outskirts of Wigan. A meeting was organised for 29 June 2017, and the local community was widely leafleted with details of the speakers and the issues that were to be addressed at the local community meeting. Strategically, it was felt that it would be helpful to draw upon the relationship between welfare and punishment to highlight the social costs of building a new mega prison. Therefore, a number of speakers were brought together to explore first of all some of the welfare issues they were confronting in Wigan and the area around it of Wigan borough (which included the village of Bickershaw) as well as issues regarding the closure of HMP Hindley and the subsequent rebuilding of the site as a new 1,300 place mega prison. Speakers were invited to talk about the NHS; the funding crisis in schools; and a platform was also provided for an account of personal experiences of ex-prisoners and the mother of a currently incarcerated prisoner. One further speaker (this author) was then planning to speak about the social and economic harms of rebuilding the prison and to give the local community as much detail as we possibly could at that point in time, given that the new prison had only been announced a number of weeks beforehand.

The first Bickershaw village meeting perhaps provided a classic illustration of misunderstandings and the difficulties that activists face both in terms of trying to read the local community. It also highlighted the democratic deficit regarding the organisation of local meetings and a public space for meetings to rationally and collectively discuss social problems and possible solutions (what I have described above as the agora). It also provides an example of an encounter in what ultimately proved to be a less than ordinarily safe space, albeit, one that could hardly be described as dangerous or unsafe. The meeting involved ordinary people coming from both the local community and also a large number of activists who had been inspired to challenge the mega prison from the previous Wigan meetings. The first speaker was the mother of a currently serving woman prisoner. She was allowed to speak, albeit with some grumblings from the gathered local residents. When, however, it came to the following three speakers – who had planned to engage with issues around social welfare education and health – the speakers were challenged by members of the local community who effectively tried to shout them down.

The local community wanted its voice to be heard and there was clear frustration in the room. The three speakers on welfare spoke more briefly than planned and directed attention more to the local issues of Bickershaw and the prison than was originally intended. To appease the situation one of the speakers (this author) then spoke directly to the most dissident voices in the room, leaving the platform and standing within almost touching distance of a number of the most rowdy members of the local community. There had been a misunderstanding. The local community had thought that the meeting had been organised by Wigan Council and that local councillors would be speaking and giving them direct and specific detailed information on the rebuilding of the prison. Some local councils were there but they remained largely silent among the angry local voices. The local community were quite vocal in their dissent – shouting: 'YES or NO is there going to be a new prison *YES or NO?*' This was something that none of the members of *Pies Not Prisons* could answer.

What was remarkable from the meeting were two things. First, it was evident that the local community was starved of a voice: we heard time and time again that there had been very limited numbers of council meetings in the local area, that many people living near HMP Hindley felt as if they had been neglected and denied a voice. Members of the local community also felt that there was a general lack of concern for their interests and indeed, that the proposed mega prison was being rolled through irrespective of their concerns. There was a palpable sense of passivity and a sense of fatalism when it came to the idea of the new prison. This frustration boiled over on the 29 June meeting and so what *Pies Not Prisons* encountered was a lot of angry people who did not really know the rules of rational dialogue in terms of a democratic discussion. Nor were they necessarily interested in issues that lay outside of their local remit: their exclusive concerns lay around HMP Hindley and the proposed new mega prison and how that would impact on the local infrastructure and community. This has been widely described in the academic literature as the 'Not In My Back Yard' (NIMBY) agenda. Second, the meeting did not end as a disaster, although it looked as though it might have on a couple of occasions. The meeting actually proved to be a great success in terms of building connections with the local Bickershaw village community over the coming months. In the first instance, once the local community had vented their anger and it was clear that we were ready to engage in reciprocal listening and started to respond in a more open manner. It was also evident that *Pies Not Prisons* was listening, and that the local activists were responding to what the local people were saying. At the end of the meeting, there was much shaking of hands, thanks for the speakers making the effort to come and also an immediate call for a follow-up meeting within only a couple of days, to be once again held at social club.

The 29 June meeting was quite well attended and highlighted more than anything else the problem of not being heard. It showed the importance of dialogical ethics and what situations can arise if such a dialogue stalls. The encounter was initially experienced in a way that the venue felt like a hostile environment. But it is important to emphasise how the meeting evolved. It was clear that understanding and engaging in dialogue with the other was starting to produce results, and that once there was clarity and a sense that the Pies Not Prisons was there to work with and alongside the local community, there was a significant change in attitude and atmosphere. A further set of local meetings in Bickershaw village were established before the first meeting closed. At the follow-up meeting, held in the first week of July 2017, 20 members of the local community attended. This encounter started in a very different way. Rather than have guest speakers, we organised organic and collective community meetings. Through this relational dialogue, we started to build a sense of what the local community actually wanted and how they thought we could help them try to stop the mega prison being built. More than this, the local community also requested quite practical advice that we could immediately and directly share with them to help build the capacity to resist. Local ordinary people wanted to know exactly what they could do in terms of challenging this through their local political channels. They wanted their local councillors to be involved; they wanted their local MP to be involved; they wanted the Mayor of Manchester to be involved: they wanted other local councillors who were well known for being dissident in council meetings, to be involved; they wanted more ordinary people who were residents in the adjoining villages to come and join them in their struggle.

Pies Not Prisons facilitated various different sets of meetings (some of which I will go into below when discussing engagement with the local political community of Wigan and Bickershaw). But one of the things that came from the follow-up meetings was a crucial connection with other communities only a short distance away, which related to a campaign group challenging the building on land adjacent to South Hindley village. This new housing estate was to be situated not far from where HMP Hindley currently stands. Through engaging with local activists in South Hindley village, who were much more organised, The South Hindley village protest group had come together for quite a number of months before the prison was announced, and while their focus was not the prison but rather on the building of new houses in a woodland area, their support and engagement allowed us to extend even further the network of local people. *Pies Not Prisons* established a small email newsletter; put local people protesting against the mega prison into direct contact with other ordinary rebels; and helped organise further meetings. Crucially, we brought together local speakers and made direct connections between the land surrounding HMP Hindley and the issues around asbestos. Through local knowledge, activists and local residents learnt about the harmful legacy of an old *Turner and Newell* asbestos factory that had been situated just north of the prison and just south of the village of Hindley itself. A further meeting was quickly organised which this time involved councillors and also a number of local people from both Hindley and Bickershaw.

Although the numbers at this 25 July 2017 meeting were much smaller than the previous big meeting in Bickershaw village, it once again provided an opportunity to hear the views of the local community and what they wanted *Pies Not Prisons* to help them with. These local meetings quite clearly were not a straightforward political community grounded in values of social justice and human rights – the opposite in fact. The moral and political frameworks held by members of the community were punitive – they wouldn't have a problem with prisons but they did have a problem with it being near to where they lived – the NIMBY approach. *Pies Not Prison* raised the harms of asbestos contamination, invited a local asbestos expert to the meeting, and also delivered information regarding the practicalities of submitting a planning application objection, all of which we hoped would be of some direct use to the local community or had been requested by them. In attendance were also representatives of the Prison Officers Association (POA) from HMP Hindley. Activists from *Pies Not Prison* had leafleted the prison and spoken with prison officers as they were leaving the jail in the days before the big meeting. At this meeting, however, it became clear that new information had been revealed that the stay of execution had been granted to HMP Hindley and that rather than close in November 2017 as being initially announced it was now to stay open until at least November 2019. This news was not officially confirmed until October 2017, when the date of closure was delayed until at least 2022 (Travis, 2017, October). Ironically then, this disjointed campaign only a few months old had achieved results. But it was a hollow victory at best and in truth possibly had very little to do with any of the issues regarding the campaign (Scott, 2018). More likely, a key factor was the broader stalling of the mega prisons that occurred in late 2017 and rising prison populations (Travis, 2017, October).

So although this third Bickershaw open meeting proved to be the last, what was interesting was that by this point there was a growing sense of community cohesion and that the campaign with the South Hindley group – and especially the concerns raised around asbestos – may actually have proved to have had some momentum. *Pies Not Prisons* had not seen the radicalisation of consciousness-raising of the community – and we certainly hadn't created any future ordinary rebels – but we laid some solid foundation work that was cut short by the announcement of the stay of execution on HMP Hindley in October 2017.

Engaging in Local Politics

The encounters with the local community of course did not just involve being involved with village residents or organising big meetings. Encounters during this form of activism also went into the local political community, which itself proved to have various positives and negatives in terms of how the local political process worked. As had been illustrated in the first big Bickershaw meeting, members of *Pies Not Prisons* found a general sense of apathy and lack of engagement in terms of some serious political support regarding many of the issues that confronted Wigan and also Bickershaw. This was perhaps best illustrated in a meeting with the local MP for the area, Rt. Hon. Yvonne Fovargue, MP. Ironically, this meeting was set up with this author and local activist Tony Broxson following the first meeting in Bickershaw by the MP. The local MP had a reputation for being on the Conservative wing of the Labour Party, but we assumed that she had some interest in at least finding out what some of the main objections to the mega prison were. We hoped that she might be interested in coming to a meeting with her constituents or engaging in the broader campaign with *Pies Not Prisons*. Yet the meeting proved enormously disappointing, at least in terms of the MP's enthusiasm for our campaign.

Almost immediately as the meeting started, the local MP said she was not prepared to talk about any policy issues regarding prison building programmes and was only prepared to talk about practical elements that could lead to an objection to the planning application. That is the 'material conditions of an objection to a prison plan'. The meeting lasted an hour and as time went on we found not only had she spoken with local coun-cillors but the local Manchester Labour Party Mayor, Andy Burnham, who had taken an interest in the campaign. The meeting proved to be an obstacle in terms of the MP's position regarding a public objection to the prison (although she did make a statement for a local newspaper about the prison and how she felt this was something that should be open to public debate), but *Pies Not Prisons* did hold follow-up meetings with the office of the local Labour Party MEP (with the hope that perhaps there could be some kind of discussion in the European Parliament) and also direct liaison with the Manchester Mayor's office, both of which provided encouragement in terms of showing interest in the kind of arguments that would have been raised against the mega prisons more broadly. There were also discussions with Labour Party councillors, who, while reluctant to engage with many of the key moral and political issues of the campaign, raised question marks about whether the planning application would even go forward and gave us some insight quite early on that they regarded the pathway to the building of the mega prison on the site of HMP Hindley as by no means clear. We also held discussions and debates outside of the local council offices, at times when the local planning committee was meeting (18 July 2017). This was done in a polite and informal manner but one which sent a message that the local community (and there are about 25 people who attended the demonstration) were not going to allow this to happen without some kind of protest (see also the discussion below).

Engagement was also made with local unions and with the *Momentum* group of the Labour Party in Wigan. Talks were given at both the Unison's main group meetings, the Unison retired meeting group, and the *Trades Council of Wigan*, to highlight issues around the problems of building a mega prison. While these talks were largely undertaken by this author, there was also direct connection with local activists – and indeed it was always local activists from *Pies Not Prisons* who established these meetings in the first instance and local activists, notably Tony Broxson, were always present and contributed to the meetings themselves. There was then a genuine attempt not only to inform the public here but also to try and build capacity in order to help the local activists themselves to build a knowledge base and encourage them to participate in direct dialogue regarding the objections to the mega prison.

There were two further aspects of the political engagement at the local level. First of all, there was a stall at the local *Diggers Festival* in September 2017 (and also *Pies Not Prisons* were represented at the festival in September 2018), which much to the delight of the local activists involved the eating of a large number of free pies. Further, there was also a fringe event organised at the local Labour Party conference (North West region which was held in November 2017 in Blackpool, Lancashire). Unfortunately, this Labour Party Conference fringe event did not attract any local MPs, but it did generate debate from a considerable number of people who are members of the Labour Party in the region.

Connecting with the Local Media

One final area also deserves some brief commentary: this is engagement with the local media. In particular, this involved connections with the local Wigan newspaper the *Wigan Post*. Over the period of around six months, there were 12 separate stories on Hindley prison that in one way or another were connected to the activities and knowledge sharing of *Pies Not Prisons*. One of these stories even made it to the front page of the newspaper (as a headline). These stories, albeit quite brief and sometimes offering also a pro prison narrative as an alleged balance to the anti-prison activism of *Pies Not Prisons*, were often informed by members of *Pies Not Prisons* and were able to give a critical narrative of the prison as the institution and also to get the message across about both the lack of need for the local prison to be any bigger – indeed we argued that the prison should be shut down – as well as highlighting the problem of asbestos in the prison and the local community (Scott, 2018). *Pies Not Prisons* therefore made direct connections between the corporate harms of asbestos-related deposits and the harms of the prison place. This actually proved to be one the most significant aspects of raising consciousness because people would start to look beyond the social death of the prisoner and to recognise that the issues that were being highlighted in terms of the rebuilding of HMP Hindley as a 1,300 space mega prison affected the wider community. Making connections, local journalists proved to be a useful way of getting our message across and crucially proved a source of credibility in terms of our direct engagement with the local community. The *Pies Not Prisons* demonstration outside Wigan Town Hall council planning committee meeting on 18 July attracted local newspaper coverage, including interviews and photographs with activists. However, a critical question was raised by local residents: 'who actually reads the *Wigan Post*?' Some of the local newspapers also picked up stories but primarily it was the *Wigan Post* that provided a platform for the voice of *Pies Not Prisons*. There was also some minor engagement with local radio in Greater Manchester and in Liverpool including *BBC*

Radio Merseyside about the mega prison; these interventions were relatively brief and did not necessarily provide the space and platform that would be required for a genuine abolitionist agora.

CONCLUSION: AN ETHICAL ENGAGEMENT?

The activist-scholar should play a key part in public engagement. The activist-scholar should provide a platform for the voice of excluded and subjugated voices (which it did do on occasion in the above illustration of the campaign by *Pies Not Prisons* with the platforming of ex-prisoner voices). The activist must also make sure that they do not silence local voices, but at the same time the activist-scholar should not be silenced – they should channel their privilege into providing resources to engage the interest of ordinary members of the community. It is important to reflect more generally on how, as an abolitionist activist-scholar, the direct interventions of *Pies Not Prisons* related to the seven rules of engagement detailed at the start of this chapter. Certainly, a number of the processes behind rules of engagement can be seen to have been followed. There was a strong building of horizontal and non-hierarchical relationships and there were genuine attempts to turn privilege into a levelling up and capacity building for local socialist activists and people living near the prison. Accountability to the local community was also evident in terms of the manner in which the agenda for engagement was decided and the commitment to supporting local residents who held views diametric to many of the members of *Pies Not Prisons*.

For all its strengths though, the activism around the Wigan Mega Prison made only a small contribution to changing outcomes. This includes: generating consciousness raising among the populace (though *Pies Not Prisons* did at least make good connections with like-minded people and highlighted how prisons are a socialist issue); did little to build new political alliances based on the recognition of difference (though dialogue between activists and ordinary people in the community was established); or create a genuine new space for rational argumentation (though local people were becoming more active and prepared to engage in direct action before the announcement of the five-year extension of the existing prison in the village).

The story of the encounter with local residents of Bickershaw then highlights a number of key issues about the importance of working with the community from where it is at. What is required is negotiating strategy that can both challenge and accommodate the opinions of local people. It is essential to try and build some kind of political momentum by both working through grassroots connections and local people's views and opinions but also by trying to mobilise local activists who are not necessarily focused on the prison. If there was one big success story of *Pies Not Prisons* it was that it was able to mobilise members of the Labour Party and in particular members of *Momentum* and associated unions in a way that meant that challenging the prison rebuilding was seen as a major local concern that should be objected to.

Alongside all of this is the enduring commitment to emancipatory politics and praxis. Through engaging in praxis, the activist-scholars in *Pies Not Prisons* aimed to build a new power base and to generate and tap into existing political consciousness in the community. This meant listening (and often carefully challenging) the ordinary voices of local people. If we are to live in a different kind of world, we need to create a mass movement that can involve or inspire millions of people. It is not just about the intellectual or those involved in grassroots movements, but reaching out to the general public. For real and lasting change, we need the support of ordinary rebels, everyone.

NOTES

1. For a further discussion of this campaign, including a detailed account of the arguments used by local activists to challenge the mega prison, see Scott (2018).
2. See discussion in Scott (2018) for further context of the campaign to rebuild HMP Hindley, Bickershaw, Greater Manchester.
3. This is an annual festival, which commemorates the life of early socialist thinker Gerard Winstanley, who was born in Wigan, and the social movement the 'Diggers', which were active in England the late 1640s.
4. Permission has been sought and granted to use the real name of this local activist.
5. Manchester No Prison was an anarchist anti-prison group formed in Manchester in 2016 and has close connections to CAPE (Community Action Against Prison Expansion), a national prison abolitionist group formed in 2014.
6. *Momentum* is a radical social group, which is closely associated with the UK Labour Party.

REFERENCES

Collini, S. (2002) Every Fruit Juice Drinker, Nudist, Sand Sandal Wearer: Intellectuals as Other People. In H. Small (ed.) *The Public Intellectual*. Oxford: Blackwell, 203–23.

Cooper, V. and Whyte, D. (eds) (2017) *The Violence of Austerity*. London: Pluto Press.

Dussel, E. (2013) *The Ethics of Liberation*. Durham, NC: Duke University Press.

Fricker, M. (2007) *Epistemic Injustice*. Oxford: Oxford University Press.

Friere, P. (1973) *Pedagogy of the Oppressed*. Harmondsworth: Penguin.

Gramsci, A. (1971) *Selections from the Prison Notebooks*. London: Lawrence and Wishart.

Haiven, M. and Khasnabish, A. (2014) *The Radical Imagination: Social Movement Research in the Age of Austerity*. London: Zed Books.

Scott, D. (2018) *Against Imprisonment*. Winchester: Waterside Press.

Sudbury, J. (2008) Challenging Penal Dependency: Activist Scholars and The Anti-Prison Movement. In J. Sudbury and M. Okazawa-Rey (eds), *Activist Scholarship*. London: Paradigms Publishers.

Travis, A. (2017, March) Four 'Supersized' Prisons to be Built in England and Wales. *Guardian*, 22 March.

Travis, A. (2017, October) Closures of Ageing Jails on Hold for Five Years as Prison Numbers Soar. *Guardian*, 12 October.

Wang, J. (2018) *Carceral Capitalism*. South Pasadena, CA: Semiotext(e).

11

Re-Imagining an End to Gendered Violence

Prefiguring the Worlds We Want

Julia Downes

INTRODUCTION

Critical analysis of feminist anti-violence movements have argued that dominant social responses to gendered violence have been shaped by a 'carceral feminist' epistemology (Gottschalk, 2006; Bernstein, 2007; Richie, 2012; Kim, 2015). This outlook invests in the use of punitive state responses, such as the law, police, courts and prison, to resolve gendered violence. However, evidence of 'anti-carceral' feminisms that resist punitive state solutions have been excavated in social movement histories in the USA and Australia (Thuma, 2019; Carlton and Russell, 2018). Black and working-class feminist movements have long recognised the state as a primary source of violence in, rather than a protector of, working-class Black, minority and migrant women's lives (Bryan, Dadzie and Scafe, 1985; Grewal, Kay, Landor, Lewis and Parmar, 1988; Prescod-Roberts and Steele, 1980). In the USA, feminists of colour have worked in coalition with penal abolitionists to develop non-state responses to interpersonal violence (INCITE! and Critical Resistance, 2005). The conceptual frames of 'community accountability' and 'transformative justice' that underpin non-state responses to gendered violence have emerged primarily from aboriginal communities and communities of colour based in the USA, Canada and Australia. These approaches reject the state as a viable partner and propose instead to expand the capacity of communities to end violence (INCITE! and Critical Resistance, 2005; Kim, 2010; Chen, Dulani and Piepzna-Samarasinha, 2011; Law, 2011). The key idea here is to prefigure a world capable of responding to violence and harm with the support, care and compassion necessary to end it, so that dominant punitive state solutions become obsolete.

In this chapter, I will explore both the potential and challenges faced in doing accountability work on gendered violence within what has been termed the 'British Left' (Dean and Maiguashca, 2018). I draw on empirical research with women and non-binary survivors who have experienced violence (such as domestic and sexual violence) from fellow activists within grassroots social movements (Downes, Hanson and Hudson, 2016; Downes, 2017). Accountability work is attempted within a punitive state, which circulates dominant ideas of thinking about and responding to violence as a problem of 'bad' individuals. Traces of this 'criminal legal imagination' can recirculate within British Left grassroots social movements faced with gendered violence within their groups. However, learning from the perspectives of survivors and experienced transformative justice practitioners and facilitators can help to map out a framework for transformative justice within the British Left. This open acknowledgement of how wider conditions can limit accountability work aims to open up pathways towards cultivating accountability as a crucial practice in dismantling the punitive state. This includes the development of an anti-carceral feminist imagination to contest the reliance on punitive state responses, such as the law, police, courts and prison, to resolve gendered violence.

SITUATING THE BRITISH LEFT AND ANTI-VIOLENCE ACTIVISMS

The British Left has been conceptualised as three key strands (Dean and Maiguashca, 2018). The first is the Labour Party: a dominant party in the political system. The second relates to smaller political parties located to the left of the Labour Party associated with Trotskyism, Marxism and revolutionary socialism. This includes organisations such as the International Marxist Group, Alliance for Worker's Liberty, Socialist Workers Party and Left Unity, who have mobilised grassroots opposition to capitalism, racism and imperialism. The third strand involves grassroots social movements that have a significant influence in cultural and political life. This includes grassroots LGBTQ, feminist, anarchist and anti-authoritarian groups, environmental and animal rights groups, DIY cultures, autonomous spaces and social centres (Wakefield and Grrrt, 1995; Downes, 2016; Pusey, 2010). In recent years, gendered violence, and inadequate responses, has been uncovered at all levels of the British Left (Cox, 2018; Downes *et al.*, 2016b). Activist-scholars have also found evidence of routine exclusions across intersections of race, class, gender, disability and sexuality within grassroots social movement groups (Montesinos Coleman and Bassi, 2011; Emejulu and Bassel, 2015; Filar, 2016; Bassel and Emejulu, 2017).

Deeply unsatisfied by how violence has been managed within organisations and wary of the state, survivors and their supporters within grassroots social movements have explored the use of creative strategies (safer space and accountability processes) to prefigure movements that are safer and inclusive of survivors of trauma. Information about these approaches has been largely disseminated to British grassroots activists in fanzines, self-published anthologies of reprinted articles and submissions (Urb and Crabb, 2011; CrimethInc, 2013; (A)Legal, 2014). Articles and zines included references to resources created by US-based organisations including INCITE!. While this offers up potential to develop non-state responses, attempts to use community accountability processes, largely envisioned by people of colour, within a white-dominated British Left is contentious. Widespread support for, and implementation of, community accountability approaches have proved difficult to realize in practice (Downes, 2016). This persistence of, and difficulty in dealing with, gendered violence within grassroots social movements is a frustrating and painful impasse for activists.

THE SALVAGE COLLECTIVE AND RESEARCH PROJECT

The salvage collective formed in November 2014 to bring together women (cis, trans and intersex), trans and non-binary individuals, who experience gender oppression, violence and abuse in grassroots social movements. The salvage collective was initially envisioned as a network to share experiences, resources, skills and build communities of belief, support and action. It emerged from a need to better understand the character of violence and the needs of survivors in activist communities. This was identified in workshops that we facilitated independently from each other in anarchist and feminist events, which is how we first met each other.[1] A small collective of three white women, the research collective and ten survivors carried out a research project to explore experiences of gendered violence, abuse and harm from the perspectives of survivors in British Left grassroots social movements (Downes et al., 2016b). Drawing on models of 'research justice' and 'participatory action research' approaches, we carried out semi-structured interviews with ten women and non-binary survivors on August 2015–January 2016 (Jolivette, 2015; Kindon, Pain and Kesby, 2009).[2]

We launched an activist-facing zine-report and toolkit at the Centre for Crime and Justice Studies in September 2016 and facilitated a series of five one-day workshops across the UK funded by the Feminist Review Trust in November and December 2016. This was followed by four capacity-building one-day workshops funded by the Harm and Evidence Research Collaborative in 2017, as we identified specific support needs and skills for activists doing accountability work in their communities. One forum event was held in Sheffield in September 2017, where the decision was made to put the collective on pause to undertake a reflective process that began in January 2018. The demands placed upon us by the wider activist community were at times overwhelming. While this confirmed the need to acknowledge gendered violence and harms within these grassroots spaces, we received many requests for us to provide a service that went beyond our capacity: to act as consultants, experts, counsellors and mediators. In short, to fix it.

This desire for an organisation to provide accountability services 'for hire' is rooted in capitalist ideas of work. The limitations of formalised models of service provision as a strategy for social change has been highlighted by feminists of colour in the USA and by European prison abolitionists (INCITE!, 2017; Kaba, 2018; Christie, 2016). This also contradicted our aim to encourage communities to develop ways to respond to harm that best made sense for them in their local contexts and networks. It became evident that *within white-dominated British Left grassroots social movements, the social conditions were not yet in place to enable accountability work to take hold*. I remember facilitating one workshop and a participant told me that we needed to develop one accountability process that really 'works'. The one that can offer us the solution. In reflecting on this, I returned to the research interview data we had generated with new questions. Paying close attention allowed me to interrogate how activists invested in punitive thinking around gendered violence and how this impacted on survivors who wanted and/

or attempted to realize accountability work. It raised the question: what is required to transform these investments into sustainable practices of transformative justice in the British Left?

THE CRIMINAL LEGAL IMAGINATION

Cultures of disbelief require a means to control what counts as truth and who can be recognised as a victim. As a dominant means to determine 'innocence' from 'guilt', the 'criminal legal imagination' can emerge in anti-authoritarian spaces as one means of achieving such 'truth'. The term 'criminal legal imagination' draws on Mimi Kim's work on 'carceral creep', in which she describes how social movement actors can go against, alongside and within legal logics to leverage movement goals (Kim, 2015). The dominance of the criminal legal imagination can crowd out creative and transformative responses. For instance, gender-based violence scholars have problematised a tendency in the field of looking 'to the state to correct injustices' and warn that a 'focus on criminal justice interventions' can occur 'often at the expense of other forms of thinking and acting on the issue' (Gill, Heathcote and Williamson, 2016: 2). Indeed, social movements are not exempt from investments in punishment to achieve movement goals, as Sarah Lamble has demonstrated in the growing endorsement of hate crime by LGBTQ activist communities in Europe and North America (Lamble, 2013). Understanding social movements as 'hybridized spaces between civil society and the state' (Kim, 2015: 5) enables comprehension of how activist groups can reject the viability of state institutions to provide justice while investing in legal action to hold the state accountable to achieve specific goals.

This approach can also help to explain how community responses to gendered violence within activist groups can fall into the trap of mimicking a criminal process. The grip of the criminal legal imagination is strong within social orders that are invested in individual punishment as the solution to social problems, especially for the most stigmatised harms such as rape and child sexual abuse. For activists attempting accountability work, the lens of punishment undermined these efforts, as Collette[3] described:

That's not what the process is for, it's not about punishment, it's about trying to get people to acknowledge what they've done [...] What they've got in their head, what they've brought into their activism from the evil outside world. They haven't got their head around transformative justice so they're still approaching it [violence in activist communities] from a punishment view.

The criminal legal imagination is embedded in Western ideas of justice rooted in systems of white supremacy, capitalism, ableism and heteropatriarchy. Characteristics of systemic power relations can show up in grassroots social movement cultures as unspoken norms and values that are brought into being, while never being explicitly named or chosen (Jones and Okun, 2001). Within grassroots movements, power relations can shape who is recognisable as a victim, whose victimhood is visible, as well as what counts as violence and how it should be responded to. The individual and systemic are therefore entwined, as activist Morgan Bassichis summarised 'the very systems we are working to dismantle live inside us' (2011: 20). In grassroots movements and in feminist anti-violence work, we are not immune from perpetuating systems of domination, however, we can work towards attending to power inequalities that emerge in our interventions. Naming abuses of power offers up the potential to dismantle oppression.

For instance, at our launch event, we received a 'call-in' (Trân, 2016) from Camille Kumar at Imkaan, a London-based Black and minority ethnic women's anti-violence organisation, who highlighted the whiteness of our research team, sample and definition of activism. Within our research project, we had perpetuated a logic in which survivors, and responses to address gendered violence, centred whiteness. Our intervention in the grassroots social movements of the British Left had perpetuated a white feminist narrative that obscured power relations between white feminists and feminists of colour (Jonsson, 2014). We had framed the problem of gendered violence and harm through a white lens and failed to attend to the racialised aspects of gendered violence. For instance, in working with white activists in grassroots anti-austerity groups, minority and migrant women have encountered racism which can show up as defensiveness, an inability to admit mistakes, and a lack of solidarity with minority and migrant women's interests, lives and activisms (Emejulu and Bassel, 2015; Bassel and Emejulu, 2017).[4] The presence of racism and sexism feeds into an inability to recognise and respond to survivors of colour, who experience racialised sexual violence within grassroots social movement spaces.[5] Paying attention to how the criminal legal imagination, embedded in systems of domination, can show up in our feminist anti-violence work and lives, by practising self-accountability,[6] is crucial in transformative justice work. In this section, I will highlight how the criminal legal imagination operates within grassroots social movements in the British Left and how this impacts on survivors drawing on data gathered in the salvage research project.

CENTRING THE OBJECTIVE 'TRUTH': INVESTIGATIONS AND EVIDENCE

Grassroots confidence in the police and the state has been decimated by state control and the discipline of activism (Gilmore, Jackson and Monk, 2016; Evans, 2018). Despite antagonistic attitudes to police conduct and state violence in grassroots activist circles, disclosures of violence within movement spaces were not commonly met with care and compassion but with denials and requests to prove it with evidence and calls for investigations. Hayley recalled how this reaction to a disclosure of sexual assault in her activist group impacted on her:

> People were saying 'no no no you need to have checks and balances you need to have an investigation you need to get evidence person A person B and you need to find out the facts of what happened' and all of this [...] He didn't even know what happened because he couldn't remember and if he'd said 'well I think you're lying' what evidence could I have brought? It made me feel dead unsafe and vulnerable.

This way of thinking values objectivity, linear and logical thinking and having one right way to get to the facts or truth of the situation (Jones and Okun, 2001). Belief is equated with having evidence. Even when survivors had gathered evidence, belief was still contingent on valida-tion of this evidence from powerful community members. For instance, Anna compiled a document on her computer to evidence the violence she was experiencing. She used this document to persuade powerful members of her social centre to believe her:

> I had quite a lot of evidence as well, so I could show people quite concrete things at the start of it [...] I showed some fairly significant people at the [social centre] some emails and stuff, which were really

hateful. I'd started, like, cataloguing them, and just had this huge text document full of everything [...] It's so difficult to communicate and explain and relive, I could just sit people down with this thing and 15 minutes later, they get it.

However, the evidence was lost. This meant that Anna had to return to telling her story, which required potentially exposing herself to re-traumatisation and disbelief. Lydia had meticulously gathered evidence of the long-term abuse she had experienced from her partner, which included police reports, photos and diaries. However, whereas Anna could use evidence to persuade significant members, influential community members refused to acknowledge or recognise Lydia's evidence, which was experienced as a painful rejection:

> I did eventually once send a message to the one who was really antagonizing online who was very openly calling me out and saying that I was lying and I sent him a message saying look I can show you arrest reports, I can show you pictures of the injuries, because I'd followed all the you know the abuse website help suggestions I had a suitcase packed under my bed I had photographs I kept diaries and I said I can show you it all and he said 'no I'm not interested' he said 'you will manipulate it to make him look bad' and that was the only time I ever reached out and said please I want to show you I said come round I want to show you what he's done.

A need or desire for evidence or an investigation to determine the objective facts of a harmful or violent situation demonstrates an inability to directly engage with the affective qualities of survivors' experiences. The discomfort that survivors who express pain and suffering directly challenges a social movement culture invested in dominant values that disregard emotions as 'inherently destructive' to a group process (Jones and Okun, 2001). This can shut down space to recognise and listen to disclosures of violence and harm experienced in social movements.

WANTING TO BE STRAIGHT BACK OUT: URGENCY IN GRASSROOTS MOVEMENTS

Grassroots social movements frequently engage in direct action, occupations and acts that can make heavy and urgent demands on the time and labour of activists. This can sideline resources required for long-term accountability work as a group prioritises more immediate goals. However, this 'continued sense of urgency makes it difficult to take time to be inclusive, encourage democratic and/or thoughtful decision-making, to think and consider consequences' (Jones and Okun, 2001). Within a constant state of urgency, survivors can be sacrificed to meet quick or highly visible goals. Survivors can be abandoned in movements, left with a stark choice of leaving or managing alone. For example, to maintain a protest camp, Leah told us how she 'just had to get on with it because I had too many other things going on [...] at the time you're too busy just getting through the next 10 minutes the next half an hour and you're just too busy surviving and it is hard'. Hayley also had to tolerate what she had been through on her own to continue direct action:

> I was determined so I wasn't going to let it stop me so I was just like wanting to be straight back out [...] it was that unifying thing of like look we're all in it for the [cause] so let's put our differences aside and that worked for a long time and I think it did in the end it was water under the bridge and it was a really horrible experience but no one held it against anyone after a while so, there are some benefits to that kind of real united against a common enemy thing like but at what cost.

The costs of this model of activism are high, and survivors' needs for care and compassion cannot be met. A continued sense of urgency places priority on maintaining the spectacle of resistance rather than long-term visionary work, deepening connections and practices of care.

Some groups, including the protest camp that Leah was involved in, did have 'safer spaces' policies, which on the surface indicated some level of understanding that violence and harm can be perpetuated in grassroots spaces. However, questions can be asked about how many were in effect merely symbolic: placed on a wall or website to signal a politic that failed to be translated into ways of relating with each other in everyday life. In times of urgency, safer spaces could be ignored or used as a last resort to remove 'bad' people from groups and venues, leaving the long-term community building function of safer spaces work to be overshadowed. This was a common trap that transformative justice facilitators have highlighted. US-based Philly Stands Up activists explained: 'safe spaces tend to function as bubbles designed to stave off folks with anti-oppression politics or to respond to people who have perpetrated assault and have not been accountable' (Bench and Peters-Golden, 2012, cited in Kim *et al.* 2012; see also Caulfield, 2013: 24–5). Violence and harm can therefore be framed as a problem of 'bad' individuals or 'outsiders' and the role of social and cultural conditions that sustain violence, including social capital and personal networks, can be obscured.

DISTANCING SURVIVORS IN ATTEMPTS TO ADDRESS VIOLENCE

Several survivors, including Breanna, Anna, Collette and Micah, decided to engage with the safer spaces, community accountability or complaints processes that were available to them. However, the criminal legal imagination, embedded in 'paternalism' (Jones and Okun, 2001), crept into these processes as powerful activists made decisions for, and in the interests of, those without power and failed to explore or engage with survivors needs or feelings. Micah, who had been sexually violated by a fellow activist, gave an account of a complaints procedure that was hastily put in place to hold the person who caused harm accountable within an activist organisation. However, this process invested in and mimicked multiple aspects of a criminal process such as taking statements, composing a jury, holding a hearing, and offering a limited role and set of pre-determined outcomes for the survivor:

> So, the guy running it, it was his job to take the statements and anonymise them and give them to the jury [...] They didn't actually see the statement until the day we had the hearing so they had the statements anonymised and given to them. [...] I don't really know what they did in the preliminaries it was going to be them talking over how the process worked but then they invited me in to like read statements and say anything I wanted to say and then they asked me what I wanted to come out of it and handed a little tick box list of options [...] They weren't particularly varied options. I was offered some support during the process but I was given an email of someone I could email but I didn't use that. It was kind of only then as well as at the hearing that they asked me how I felt the complaints procedure

had gone like that was the only time I'd been asked that and I was like 'pretty shit actually' [...] The fact that the whole thing just mirrored a court process and was really weird. How long it took, it took two months. I'd found it quite hard to make a complaint because it is hard to balance confidentiality with getting something done about it. Also, there was no like waiting area for me at the meeting so we had to go down the road while they made their decision. Lack of support during the process.

It is particularly striking that this procedure progressed despite an early admission and validation of harm made by the person who caused harm at the statement stage. Instead of exploring survivors needs and imagining creative solutions, activists collectively replicated the procedural harms commonly experienced by 'complainants' in a criminal process. These harms included a lack of sensitivity, support and control in the process. The complaint that Anna made about a person who had harmed her triggered a review of the social centre's safer spaces policy, in which she was invited to attend:

I went into it expecting something very different, I'll say that much. I was, expecting it to be like 'right, so, this has happened, and this is why I feel like this' and I was kind of presented with quite a lot of bureaucracy. Which is quite a strange response when you're feeling so emotional about a thing [...] But yeah, it was just, for their sake. Trying to cover themselves, but there seems to be a sort of conflict of interest there, if your main priority is making sure that you can account for everything, and you don't act until you absolutely need to, that's not my top priority, my top priority wasn't them keeping a cool front.

In this example, there was little exploration of what Anna may potentially want or expect from the process. The latter part of the quote brings us to the heart of issue, a process constrained in this way can assist the powerful in avoiding accountability for creating and sustaining the conditions that enable violence and abuse. The bare minimum can be done (removal of the person who has caused harm) to maintain a reputation or image of inclusion. This links with Sara Ahmed's recent work on complaint, in which complaint procedures can come into existence without coming into use (Ahmed, 2018). Processes can be slow, bureaucratic and complicated to exhaust and wear down survivors. Without critical interrogation of the unspoken cultural values and norms that produce violence, safer spaces policies can be used to create evidence of doing something without doing anything. Within activist groups and organisations, belief remains firmly in the hands of the powerful, who are invested in maintaining the status quo. The ability for community leaders to abuse power and silence survivors has been recognised as a key internal barrier for feminists of colour working with Black and minority women.[7]

DEMANDING A ONE-SIZE-FITS-ALL SOLUTION

The idea that one 'effective' safer spaces policy or a single solution can exist was a consistent pressure in our work. This brings me back to the workshop participant I mentioned above and his frustrated plea to me for one accountability process that can fix it. Beth also picked up on this pressure: 'there's an idea that there's a right way and wrong way to deal with this and follow these few simple steps and this problem won't arise anymore'. There is a distinct inability to sit with discomfort and uncertainty when violence happens.

A desire for a linear solution in grassroots activist groups was also recognised by Erin, however, she argued that the viability of any 'solution' remains impossible without basic support and care for survivors:

I think what we need to do first is all the stuff that goes around the accountability process because otherwise we try and do the accountability process on its own and it all falls apart because there's nothing to hold it together.

In what is needed to 'hold it together', Erin is referring to the social and cultural conditions that allow survivors to be recognised as worthy of care and compassion. Investing in a 'step-by-step' guide that is isolated from broader systemic change to 'fix' violence is limited. As explored above, the use of linear complaints procedures to resolve violence without space for the needs, feelings or due care and compassion for individual survivors can amplify harm. This is a lesson that survivors and activists involved in safer spaces and accountability work have learned, as Hayley discussed in her own practice:

> Something I've learned in mediation and accountability [is] it can do harm to the person who's being harmed and actually we've put that into practice in dealing with situations in activism because I've learned that from my own experience that sometimes trying to fix things can make it worse, trying to fix things doesn't always work.

CULTIVATING ACCOUNTABILITY IN THE BRITISH LEFT: TRANSNATIONAL LESSONS

To move towards a framework for accountability work for British Left grassroots activists, I draw on work primarily led by women of colour and migrant, queer and trans people of colour and aboriginal communities, who have developed transformative justice approaches in the USA and Australia.[8] The practice of 'transformative justice', articulated by Canadian activist-scholar Ruth Morris in the 1980s and 1990s, was reinvigorated by communities of colour in the early 2000s, keen to re-politicise a stagnant feminist anti-violence movement in the USA (Morris, 2000; INCITE! and Critical Resistance, 2005; Russo, 2019). The collective political task at hand is in how to use these lessons to shift from a criminal legal imagination that centres on *punishment* to an anti-carceral feminist imagination that values *accountability* in other places and socio-political contexts.

SUPPORTING SURVIVORS: HOW NEEDS CAN BE MET

Any response to a person who has been violated should enable them to reclaim their agency and regain control over their life. Instead of distancing survivors, as Anna and Micah experienced, transformative responses to violence hold space with survivors to explore their needs, wants, feelings, options and choices. This may require community members to confront common misconceptions of survivors. The assumption of survivors as damaged and fragile can lead to community members feeling insufficiently skilled to support survivors, unable to identify what they can do to help or frozen by a fear of causing further harm. Chicago-based transformative justice facilitator Mariame Kaba challenges these perceptions: 'what I always tell people is that as a survivor and as someone who has been around survivors my entire life in my community we are actually not fragile beings we are incredibly pragmatic and resilient because we've survived a lot' (Kaba, 2018). Therefore, the first critical lesson is, as Erin said above – to 'go be there for them' – to support survivors. This can take many different forms including emotional care, material support (including food, companionship, housing, transportation and financial support), creating and holding spaces to grieve, feel and heal in, and actively listen. While it can be difficult for survivors to clarify their needs, particularly in crisis situations, giving space and time to sit with pain and suffering without jumping to an answer or resolution (to fix or rescue) is more empowering for the survivor, and more transformative for a community, who can gain confidence, skills and political awareness of the impacts of harm and trauma (Kim, 2015).

In exploring what a survivor's needs look like, the next challenge to consider is whether these needs can be addressed in an accountability process? Or does a survivor, particularly an activist with privilege (e.g. white, high income, non-disabled, secure immigration status), have short-term or long-term needs that can be adequately met by state agencies, an independent advocacy service or a helpline (such as Rape Crisis, Trans Survivors Switchboard or Women's Aid)? We do not yet live in a world with accountable communities and survivors living with violence in the here and now do not have time to wait. Some survivors may have had contact with state agencies and companionship may be needed to navigate these systems (particularly those at risk of being criminalised by these systems) to access justice. It is crucial to walk alongside a survivor rather than pressure them to pursue a specific path; this requires supporters to hold space for pain, discomfort and uncertainty. Accountability is not suitable to address every harm and meet all survivors' needs. For instance, it does not best serve a survivor's need for healing and can be a very difficult and time-consuming process for all involved, as Mariame Kaba explains:

> Many times processes feel terrible because the harm is so central and if you are engaged in the process with the person who harmed you. My god! It's bringing up so much stuff that if you're constantly trying to grab at the healing you're not in the harm processing that. You're outside looking for that destination that's somewhere down the road

but no actually we have to be right here right now handling all that the fear, the anger, the vengeance feelings, the back and forth sliding against one day you'll want them dead the next day you're ok, we just have to be here holding this right now. So that's what I mean by it's not often [that it] feels like a healing space because healed is not a destination you're always in process.

(Kaba, 2018)

This underscores the need for all involved to be clear about the goals of accountability processes and what needs a process can hold. For Mariame Kaba, accountability work can hold 'an acknowledgement of the harm that occurred, to insist that this person never do this again, to address issues around trust and figuring out how to trust people' (Kaba, 2018). For instance, the accountability process that Breanna, a participant in the salvage research project, experienced was considered by many to be a 'failure' as the person who caused harm was not able to acknowledge the harm they had caused. However, the support that Breanna received did address her need to be heard and believed, to connect with and trust others again:

They've been amazing. They've restored my hope in people. They've made me believed which a lot of people didn't. [...] they had me tell all the harm stories about what had happened with details as much as I was comfortable and it was really traumatic and then afterwards it was like being a phoenix. They've un-sprung me. [...] They were the change they un-sprung me. Literally. It's like being carried and I don't think they'll ever know ever ever know exactly how much they've done [...] They've given me confidence they've given me strength and knowing that I can go 'look this man did this shit and there's an accountability process they can answer any questions' makes me feel less like a lone screaming delusional nutter. No [abuser] has been questioning their credibility and my credibility and they've given me my credibility that I need.

Therefore, while accountability work cannot address all harms and meet all needs, it can offer opportunities to meet needs for acknowledgement, trust and connection. However, accountability cannot be forced onto a person who caused harm and the process can be emotionally distressing and challenging for those involved. The expectations of what needs a process can hold for all involved needs to be acknowledged and adjusted accordingly.

A SITUATED FRAMEWORK FOR TRANSFORMATIVE JUSTICE

In this section, I outline four key avenues for grassroots activists located in the British Left to develop a situated framework for transformative justice to shift towards responses to gendered violence grounded in accountability. This involves: (i) developing understandings of, and responses to, gendered violence as a *collective* process; (ii) centring *relationships* and ways of relating; (iii) *accepting mistakes* as moments for learning/transformation; and (iv) learning from the strengths and weaknesses of diverse anti-violence strategies in British social movement *histories*.

In salvage workshops, we used a scenario-based activity that involved different groups responding to a hypothetical situation of harm from different standpoints. The group that struggled the most were the group who were designated to be close friends of the person who caused harm. The initial impulse tended to be for the group to exclude the person who caused harm from their organising spaces and terminate friendships. It was challenging to imagine other courses of action beyond exclusion. What we need to let go of here is 'the notion that there are "good" and "bad" people [...] We all harm people and are harmed ourselves, in different contexts and conditions and with different levels of power behind us' (Bassichis, 2011). While an impulse to exclude and shun those who harm us and/or those we care about is understandable in a world that disposes of people in prisons, detention centres and secure institutions as Philly Stands Up activists urge, we need to 'find ways to build community with each other without connecting our safety to somebody's exile' (Bench and Peters-Golden, 2012, cited in Kim *et al.*, 2012). In terms of complicating ideas of 'good' and 'bad' people, Common Justice founder, Danielle Sered recognises that 'nearly everyone who commits violence has also survived it, and few have got formal support to heal' (Sered, 2019: 4). Assumptions of safety and sameness can be shifted in a collective naming of the power inequalities, harms and traumas we enter communities and groups with as survivors, supporters or bystanders. The sharing of stories of harm, resilience and resistance in 'community support circles' can allow groups to deepen understandings of how violence shapes all our lives and nurture a commitment to building collective strategies to address harm (Russo, 2019).

Prefiguring liberatory ways of relating to each other lies at the heart of social transformation. Accountability work is a long-term political orientation that questions the ways in which we understand and respond to harm with those we are in community with. Accountability work is an active process that creates and transforms community and different ways of relating to each other, as Mariame Kaba reflects upon in her practice:

> I keep reminding myself and the people I'm in community with in a process that we're doing this because we have a political commitment towards bigger things, ideals for how we treat each other, the interest we all have, the animating question we all have which is how we adjudicate and evaluate harms in a way that is just? How do we do this? And we are testing that out by practicing together being in relationship with each other, transforming our human relationships so that we have a transformed world that's why we're doing it.
>
> (Kaba, 2018)

This can look like many things including: sitting with difficult feelings and experiences without jumping to resolution, figuring out the needs and boundaries of ourselves and others, finding more equitable ways of relating to each other, naming power, learning to actively listen and addressing violence at its small stages (Kim, 2015). Transformative justice is not 'a replacement for police or prisons or a one-size-fits-all fix, but instead [is about] infusing our communities with skills to create resilient, honest, loving relationships' (Bassichis, 2011). The relationship is central in Mariame Kaba's transformative justice work:

> Everything is about the relationship, that is the unit that matters here is the relationship that we build with each other that allows us to build trust over time so that I am accompanying you and you are coming along.
>
> (Kaba, 2018)

Instead of framing activist work around scarcity and urgency, reorienting work around values of abundance and connection, as adrienne maree brown's principles of emergent strategy remind us 'there is always enough time for the right work' and to 'move at the speed of trust' (adrienne maree brown, 2017: 41–2), offers up a framework for a more sustainable activist practice.

Accountability work is emergent, unpaid work in which projects function with limited budgets (if any) and resources. However, the scrutiny that accountability work can face from the wider community can mean that activists feel a high level of responsibility for the outcome of interventions (Caulfield, 2013). This can fuel a culture of perfectionism that positions 'mistakes as personal failings' and 'doing wrong with being wrong' (Jones and Okun, 2001). Activists involved in accountability work can struggle to navigate the demands of the work. However, experienced movement facilitators argue that transformative justice work is primarily about learning and mistakes are central to this process: 'never a failure, always a lesson' (adrienne maree brown, 2017: 41). It may seem counter-intuitive to expect mistakes to be made when responding to violence given additional pressure to be perfect, avoid 'failure' or deepen harm, however, accepting mistakes is an important lesson, as Mariame Kaba explained:

> if you go into it with the idea that the person you are working with is a fragile china doll who's going to crack under any pressure so you can't make a mistake well then you're already set up for failure and failure not in the sense of learning but failure in the sense of catastrophic hurt [...] So the binary of success and failure get rid of that, that's number one.
>
> (Kaba, 2018)

Finding ways to accept mistakes as part of the process and devote time and resources into reflection and identifying lessons learned can be more transformative. As Beth summarised:

> I think there's something to be learned from the thing you're trying to cut out or there's something to be learned from the things you're trying to shun and trying to shut it down, doesn't make it go away for a start. There's no possibility for transforming it when that happens.

The fourth area involves connecting with and learning from our, often messy and conflicted, movement histories: to learn from our elders; to uncover diverse tactics in anti-violence work that have so far been hidden in British feminist histories (Williamson, 2017). For instance, Women Against Rape (WAR), an advocacy and campaign group established in 1976, developed an understanding of the state as a sexist and racist institution, evident in slogans such as 'Racism is Rapism' and research on racialised sexual violence (Hall, 1985). Their intersectional approach to understanding and challenging sexual violence has been shaped by a long-term relationship of organising alongside Black Women's Rape Action Project (BWRAP) and in coalition with English Collective of Prostitutes (ECP) and Wages for Housework (WFH) at Crossroads Women's Centre in London.[9] Divestment from the police, as a source of racist, sexist and homophobic state violence, was a central political tactic for the Lesbians and Policing Project (LESPOP). This London-based project, set up in 1985, conducted research on how lesbians were being treated by the police and educated Black and white lesbians of their legal rights to defend themselves from police harassment in protests, arrest and raids. Nonetheless, a growing 'carceral feminist' agenda, as the British state incorporated feminist demands in criminal justice reforms, has been 'at the price of a radical analysis of the role of state violence in the lives of women of colour' (Sudbury, 2006: 22). These reforms have arguably benefited the most privileged women to the detriment of working-class Black and minority women (Walklate, Fitz-Gibbon and McCulloch, 2018). The challenge here for activists is in how to pick up the call for non-state alternatives to harm that was largely abandoned by the women's specialist sector from the 1990s onwards (Sudbury, 2006). Working in coalition across arenas of activism and specialist support services offers the potential to learn from a British legacy of diverse tactics to gendered violence that oppose state regulation and control.

CONCLUSION

Given global conversations of the harms of state violence, carceral feminism and prison expansion, it is time for a shift of imagination in how to address gendered violence. Transformative justice offers a framework to strengthen our collective capacity to end violence and harm in the networks, spaces and places in which it occurs. However, this requires careful translation into the peculiarities of Britain and its social movements that are shaped by enduring legacies of imperialism and racism. Accountability requires the cultivation of spaces to gather those invested in understanding and ending violence together to gather/ sharpen tools, accounts, stories and experiences of challenging harm. To learn from each other and develop the skills and practices that we need to realize the world we want – the world in which we no longer solely rely on punitive state institutions to resolve gendered violence and harms for us. We can wait no more.

NOTES

1. 'Victim-Survivor led Challenges to Violence and Abuse in our Communities' and 'Accountability Processes', 19 October 2014, Queen Mary's University, London; and 'Gendered Abuse & Violence in Radical Activist Communities', 29 November 2014, Quaker Meeting House, Sheffield.
2. For more information about our sample and research project, see Downes, Hanson and Hudson (2016a).
3. Pseudonyms are used for all participants.
4. See also, Unfollow Movement for Justice, https://unfollowmfj.wordpress.com (accessed 10 April 2019).
5. See, for example, Anonymous, Wharf Chambers Statement Response – Abuse Apologism and Racism, http://wharfabuseandracism.tumblr.com (accessed 10 April 2019).
6. For further information on self-accountability, see K. Fujikawa and S. Perez-Darby, 27 September 2018, 'What is Self-Accountability', Part 2 Building Accountable Communities video series published by Survived & Punished on https://youtu.be/kZIEYuYZ1sw (accessed 10 April 2019).
7. P. Patel, Southall Black Sisters, 11 October 2018, Unpublished interview.
8. These lessons are only possible because of the work of many individuals and groups, primarily people of colour, including: adrienne maree brown, Alisa Bierria, Ana Clarissa Rojas Durazo, Ann Russo, AORTA, The Audre Lorde Project, Bay Area Transformative Justice Collective, Beth Richie, Challenging Male Supremacy Project, Creative Interventions, Critical Resistance, Communities Against Rape and Abuse (CARA), Communities United Against Violence (CUAV), Danielle Sered, Generation 5, INCITE!, Jennai Bundock, Jennifer Patterson, Lauren Caulfield, Leah Lakshmi Piepzna-Samarasinha, Mariame Kaba, Mia Mingus, Mimi Kim, Morgan Bassichis, Northwest Network, Rachel Herzig, Revolution Starts at Home collective, Philly Stands Up, Support New York, Undercurrent, Victoria Law and many more.

9. For further information on the work of Women Against Rape and Black Women's Rape Action Project, see http://againstrape.net (accessed 10 April 2019).

REFERENCES

adrienne maree brown (2017) *Emergent Strategy: Shaping Change, Changing Worlds.* Chico, CA: AK Press.

Ahmed, S. (2018) Complaint as Feminist Pedagogy. 11 May 2018, University of Leeds.

(A)Legal (2014) *What About the Rapists? Anarchist Approaches to Crime and Justice.* Self-published.

Bassel, L. and Emejulu, A. (2017) *Minority Women and Austerity: Survival and Resistance in France and Britain.* Bristol: Policy Press.

Bassichis, M. (2011) *Reclaiming Queer & Trans Safety: The Revolution Starts at Home.* New York: South End Press.

Bernstein, E. (2007) The Sexual Politics of the 'New Abolitionism'. *Differences,* 18(5): 128–51.

Bryan, B., Dadzie, S. and Scafe, S. (1985) *The Heart of the Race: Black Women's Lives in Britain.* London: Virago.

Carlton, B. and Russell, E.K. (2018) *Resisting Carceral Violence: Women's Imprisonment and the Politics of Abolition.* London: Palgrave Macmillan.

Caulfield, L. (2013) To Research Community-Based Safety Projects and Strategies to Combat Gender Violence, USA. Winston Churchill Memorial Trust of Australia Report.

Chen, C-I, Dulani, J. and Piepzna-Samarasinha, L.L. (2011) *The Revolution Starts at Home: Confronting Intimate Violence Within Activist Communities.* New York: South End Press.

Christie, N. (2016) *Crime Control As Industry.* London: Routledge.

Cox, L. (2018) *The Bullying and Harassment of House of Commons Staff: Independent Inquiry Report.* London: Cloisters.

CrimethInc (2013) Accounting for Ourselves: Breaking the Impasse Around Assault and Abuse in Anarchist Scenes. Self-published.

Dean, J. and Maiguashca, B. (2018) Gender, Power, and Left Politics: From Feminization to 'Feministization'. *Politics & Gender,* 14(3): 376–406.

Downes, J. (2016) DIY Queer Feminist (Sub)Cultural Resistance in the UK. Unpublished PhD Thesis: University of Leeds.

Downes, J. (2017) 'It's Not the Abuse that Kills You, It's the Silence': The Silencing of Sexual Violence Activism in Social Justice Movements in the UK Left. *Justice, Power & Resistance,* 1(2): 200–32.

Downes, J., Hanson, K. and Hudson, R. (2016a) Salvage: Gendered Violence in Activist Communities. https://projectsalvage.wordpress.com/research (accessed 10 April 2019).

Downes, J., Hanson, K. and Hudson, R. (2016b) *Salvage: Gendered Violence in Activist Communities*. Leeds: Footprint Workers Co-Op.

Emejulu, A. and Bassel, L. (2015) Minority Women, Austerity and Activism. *Race & Class*, 57(2): 86–95.

Evans, R. (2018) UK Political Groups Spied on by Undercover Police. *Guardian*, 15 October.

Filar, R. (2016) Notes Towards a Theory of the Manarchist. *Strike! Magazine*, 14.

Gill, A.K., Heathcote, G. and Williamson, E. (2016) Introduction: Violence. *Feminist Review*, 112(1): 1–10.

Gilmore, J., Jackson, W. and Monk, H. (2016) Keep Moving: Report on the Policing of Barton Moss Community Protection Camp. November 2013–April 2014, Centre for the Study of Crime, Criminalisation and Social Exclusion, Liverpool John Moore University Centre for URBan Research (CURB), University of York.

Gottschalk, G. (2006) *The Prison and the Gallows: The Politics of Mass Incarceration in America*. Cambridge: Cambridge University Press.

Grewal, S., Kay, J., Landor, L., Lewis, G. and Parmar, P. (1988) *Charting the Journey: Writings by Black and Third World Women*. London: Sheba.

Hall, R.E. (1985) *Ask Any Woman: A London Inquiry into Rape and Sexual Assault*. Bristol: Falling Wall Press.

INCITE! and Critical Resistance (2005) Gender Violence and the Prison Industrial Complex: Interpersonal and State Violence Against Women of Color. In N.J. Sokoloff (ed.), *Domestic Violence at the Margins: Readings of Race, Class, Gender and Culture*. New Brunswick, NJ: Rutgers University Press, 102–14.

INCITE! (2017) *The Revolution Will Not be Funded: Beyond the Non-Profit Industrial Complex*. Durham, NC: Duke University Press.

Jolivette, A.J. (2015) *Research Justice: Methodologies for Social Change*. Bristol: Policy Press.

Jones, K. and Okun, T. (2001) *White Supremacy Culture. Dismantling Racism*: A Workbook for Social Change Groups 2001. www.showingupforracialjustice.org/white-supremacy-culture-characteristics.html (accessed 10 April 2019).

Jonsson, T. (2014) White Feminist Stories. *Feminist Media Studies*, 14(6): 1012–27.

Kaba, M. (2018) How to Survive the End of the World. Podcast, interviewed by Autumn Brown and adrienne maree brown. The Practices We Need: #metoo and Transformative Justice Part 2, 7 November.

Kim, M. (2010) Alternative Interventions to Intimate Violence: Defining Political and Pragmatic Challenges. In J. Ptacek (ed.), *Restorative Justice and Violence Against Women*. Oxford: Oxford University Press, 193–217.

Kim, M. (2015) Dancing the Carceral Creep: The Anti-Domestic Violence Movement and the Paradoxical Pursuit of Criminalization, 1973–1986. ISSI Fellows Working Paper, Institute for the Study of Societal Issues UC Berkeley.

Kim, M., Bassichis, M. (CUAV), Hernandez, F., Maccani, R.J., Jashnani, G., Bench and Peters-Golden, J. (2012) A World Without Walls: Stopping Harm and Abolishing the Prison Industrial Complex. *The Abolitionist*, 6 February, www.cuav.org/a-world-without-walls-stopping-harm-abolishing-the-prison-industrial-complex (accessed 10 April 2019).

Kindon, S., Pain, R. and Kesby, M. (2009) Participatory Action Research. International Encyclopaedia of Human Geography. In R. Kitchin and N. Thrift (eds), *International Encyclopaedia of Human Geography*. Oxford: Elsevier, 90–5.

Lamble, S. (2013) Queer Necropolitics and the Expanding Carceral State: Interrogating Sexual Investments in Punishment. *Law Critique*, 24: 229–53.

Law, V. (2011) Protection Without the Police: North American Community Responses to Violence in the 1970s and Today. *Upping the Anti*, 12: 91–104.

Montesinos Coleman, L. and Bassi, S.A. (2011) Deconstructing Militant Manhood: Masculinities in the Disciplining of (Anti-)Globalisation Politics. *International Feminist Journal of Politics*, 13(2): 204–24.

Morris, R. (2000) *Stories of Transformative Justice*. Toronto: Canadian Scholars' Press.

Prescod-Roberts, M. and Steele, N. (1980) *Black Women: Bringing It All Back Home*. Bristol: Falling Wall Press.

Pusey, A. (2010) Social Centres and the New Cooperativism of the Common. *Affinities*, 4(1): 176–98.

Reiner, R. (2016) Foreword. In Mark Brunger, Stephen Tong and Denise Martin (eds), *Introduction to Policing Research: Taking Lessons from Practice*. London: Routledge.

Richie, B.E. (2012) *Arrested Justice: Black Women, Violence and America's Prison Nation*. New York: New York University Press.

Russo, A. (2019) *Feminist Accountability: Disrupting Violence And Transforming Power*. New York: New York University Press.

Sered, D. (2019) *Until We Reckon: Violence, Mass Incarceration and a Road to Repair*. New York: The New Press.

Sudbury, J. (2006) Rethinking Antiviolence Strategies: Lessons from the Black Women's Movement in Britain. In *Color of Violence: The INCITE! Anthology*. Cambridge, MA: South End Press.

Thuma, E.L. (2019) All Our Trials: Prisons, Policing and the Feminist Fight to End Violence. Urbana, IL: University of Illinois Press.

Trân, N.L. (2016) Calling IN: A Less Disposable Way of Holding Each Other Accountable. In Mia McKenzie, CeCe McDonald and Patrisse Cullors (eds), *The Solidarity Struggle: How People of Color Succeed*. Oakland, CA: BGD Press, 59–63.

Urb, C. and Crabb, C. (2011) *It's Down to This: Stories, Critiques and Ideas on Community and Collective Response to Sexual Violence and Accountability*. Chico, CA: AK Press.

Wakefield, S. and Grrrt (1995) *Not for Rent: Conversations with Creative Activists in the UK*. Amsterdam: Evil Twin Publications.

Walklate, S., Fitz-Gibbon, K. and McCulloch, J. (2018) Is More Law the Answer? Seeking Justice for Victims of Intimate Partner Violence Through the Reform of Legal Categories. *Criminology & Criminal Justice*, 18(1): 115–31.

Williamson, A. (2017) The Law and Politics of Marital Rape in England, 1945–1994. *Women's History Review*, 26(3): 382–413.

12

Challenging Prevent

Building Resistance to Institutional Islamophobia and the Attack on Civil Liberties

Robert Ferguson

CHALLENGING PREVENT: DEFIANCE, DISSENT AND RESISTANCE

The Prevent programme was first introduced under Tony Blair in 2003, as a strand of the government's counter-terrorism strategy, 'CONTEST'. Following the 7/7 bombings in 2005, state funding for the Prevent programme increased steadily and Prevent now occupies a pivotal role in the British state's 'counter-extremism' strategy. In 2015, David Cameron's government placed Prevent on a statutory footing, institutionalising Prevent's role across wide reaches of the public domain by imposing a statutory 'duty' on public sector institutions to pay 'due regard to the need to prevent people from being drawn into terrorism' (HM Government, 2015). Placing Prevent on a statutory footing had a major impact on the Muslim community, and on the relationship between public institutions and those they served. In the wake of the government announcement in March 2015, widespread opposition emerged, spanning the Muslim community, the education sector, public sector employees, civil liberties organisations and anti-racist campaigners.

Within months of its introduction, Prevent's credibility and reputation was severely damaged, particularly within the Muslim community. In January 2016, David Anderson QC, the government-appointed independent reviewer of terrorism legislation, in a submission to the Home Affairs Select Committee, recommended an independent review. He noted Prevent had become a 'significant source of grievance' in the Muslim community and had encouraged 'mistrust to spread and to fester'. Anderson documented wide-ranging condemnations of the Prevent duty across civil society (Home Affairs Select Committee, 2016).

There is a wide body of writing and commentary that systematically critiques Prevent and its impact (see, for example, Kundnani, 2009, 2014, 2015; Holmwood and O'Toole, 2017; Belaon, 2015; Open Society Justice Initiative, 2016; Just Yorkshire, 2017; CAGE, 2011, 2014). However, there has been little study of the movement against and opposition to Prevent. The aim of this chapter is to explore the successes, limits and challenges that the various movements and campaigns against Prevent faced in education institutions. Education forms one of the state's central terrains for combatting 'extremist' ideas and promoting 'British values'. Education is the main sphere for Prevent's surveillance role, accounting for the single highest number of referrals to Channel: panels, co-ordinated by the police, charged with 'supporting' individuals deemed vulnerable to 'radicalisation'. Above all, education has been the foremost site of resistance to Prevent.

PREVENT: STATE-SPONSORED ISLAMOPHOBIA

Prevent rests on the premise that ideology is the key driver of terrorism and is characterised by an 'extremist' worldview that divides society into 'them' and 'us'. The Prevent strategy therefore, is to identify the alleged proponents of 'extremism' on one hand and those individuals whose pathological and psychological vulnerabilities they exploit, leading to 'radicalisation' and violence.

The Prevent narrative itself disregards any analysis of terrorism as a *political* strategy. Its core categories such as 'extremism' and 'radicalisation' evade any positive definition. They are in themselves arbitrary and defined negatively, primarily in relation to 'British values' that are assumed as self-evident and uncontested. The effect is to de-contextualise and de-politicise analyses of terrorism. In an early, comprehensive analysis of Prevent, Arun Kundnani demonstrates how the programme constructs Muslims as a 'suspect community', 'depoliticising young people and restricting radical dissent'. Kundnani argues that Prevent assumes that '… the government needs to combat extremism through "a battle of ideas" which aims at isolating "mainstream Muslims" from a global insurgency.' He further notes that a 'form of ideological campaigning for "British values" and "moderate Islam" has come to be seen as a matter of national security. Notions of multiculturalism are seen as a threat to this campaign' (Kundnani, 2009: 6–7).

The features of Prevent identified by Kundnani recur throughout the literature on Prevent and 'counter-extremism'. This includes Kundnani's later work, Holmwood and O'Toole's important study of the Trojan Horse affair in Birmingham schools, and a range of specific case studies (Kundnani, 2014, 2015; Holmwood and O'Toole, 2017). The same critiques also arise in campaigning literature and in campaign meetings, conferences and protests.

The Impact of Prevent: Referrals to Channel

The targeting of individuals under the Prevent duty has provided a key focus of opposition. Referrals to Channel rose from five in 2006/7 to 1,281 in 2013/14 (National Police Chiefs' Council, n.d.). In 2015/16, after the introduction of Prevent as a statutory duty, the referral rate escalated six-fold to a total of 7,631 individuals subject to a referral to Channel (Home Office, 2017). This has had human consequences. In the majority of cases, any concern regarding terrorism proved unfounded. In 2017/18, of 7,318 individuals referred, only 18 per cent were deemed appropriate for discussion by a Channel panel and, of those, only 5 per cent were deemed as requiring 'support' (Home Office, 2018).

While much is recently made of the rise in referrals for right-wing extremism, referral rates are grossly disproportionate. The Muslim population of Britain at the 2011 census was 4.8 per cent (Office for National Statistics, 2011/2012). If we extrapolated the referral rate of Muslims to the 'white British' population, the latter would have run to many tens of thousands. Furthermore, referrals of individuals from white British backgrounds do not reflect on British nationality, culture, white ethnicity or religion. Islamophobic stereotyping dominates the individual case profiles of those referred.[1]

This has to be understood in the context of Prevent as a disguised but systemic form of institutionalised Islamophobia. Each year, hundreds of thousands of teachers, academics, health staff, police and public sector staff are funnelled through WRAP 'training'; the core message is a 'statutory duty' to report 'concerns'. The parameters of 'suspect' behaviour are so broad that subjective prejudices are potentially allowed free reign. A typical resource notes that cause for concern in child behaviour may include: '*trying to make sense of world events*'; '*personal grievance or experience of racism or discrimination*'; '*out of character changes in dress, behaviour*'; '*changes in friendship group*'; '*appearing angry about government policies, especially foreign policy*' (Camden Safeguarding Children Board, 2015).

Prevent referrals thus reflect a systematic embedding of racial profiling and discriminatory practice behind which lie countless individual instances of distress, anger, alienation, even trauma, that impact on individuals, classmates, families and communities.

Universities and Prevent

Prevent's impact on campuses was felt immediately on its introduction as a statutory duty. Individual Muslim students and Islamic societies fell under suspicion; in at least one instance, CCTV cameras were installed to monitor a prayer room (Faith Matters, 2016). Muslim and non-Muslim campaigners were vilified in the media and arenas of legitimate debate and campaign activity became circumscribed, monitored or even banned (Nagdee, Ghani and Ibrahim, 2017: 31–4). The pressure was exacerbated further as criticism of the State of Israel, and pro-Palestine solidarity was deemed 'anti-Semitic' (*Guardian*, 2017).

Right-wing think-tanks, such as the Henry Jackson Society, and their front organisation, the misnamed 'Students Rights', mounted regular witch hunts of Prevent's critics (Fox, 2019). Malia Bouattia, National Union of Students (NUS) Black Students Officer (later elected NUS President) and Shelly Asquith, an NUS vice-president, both at the forefront of the Students Not Suspects campaign, came under particular attack. As campuses became one of the most important sites of resistance to Prevent, student activists, both Muslim and non-Muslim, became key targets for a joint assault by government ministers, the racist right, right-wing media and Prevent advocates.

Schools and Community

Schools bear a unique relationship to the communities they serve, and state education has been a uniquely contested social sphere since its inception. It is no accident, therefore, that Prevent takes on its most institutionalised form in our schools and colleges. The education sector as a whole accounts for the single largest number of Channel referrals, closely followed by the police, from whom referrals include school pupils and students. The median age of referrals from the education sector is 14 (Home Office, 2018: 11).

While the extent of referrals points to the structural discriminatory character of Prevent, the implementation of Prevent extends well beyond monitoring and reporting individuals. Schools form a bridgehead across which the state reaches into the community and society. In 2014, Birmingham schools became the site of a state-induced 'moral panic', riven with Islamophobic narratives, directed at the largest Muslim community in the UK.

The nationwide furore that became known as the Trojan Horse affair surfaced in the form of a letter purporting to be part of a correspondence between a group of 'Islamists', which was sent to Birmingham City Council and leaked to the media. The 'letter' appeared to reveal an Islamist plot to take over Birmingham schools. It was soon identified as a hoax. Nonetheless, a series of investigations into 21 Birmingham schools was launched by Ofsted, the Education Funding Authority, Birmingham City Council and a government investigation under former counter-terrorism chief Peter Clarke.

Of the schools investigated, five were placed in special measures and one labelled inadequate. The chair of governors of Park View Educational Trust and 14 teachers were banned from the teaching profession for life. In the aftermath of Trojan Horse, Muslim governors and parents were effectively purged from Birmingham schools (Holmwood and O'Toole, 2017). The Trojan Horse affair was mobilised as explicit justification for the government's introduction of the Prevent duty. It marked out education as a frontline for the state in enforcing compliance upon Muslim communities.

The run up to the new legislation coming into force saw further state intervention in the east London borough of Tower Hamlets, as Ofsted mounted unannounced inspections in a number of local schools, again framed in the context of 'extremism' and British Values; clashes also developed in the neighbouring boroughs of Waltham Forest and Newham between institutions, local authorities and local Muslim communities.

In addition to state interventions targeting individuals and schools, Prevent has a particularly discriminatory influence on pedagogy and pastoral provision. Ofsted inspectors are specifically charged with interrogating lesson plans and schemes of work for compliance with Prevent and 'British Values' (Ofsted, 2018: 48). This forms a key 'line of enquiry' for inspectors, particularly for schools with a high Muslim intake. A school judged 'inadequate' on such grounds, faces the threat of 'special measures' and possible suspension of funding. As a consequence, the presumption that young Muslims may be non-reflective, liable to prejudice, or a potential danger to themselves and others, can seep into pedagogy itself. This is most evident when approaches to equality and diversity issues become racialised under a Prevent umbrella or as religious observance, prayer and dress become viewed through the prism of 'British Values'.

The sum effect of prevent interventions and approaches is to 'chill' critical areas of discussion. These include the role of the state, political parties and mainstream media in fomenting Islamophobia; the role of foreign policy and military intervention in fuelling the spread of terrorism; open discussion of Palestine and any open criticism of Prevent itself. The resources on the government sponsored 'Educate Against Hate' site for school leaders and staff are framed to divert away from any such discussions and onto individual behaviours and 'ideology'. Muslim students often feel constrained even in discussing recent acts of terror in a school environment. Education unions in particular have been prominent in highlighting such 'chilling' influences (Courtney, 2016).

There is a telling absence of research on Prevent. One rare project that examines educationalists' experiences indicates a relatively high level of confidence among those surveyed in *implementing* the duty (Busher, Choudhury, Thomas and Harris, 2017: 22).[2] However, 57 per cent of staff surveyed thought Prevent made it more likely that Muslim students might feel stigmatised whereas only 9 per cent thought the reverse (Busher *et al.*, 2017: 55). Perceptions of BME staff varied significantly from white colleagues: so 29 per cent of Black Ethnic Minority (BME) staff thought discussions with students on issues such as extremism and inequality were less open as a consequence of Prevent; only 9 per cent of white staff were of this view. Whereas 43 per cent of white teachers thought discussions were more open, only 25 per cent of BME staff did so (Busher *et al.*, 2017: 53). Almost 40 per cent of BME staff thought the Prevent duty made it more difficult to create an environment in which students from different backgrounds get on well with one another, as opposed to 25 per cent of white staff (Busher *et al.*, 2017: 56).

Such differentiated responses from white and BME staff serve to signal the institutionally racist character of Prevent. The voices of Muslim staff and students are effectively excluded from any consideration of discriminatory practice or equality impact assessment. The framing of Prevent as a 'rational' appeal to collective security and 'safeguarding' is deeply insidious; the effect is to depoliticise state policy and mask the institutionalised Islamophobia at its core. Introducing a specific Prevent 'duty' has also served to suppress discussion and debate over Prevent within institutions. Objections are dismissed as at best, 'personal opinion' that must be put aside in meeting 'safeguarding' responsibilities and, at worst, an attempt to obstruct employers' and employees' obligations under law.

The advocates of Prevent had significant success in disguising its inherent 'othering' of the Muslim community and in presenting Prevent as a 'safeguarding' measure. Second, Prevent appropriated 'liberal' values around equality themes as a vehicle for differentiating between 'British' values and those of a Muslim 'other'. However, crucially, in the final analysis, Prevent rests on enforcement and threat, both implicit and explicit. The Trojan Horse Affair, the thousands of referrals of entirely innocent individuals, the suppression of free speech on campus, the interventions by Ofsted, local Prevent officers, Channel and the police all set a marker of state expectations for public institutions. The pressure to self-police and to conform to a state narrative is intense. It is against this background that resistance to Prevent has to be understood.

OPPOSITION: BUILDING ALLIANCES, FORGING UNITY

Resistance to Prevent was both diverse and unifying, and the alliances that formed as the movement took shape, displayed a distinctive character. This was not a movement focused on mass public opposition to foreign policy, such as the mass anti-war movement led by the Stop the War Coalition against the Iraq War, or earlier movements for nuclear disarmament. Nor did it follow the same trajectory as mass movements against racism and fascism, such as the Anti-Nazi League, nor that of social movements around the environment or womens' rights and LGBTQ rights.

The movement against Prevent is shaped in large part by the nature of the legislation itself. First, Prevent is extra-judicial in character and even participation (for instance, Channel is nominally 'voluntary').

Second, the state has been at pains to present Prevent in 'liberal' clothing. Unlike, for example, the openly reactionary character of Clause 28 of the Local Government Act (1988), which similarly imposed a 'duty' on local authorities, in this case not to 'intentionally promote homosexuality or publish material with the intention of promoting homosexuality' or 'promote the teaching in any maintained school of the acceptability of homosexuality as a pretended family relationship.'[3] Third, Prevent isolates, intimidates, silences and disempowers in ways that mitigate against seeking solidarity or support.

The narrative of 'safeguarding' has to a significant extent been effective in disguising Prevent's institutionally racist character. Many public sector workers, who would oppose outright any open expression of Islamophobia or racism, have been persuaded the policy is benign. Those who are sceptical, feel under pressure to comply with a duty whose declared aim is to counter the threat of terrorism. Ultimately, however, there is the very real threat of sanction, both against individuals and institutions.

The comparison with the opposition to Clause 28 is instructive. The effect of the 1988 legislation was to reinforce discrimination and prejudicial attitudes. As with Prevent, the key focus was education and 'safeguarding' children from perceived 'malign' influences that undermined 'family values'. The legislation served to legitimise and reinforce views of gay men as a threat to society. Opposition to Clause 28 first emerged from within the LGBT+ community. However, their campaigns won support from education unions, teachers, the wider trade union movement, including the National Union of Miners and the Labour Party.

However, whereas Prevent has taken pains to cloak itself as a *defence* of 'liberal' values and equality, the narrative underpinning Section 28 was openly reactionary and regressive. Opposition to Section 28 was shaped by major demonstrations and protests by the LGBT+ community and their supporters, in a way that the movement against Prevent has not.

For all these reasons, the opposition to Prevent has not taken the form of a single mobilising organisation such as the movements referred to above but rather of alliances between discrete organisations and campaigns that would come together in joint initiatives and to share platforms, while focusing on their own independent remit.

Opposition has taken the form of community and campaign meetings, trade union events, public statements, open letters, petitions and a high level of online and social media campaigning. The formation of alliances has been highly significant, not least between Muslim and non-Muslim activists and organisations.

One feature of the opposition that is important to note are the common roots in wider social movements that many of these activists did share. Particularly significant here is the continuing political legacy of the anti-war movement and Stop the War Coalition and its role in forging mass opposition to war on the premise of an explicit rejection of Islamophobia on the part of the state and within society as a whole. Its mass demonstrations were marked by an unprecedented unity between Muslim and non-Muslim, with Muslim communities mobilising tens of thousands from across Britain.

The impact of the anti-war movement and its unifying character cannot be underestimated in forging a political basis for unity in combatting the divisive effects of Islamophobia and Prevent. That spirit of unity, which was a unique feature of the anti-war movement in Britain, was explicitly invoked among campaigners as former alliances and collaboration were renewed or reforged.

Universities

A key component of the coalitions and alliances against Prevent was the campaign launched by activists in the National Union of Students (NUS). The 'Students Not Suspects' (SnS) tour, initiated by NUS Black Students, began at the start of the academic year in October 2015, providing a major focus for opposition to Prevent. The student-led campaign was complemented and reinforced by independent initiatives on the part of hundreds of academics including an open letter signed in July 2015 by 280 leading academics, campaigners and student leaders, followed by a number of other high-profile initiatives (*Independent*, 2015).

A keynote speaker of the SnS tour was former Guantanamo prisoner, Moazzam Begg, also Outreach Director for the advocacy and campaign group, CAGE whose presence attracted a large number of Muslim community activists who were joined by anti-racist campaigners, left activists, teachers and others. Important links were forged between these different activists that in turn led to collaboration beyond the campuses themselves. This process led to the formation of 'Challenging Prevent', reaching a peak with a national conference in 2016 at Goldsmiths University. Over 400 activists attended including a wide range of Muslim community organisations, trade unions, academics, anti-racist organisations and individuals who had been targeted by Prevent.[4]

The SnS campaign was met with ferocious attack by right-wing media, far-right commentators and think-tanks, and advocates of Prevent, often characterised by Islamophobic hate mongering and demonisation. Indeed, it is a characteristic of Prevent that for all its 'liberal' veneer, when faced with opposition, it has relied on the racist right and Islamophobic sections of the media to demonise its critics. Muslim voices and organisations bore the brunt. Two advocacy organisations in particular, CAGE and Muslim Engagement and Development (MEND), were continually targeted as 'extremists'. The SnS campaign and its leadership were attacked relentlessly for their collaboration with Muslim voices.

The attempt to divide and undermine opposition to Prevent was not without effect. Nonetheless, this phase of the movement against Prevent had a formative and long-lasting impact. The SnS' initiative provided a focus for students, academics and community and trade union opposition that continues to prove a thorn in the side of state policy.

Resistance: Schools and Communities

It was the imposition of the Prevent duty in schools that gave rise both to the most bitter and open rifts between the state and Muslim communities. The Trojan Horse affair encapsulated the way in which the state sought to use education and schools to bring entire communities into line. Massive punitive resources were brought to bear in the form of three separate enquiries and intense media pressure. Beyond the five schools and 14 teachers and governors targeted, the underlying narrative was of a Muslim community importing 'alien' values into British schools, posing a threat to society as a whole.[5]

Nonetheless, despite the state achieving its initial aims, it certainly did not win hearts and minds – quite the reverse. Community opposition took the form of a sustained, determined campaign. By 2017, the teaching bans imposed on Tahir Alam, chair of governors at Park View, and 13 teachers were overturned, dismissed in the courts or dropped. Alliances formed during the campaign, anticipated those that emerged after 2015.

Over three years after Trojan Horse, a meeting in Birmingham saw several hundred local people in attendance, despite the original venue being placed under pressure and cancelling at the last moment. The platform reflected the alliances characteristic of the movement against Prevent: Salma Yaqoob, a leading political figure in Birmingham and in the movement against the Iraq War; Azad Ali of MEND; Kevin Courtney, General Secretary of the NUT; Tahir Alam, former chair of governors at Park View; John Holmwood, professor at Nottingham University; and Peter Oborne, journalist and writer for the *Spectator*. The meeting was hosted by MEND and supported by Birmingham Stand Up To Racism and the Association of Muslim Parents.

The opposition to Trojan Horse was not able to stop the immediate assault by the state on the Muslim community in Birmingham. It was nonetheless vindicated by the dismissal of the lifetime bans on those targeted, even if justice could not be said to be won. The campaign had a lasting impact on the community in Birmingham and fed into the wider campaign against Prevent after 2015. As Salma Yaqoob expressed,

> I feel a whole generation has been written off. The young people from those schools affected will be tainted forever with the label of 'potential extremist'. It will stay with them for a long time, as they grow up, go to university and apply for jobs in coming years. The accusations and image being banded around in recent months of Birmingham – both nationally and internationally – have been destroyed.
>
> (University News, 2015)

Resistance Spreads

After Parliament approved the government Prevent guidance in March 2015, local authorities and schools began revising their policies and procedures, keen to pre-empt the 2015/16 round of Ofsted inspections and demonstrate compliance. The scene was set for a series of conflicts.

In May 2015, a survey of primary school children at a mainly Muslim school in Waltham Forest led to a campaign by parents that spread across the community. The survey questions not only evoked anti-Muslim prejudices and stereotypes but identified the children taking the survey with the apparent intention of identifying those who might be seen as 'vulnerable to extremism' (Faith Matters, 2015). Parents were not informed of the survey which signposted Prevent and Channel Guidance (Belaon, 2015: 14).

As a direct result, Waltham Forest Council of Mosques (WFCOM) resolved to boycott Prevent, declaring the programme to be an attack on the Islamic community (Taylor, 2015). Waltham Forest Council was forced to disown the questionnaire but nonetheless refused to jettison the project under which the survey had been promoted, 'BRIT' (Building Resilience Through Integration and Trust). In December, campaigners, including WFCOM, MEND and anti-racist campaigners lobbied a council meeting to demand the BRIT project be suspended. They were joined by family members, who had a few days earlier been turned off a flight for a holiday in Disneyland (BBC News, 2015).

The Waltham Forest council lobby was joined by campaigners from neighbouring Newham. In June 2015, three Muslim women students from Newham Sixth Form College were suspended after sending a long email to students and staff, complaining about the response of college management to the implementation of Prevent (Thomas-Johnson and Milmo, 2015).

The introduction of the Prevent duty had heightened tensions and focussed anger at rising levels of institutional Islamophobia across Muslim communities in east London. In Newham, the case of the 'NewVIc 3' surfaced as some schools attempted to restrict uniform options and preclude previously permitted forms of Muslim dress. The appointment of Ghaffar Hussain, former managing director of the Quilliam Foundation, as Newham Prevent lead fuelled local animosity intensely. Quilliam had been condemned for associations with the far-right and for promoting a blacklist of Muslim organisations, including the Muslim Council of Britain (Ahmed, 2016). In 2013, Hussain himself declared he did not believe the fascist founder of the English Defence League, Tommy Robinson, to be either a 'racist' or that he hated ordinary Muslims (Hussain, 2013).

Well-attended meetings were held in Newham, Ilford and Waltham Forest against Prevent, attracting Muslim audiences of up to 250; the majority were parents but also included teachers, local faith leaders, trade unionists and anti-racist activists. Organisers included MEND, WFCOM, Prevent Watch and Stand Up To Racism with a wide range of speakers including Moazzam Begg; Professor David Miller; Sufiyan Ismail (CEO of MEND); representatives of the NUT; and Stand Up To Racism (Nair, 2015).

In December, a Newham statement condemning the divisive impact of Prevent in the community was sent to all Newham councillors and received national and local press coverage. Over 40 local signatories included: 18 Imams from Newham mosques; Malia Bouattia, national officer of the NUS; local officers of the students' union at UEL, including the president and the LGBT officer; Newham MEND; local officers of the NUT and the University College Union (UCU); the Green Party; Stand Up To Racism and others (Stand Up To Racism, 2015).

Opposition to Prevent was framed within a general climate of anti-Muslim prejudice, discrimination and hate crime. Many of the campaigners against Prevent play leading roles in protests against hate crime and the far-right. The political and media proponents of Prevent have themselves mobilised its 'counter-extremism' narrative to target forms of religious observance, particularly female dress, prayer and the observance of Ramadan.

This was exemplified when St Stephen's Primary school in Newham became the focus of a national campaign to ban the hijab at the start of the academic year in 2017 (*Sunday Times*, 2017). This echoed the anti-Muslim climate fuelled by bans on the headscarf in France and elsewhere, and the targeting of Muslim women and girls in Britain in rising levels of hate crime and violence. The hijab ban campaigners met with and received a positive reception from the head of Ofsted and Chief Inspector of Education, Amanda Spielman, who publicly supported the St Stephen's head and chair of governors and denigrated the parents' campaign as the work of outside extremists (Weale, 2018). Spielman had already suggested that her inspectors would question primary girls who wore headscarves; she repeatedly and insistently framed issues of Muslim dress in the context of extremism and 'British Values'. Inevitably, opposition to Prevent was seen in the wider context of Islamophobia and anti-Muslim prejudice.

Despite the powerful forces ranged against the parents at St Stephen's and their supporters, their opposition to the ban was victorious. The head was finally forced to concede to a meeting of over 100 parents that the school had made 'a huge error of judgement' and she announced the ban had been withdrawn (Thomas-Johnson and Hooper, 2018). The chair of governors resigned after it was revealed that he had posted abuse on social media and had circulated an email attacking a local Imam as 'an unholy bastard' (Thomas-Johnson and Hooper, 2018).

The importance of the St Stephen's campaign should not be under-estimated. Calls for a national ban were dropped once the extent of community opposition at the school became evident. A national ban on the hijab in schools could only have reinforced the demonisation of Muslim women, already vulnerable to hate crime and violence.

Amanda Spielman was herself put on the defensive at Education Sub-Committee hearings in Parliament. The national conference of the NEU (NUT Section) passed a resolution condemning Spielman for her statements that threatened to 'lead to further marginalisation of, and increased physical and verbal attacks on, Muslim girls and Muslim women' (Education Committee, 2018; Hooper, 2018). The vote was overwhelming and followed electric contributions from Muslim women teachers, videos of which went viral.

The St Stephen's campaign proved the potential of a local campaign. The parents had been supported by campaigners from MEND, local councillors, faith leaders and anti-racist campaigners, many of whom saw the 'hijab ban' as an extension of state's 'counter-extremism' Prevent agenda. What had been begun as a concerted campaign to ban the hijab in schools at the start of the academic year in 2017, foundered.

Inside the Classroom Walls

Unorganised, individual and informal forms of resistance are by defi-nition difficult to quantify, particularly where punitive action may be brought to bear, if such opposition is exposed. Yet the extent to which education staff, students and even institutional managers circumvent, adapt or even undermine the intentions of the state should not be under-estimated. This is hinted at by Busher et al., who note that teachers are highly aware of the 'possible negative consequences of the Prevent duty on student–staff interactions' and of the potential for Muslim students to be stigmatised. Consequently, they observe that: 'schools, colleges and individual staff have developed a variety of strategies to counter or at least mitigate such consequences' (Busher et al., 2017: 54).

Underlying this observation, there lies a contested process, sometimes conscious and deliberate, sometimes reactive grounded in a strong anti-racist, inclusive ethos within the teaching profession. Ultimately, neither Prevent leads Ofsted inspectors nor can managers police every classroom. Indeed, the Prevent narrative had to adapt over time in order to gain purchase and acceptance. Even so, individual teachers may ignore materials they perceive as problematic, or adapt and develop their own, sometimes with managers' agreement. These may include discussions on discriminatory legislation, media attacks on Muslims, discussion on the causes of terrorism and the role of foreign policy.

In some institutions an excessive diet of Prevent and British Values is allowed to pass as simply a tiresome tick box exercise. In an informal conversation one teacher commented, 'We pretend to talk about it ... and they pretend to listen'.

In staff settings, Muslim staff hold their peace. They are acutely aware of debates on Prevent and are generally more informed than the often all-white and non-Muslim leadership teams who lecture them on Islamophobia. Discussion on Prevent that is suppressed within formal settings often re-emerges in union forums, in informal spheres or outside the school walls.

Individual and Community Resistance

The introduction of Prevent as a statutory duty was marked by highly publicised examples of individual targeting. These were generally the result of spontaneous acts of opposition by individual parents and students (*Independent*, 2016; Prevent Watch March and June 2016). While such individual acts of defiance have only involved a small number of individuals, these played an important part in shaping public perceptions and generalising opposition, including within the education unions and the civil liberties' organisation 'Liberty' (Whittaker, 2016; UCU, 2015; Liberty, 2017). Their cases were given very wide social media coverage by Muslim advocacy organisations in particular, such as CAGE, MEND and Prevent Watch, and campaign meetings and conferences frequently provided a platform to individuals such as Mohammed Umar Farook, Ifhat Smith and others.

Muslim advocacy organisations acted as important 'go to' platforms for a wide section of the Muslim community. Community leaders and mosque committees that had relationships with their local authorities and felt under the watchful eye of Prevent were often reticent in voicing opposition or criticism. Campaign materials, news reports and resources from MEND and CAGE provided an important avenue for raising awareness and discussion of Prevent within the Muslim community.[6] Online platforms such as *5Pillars* and organisations such as the Islamic Human Rights Commission and MPACUK also commanded a significant audience).[7] NUS Black Students produced a handbook on combatting Prevent and Stand Up to Racism produced a pamphlet, 'Prevent: Why We Should Dissent' (Nagdee *et al.*, 2017; Ferguson, Ali and Richardson, 2017).

There has been an ongoing cost for those taking a stand against Prevent and more generally against mainstream Islamophobia. Muslim organisations have been subject to vilification by right-wing think-tanks, politicians and the media. The Tory government refuses to have any formal relation even with the MCB; Trade unionists and anti-racist campaigners who express solidarity with Muslim communities against Prevent also find themselves a target.

RESISTING PREVENT: THE CHALLENGES AND THE FUTURE

The movement against Prevent has had considerable success in highlighting the Islamophobic narrative at its centre and in challenging its claims as an effective means of countering terrorism. Prevent has been widely discredited. The announcement of an 'independent review' by the current government is evidence of a recognition, however partial, of Prevent's failures.

However, the movement against Prevent continues to face significant challenges. The duty itself is deeply institutionalised within state and public institutions. Prevent's 'chilling effect' on dissent remains significant, particularly within Muslim communities and in education. Opponents face demonisation at the hands of government ministers, the media, Ofsted, right-wing 'think-tanks' and Prevent professionals (Gilligan, 2016). These campaigns foster a climate of intimidation that inhibits open dissent, despite individual apologies and retractions (*Daily Telegraph*, 2016; 2017). Each year, thousands of innocent individuals are cast under suspicion and referred through an extra-judicial process administered by the police.

The opposition to Prevent also faced broader challenges. The Students Not Suspects (SnS) campaign reached a peak with the 'Prevent, Islamophobia and Civil Liberties Conference' in June 2016. However, following her election victory as NUS president that year, Malia Bouattia and the left in the NUS faced a virulent campaign from the right, resulting in her defeat the following year. As a Muslim woman president and a vocal supporter of the Palestinian struggle, Bouattia soon found herself caught up in the charges of anti-Semitism being mounted against Jeremy Corbyn's supporters and the left, putting the left in the NUS on the defensive.

Even on the part of anti-Prevent campaigners within the Muslim community, there is an underlying tension between gaining acceptance and a 'voice at the table', and maintaining an activist stance that estranges them from local and national political support. Such tensions were at the root of emergent differences that led to the departure of a number of leading activists from MEND in early 2018.

Similar pressures are evident in the reluctance of Labour Party figures in calling for the complete withdrawal of Prevent, who otherwise play an active and prominent role against racism and Islamophobia. While education unions have declared their opposition to Prevent and called for the statutory duty to be repealed, this does not extend to non-compliance.

CONCLUSION

The anti-Prevent movement has had lasting resonance and impact. The primary role has come from within the Muslim community and Muslim organisations. However, opposition to Prevent from non-Muslim organisations, education unions, academics, civil liberty organisations and anti-racist activists has been a central and critical feature. Opposition from non-Muslim voices and organisations has been important in and of itself, however, the solidarity, joint platforms and coalitions of resistance that emerged between Muslim and non-Muslim were important in another key respect.

While such alliances could not entirely dissipate the sense of siege in Muslim communities, non-Muslim opposition was an important counter to the charge that opposition to Prevent was restricted to 'Muslim extremists'. Attempts by the state, media and the Islamophobic right to isolate and silence Muslim voices would have been far more successful if Muslim organisations had been left to fight alone.

So the NUS and the SnS campaign played an important role on the campuses and as a focus for wider networks of opposition. Activists and representatives in the education unions helped counter and limit anti-Muslim racism fuelled by the Prevent narrative and at local level, trade union opposition reinforced community opposition where anti-racist organisations such as Stand Up To Racism also played a role. Opposition from academics, while focusing on defending free speech, lent important authority to criticisms of the Prevent narrative.

What is the way forward then for the movement against Prevent? Significant challenges remain. The architects of Prevent in its current form have had some success in masking the underlying racist narrative in 'liberal' colours, or even as a vehicle of opposition to racism, prejudice and inequality. The terrorism threat is real and there is thus an understandable apprehension at being tarred as complicit in failing to address it. Institutions and leaders fear the array of punitive measures the state has at its disposal. Some left political figures and sections of the anti-racist movement that have been robust in opposing anti-Muslim racism and hate crime, display greater hesitancy when it comes to Prevent.

Paradoxically, these challenges may point to one way forward. The introduction of Prevent as a statutory duty did not emerge in a vacuum. From the outset, Prevent was framed within a wider narrative of Muslims as a 'suspect community'. This narrative has fuelled the rise of prominent, racist 'populist' politicians, parties and movements that present themselves as their nations' defence against Muslim and migrant 'invaders'. This theme has been played across Europe, the Americas and beyond by voices ranging from Donald Trump and Viktor Orbán, prime minister of Hungary to far-right and fascist street movements including the followers of Tommy Robinson in Britain.

Yet here, paradoxically, there is perhaps a pointer towards how the movement against Prevent can reinforce itself and engage with wider forces. The rise of racism, Islamophobia and the far-right has evoked widespread opposition. There is rising opposition both to the Conservative government's 'hostile environment', not least in targeting the Windrush generation, and to the far-right street movements of Tommy Robinson and others. The shock and horror at the Nazi terror attack in Christchurch has brought the anti-Muslim character of both far-right and mainstream politics under scrutiny. There is growing awareness and hostility to the use of demonising narratives of Muslims as 'invaders' – an alien threat or a suspect community.

Opposition to Prevent retains its specific importance in challenging state and institutionalised Islamophobia, however, the wider movement against racism and the far-right also offer avenues to root that opposition more widely and to potentially greater effect. This should not be a huge leap; opposition to Prevent took shape from networks of activists and organisations that, despite their diverse character, often shared common roots in movements against war, Islamophobia and racism. Success in winning broader support and widening opposition to Prevent will in large part rest with the growing battle against Islamophobia, racism and the far-right.

NOTES

1. See the numerous case histories identified by Prevent Watch, an advocacy organisation for individuals and families who have been targeted under the auspices of Prevent: www.preventwatch.org/cases (accessed 13 January 2019).
2. The researchers acknowledge that self-selection may have biased their sample against potentially critical respondents. Crucially there has been no study of students' views of Prevent.
3. See Local Government Act 1988, www.legislation.gov.uk/ukpga/1988/9/contents (accessed 18 January 2019).
4. Prevent, Islamophobia and Civil Liberties Conference, Conference Timetable, June 2016. https://challengingprevent.com/conference-programme (accessed 10 November 2018).
5. The details of the Trojan Horse affair and its political setting are extensively and forensically examined by John Holmwood and Therese O'Toole (2017) in *Countering Extremism in British Schools?*
6. CAGE, www.cage.ngo; MEND, www.mend.org.uk.
7. *5 Pillars*, https://5pillarsuk.com; IHRC, www.ihrc.org.uk; MPACUK, https://mpacuk.org.

REFERENCES

Ahmed, N. (2016) The Quilliam Foundation is Financed by Tea-Party Conservatives Investigated by Sam Harris. *Insurge Intelligence*, 8 January. https://medium.com/insurge-intelligence/the-quilliam-foundation-is-financed-by-tea-party-conservatives-investigated-by-sam-harris-1e43d54f0bee (accessed 30 November 2018).

BBC News (2015) Muslim Family's Halted Disneyland Trip is Raised with PM. 24 December. www.bbc.co.uk/news/uk-35167511 (accessed 10 October 2019).

Belaon, A. (2015) *Building Mistrust, Ethnic Profiling in Primary Schools: A Critical Analysis of the Prevent Counter-Radicalisation Model Implemented in Primary Schools*. London: Claystone.

Busher, J., Choudhury, T., Thomas, P. and Harris, G. (2017) What the Prevent Duty Means for Schools and Colleges in England: An Analysis of Educationalists' Experiences. Aziz Foundation, July.

CAGE (2011) *Good Muslim Bad Muslim: A Response to the Revised Prevent Strategy*. London: CAGE.

CAGE (2014) *The Prevent Strategy: A Cradle to Grave Police-State Report*. London: CAGE.

Camden Safeguarding Children Board (2015) Keeping Children and Young People Safe from Radicalisation and Extremism: Advice for Parents and Carers. www.cscb-new.co.uk/wp-content/uploads/2015/12/CSCB_Radicalisation_and_Extremism_Leaflet_Update_Single_Pages.pdf (accessed 20 November 2015).

Courtney, K. (2016) The Problems with Prevent. SecEd, 9 March. www.sec-ed.co.uk/blog/the-problems-with-prevent (accessed 20 November 2018).

Daily Telegraph (2016) Ifhat Smith – An Apology. 29 October. www.telegraph.co.uk/news/2016/10/29/ifhat-smith--an-apology (accessed 10 January 2019).

Daily Telegraph (2017) Haras Ahmed – An Apology. 6 August. www.telegraph.co.uk/news/2017/08/06/haras-ahmed-apology2 (accessed 10 January 2019).

Education Committee (2018) Accountability Hearings, 7 March 2018. https://goo.gl/sRj7H3.

Faith Matters (2015) Circulating 'Cohesion' BRIT Questionnaire in Buxton School Raises Eyebrows. 23 May. www.faith-matters.org/2015/05/23/circulating-cohesion-questionnaires-in-buxton-school-raises-eyebrows (accessed 20 November 2018).

Faith Matters (2016) Cameras in Prayer Rooms in Westminster University Leads to Concern. 13 February. www.faith-matters.org/2016/02/13/cameras-in-prayer-rooms-in-westminster-university-leads-to-concern (accessed 11 January 2019).

Ferguson, R., Ali, A. and Richardson, B. (2017) Prevent: Why We Should Dissent. *Stand Up To Racism & MEND*, January.

Fox, E. (2019) *Extreme Speakers and Events: In the 2017/18 Academic Year*. London: Henry Jackson Society.

Gilligan, A. (2016) NUT Leaders 'Colluding to Undermine Anti-Terror Policies'. *Daily Telegraph*, 23 January, www.telegraph.co.uk/news/uknews/terrorism-in-the-uk/12117736/NUT-leaders-colluding-to-undermine-anti-terror-policies.html (accessed 10 October 2018).

Guardian (2017) Letters: Free Speech on Israel Under Attack in Universities. 27 February. www.theguardian.com/education/2017/feb/27/university-wrong-to-ban-israeli-apartheid-week-event (accessed 22 November 2018).

HM Government (2015) Revised Prevent Duty Guidance for England and Wales. 16 July.

Holmwood, J. and O'Toole, T. (2017) *Countering Extremism in British Schools? The Truth about the Birmingham Trojan Horse Affair*. Bristol: Policy Press.

Home Affairs Select Committee (2016) Supplementary written evidence submitted by David Anderson Q.C. (Independent Reviewer of Terrorism Legislation), 29 January. http://data.parliament.uk/writtenevidence/committeeevidence.svc/evidencedocument/home-affairs-committee/countering-extremism/written/27920.pdf. (accessed 25 November 2018).

Home Office (2017) Individuals Referred to and Supported Through the Prevent Programme, April 2015 to March 2016. *Statistical Bulletin* 23(17), 9 November. https://assets.publishing.service.gov.uk/government/uploads/system/uploads/attachment_data/file/677646/individuals-referred-supported-prevent-programme-apr2015-mar2016.pdf (accessed 15 December 2018).

Home Office (2018) Individuals Referred to and Supported Through the Prevent Programme, April 2017 to March 2018. *Statistical Bulletin*, 31(18), 13 December. https://assets.publishing.service.gov.uk/government/uploads/system/uploads/attachment_data/file/763254/individuals-referred-supported-prevent-programme-apr2017-mar2018-hosb3118.pdf (accessed 10 January 2019).

Hooper, S. (2018) Schools Hijab Ban Could Lead to Attacks on Muslim Girls, Teachers Warn. *Middle East Eye*, 1 April. www.middleeasteye.net/news/schools-hijab-ban-could-lead-attacks-muslim-girls-teachers-warn (accessed 15 January 2018).

Hussain, G. (2013) Criticise if you will, but Tommy Robinson's Leaving the EDL is a Positive Move. *Left Foot Forward*, 9 October. https://leftfootforward.org/2013/10/tommy-robinson-leaving-edl-positive/ (accessed 30 November 2018).

Independent (2015) Prevent will have a Chilling Effect on Open Debate, Free Speech and Political Dissent. *Independent*, 10 July. www.independent.co.uk/voices/letters/prevent-will-have-a-chilling-effect-on-open-debate-free-speech-and-political-dissent-10381491.html (accessed 20 November 2018).

Independent (2016) Anti-Terror Police Question Schoolboy for Wearing Pro-Palestine Badge. *Independent*, 14 February 2016, www.independent.co.uk/news/uk/anti-terror-police-question-schoolboy-for-wearing-pro-palestine-badge-a6873656.html (accessed 30 November 2018).

Just Yorkshire (2017) *Rethinking Prevent: A Case for an Alternative Approach*. Rotherham: Just Yorkshire.

Kundnani, A. (2009) *Spooked! How Not to Prevent Violent Extremism*. London: Institute of Race Relations.

Kundnani, A. (2014) *The Muslims are Coming! Islamophobia, Extremism, and the Domestic War on Terror*. London: Verso.

Kundnani, A. (2015) *A Decade Lost: Rethinking Radicalisation and Extremism*. London: Claystone.

Liberty (2017) Prevent Duty Must be Scrapped: LEA Admits Discrimination After Teachers Call Police Over Seven-Year-Old Boy's Toy Gun. *Liberty*, 27

January 2017, www.libertyhumanrights.org.uk/news/press-releases-and-statements/prevent-duty-must-be-scrapped-lea-admits-discrimination-after (accessed 20 November 2018).

Nagdee, I., Ghani, H. and Ibrahim, Z. (eds) (2017) Preventing Prevent: Handbook 2017. NUS Black Students (updated). www.nusconnect.org.uk/resources/preventing-prevent-handbook-2017 (accessed 30 November 2018).

Nair, A. (2015) Professor at Ilford Event: We are Combating Islamophobia at a Time of Political Optimism. Newham Recorder, 28 September. www.ilfordrecorder.co.uk/news/professor-at-ilford-event-we-are-combating-islamophobia-at-a-time-of-political-optimism-1-4239005 (accessed 11 November 2018).

National Police Chiefs' Council (n.d.) National Channel Referral Figures. www.npcc.police.uk/FreedomofInformation/NationalChannelReferralFigures.aspx (accessed 10 September 2018).

Office for National Statistics (2011/2012) Religion in England and Wales 2011. www.ons.gov.uk/peoplepopulationandcommunity/culturalidentity/religion/articles/religioninenglandandwales 2011/2012 (accessed 15 November 2018).

Ofsted (2018) School Inspection Handbook: Handbook for Inspecting Schools in England Under Section 5 of the Education Act 2005. September.

Open Society Justice Initiative (2016) Eroding Trust: The UK's Prevent Counter-Extremism Strategy in Health and Education. New York: Open Society.

Prevent Watch, The Cucumber Case, 6 March 2016. www.preventwatch.org/the-cucumber-case (accessed 30 November 2018).

Prevent Watch (2016) The Terrorist House Case. 12 June. www.preventwatch.org/terrorist-house-case (accessed 30 November 2018).

Stand Up To Racism (2015) Statement on Prevent. December. www.standuptoracism.org.uk/wp-content2015/uploads/2015/12/Newham-Statement-on-Prevent-15.pdf (accessed 30 November 2018).

Sunday Times (2017) Letters, The Hijab has No Place in Our Primary Schools. 10 September. www.thetimes.co.uk/article/1a3c2350-9567-11e7-bebd-80ab3cacd299 (accessed 8 October 2018).

Taylor, D. (2015) Waltham Forest Council of Mosques Says Policy is an Attack on Islamic Community. Guardian, 17 December. www.theguardian.com/world/2015/dec/17/society-of-mosques-to-boycott-anti-terror-prevent-programme (accessed 20 November 2019).

Thomas-Johnson, A. and Hooper, S. (2018) Sunday Times 'Twisted' Hijab Ban Story to Stoke Debate, Teachers Say. Middle East Eye, 9 February. www.middleeasteye.net/news/exclusive-sunday-times-twisted-hijab-ban-story-stoke-debate-teachers-say (accessed 5 October 2018).

Thomas-Johnson, A. and Milmo, C. (2015) Muslim Students Threaten to Sue College After Being Suspended for Complaining of Islamophobia. Independent, 11 June. www.independent.co.uk/news/uk/home-news/muslim-students-threaten-to-sue-college-after-being-suspended-for-complaining-of-islamophobia-10313977.html (accessed 8 November 2018).

UCU (2015) The Prevent Duty: A Guide for Branches and Members. December 2015, www.ucu.org.uk/media/7370/The-prevent-duty-guidance-for-branches-Dec-15/pdf/ucu_preventdutyguidance_dec15.pdf (accessed 30 November 2018).

University News (2015) A Generation has been Written Off Due to Muslim–Western Tensions, says Leading Female Campaigner. 27 January, Birmingham City School of Social Sciences. www.bcu.ac.uk/social-sciences/news/a-generation-has-been-written-off-due-to-muslim-western-tensions-says-leading-female-campaigner (accessed 15 April 2019).

Weale, S. (2018) Ofsted Chief Accuses Minority Groups of 'Entitlement' in Hijab Row. *Guardian*, 9 July. www.theguardian.com/education/2018/jul/09/ofsted-amanda-spielman-accuses-minority-groups-entitlement-hijab-row-schools (accessed 5 October 2018).

Whittaker, F. (2016) NUT Prevent Strategy Motion: What it Actually Says. *Schools Week*, 28 March 2016. https://schoolsweek.co.uk/nut-prevent-strategy-motion-what-it-actually-says (accessed 30 November 2018).

Notes on Contributors

Peter Beresford is Professor of Citizen Participation at the University of Essex and Co-Chair of Shaping Our Lives, the national disabled people's and service users' organisation. He is a long-term user of mental health services, author of *All Our Welfare* and many other publications concerned with democratising public policy.

Julia Downes is a Lecturer at The Open University (UK). Her research critically examines the continuum of diverse 'carceral' and 'anti-carceral' activist strategies used in struggles to end gendered harms. She is also the coordinator of Sheffield Transformative Justice Learning Group and co-founder of the salvage collective.

Robert Ferguson is a trade union and community campaigner against Prevent. Until 2017, he managed tutorial provision in a large sixth form college, with a majority intake of Muslim students. He is a long-standing anti-racist activist, convenor of Newham Stand Up To Racism and officer of Newham National Education Union.

Joe Greener is Lecturer in Social Policy and Criminology at the University of Liverpool in Singapore. Joe has been an active campaigner in several anti-austerity campaigns in Liverpool. His research interests address critical perspectives on welfare policy and criminology in Singapore and the UK.

Emily Luise Hart is a Lecturer in Criminology at the University of Liverpool. Her research takes a critical and abolitionist approach to the study of prisons, women offenders, resettlement and desistance from crime. She is co-editor of *New Perspectives on Desistance: Theoretical and Empirical Developments* (Palgrave, 2017) and is a campaigner for Community Action on Prison Expansion (CAPE) and a trade union activist for the UCU.

Lisa Mckenzie is a sociologist at the University of Durham and a working-class academic. Her work builds upon the narratives of working-class communities collected through political ethnographic research. Lisa brings an unusual and innovative approach to research as an activist and by means of her extensive experience of bringing the academic world and local community together.

Rich Moth is a Senior Lecturer in Social Work at Liverpool Hope University. Rich has been involved in a number of mental health, welfare and anti-austerity campaigns over recent years, and is a member of the national steering committee of Social Work Action Network (SWAN). He is author of *Understanding Mental Distress: Knowledge and Practice in Neoliberal Mental Health Services* (Policy Press, 2019), and an Associate Editor of *Critical and Radical Social Work* journal.

Laura Naegler is a Lecturer in Criminology at Northumbria University. Her research interests are in critical and cultural criminology, with a focus on urban control and city politics, gender and resistance. She has conducted various ethnographic studies with social movements, including US movements 'post-Occupy' and anti-gentrification movements in Germany.

Ken Olende is researching a PhD on 'Rethinking "Blackness" as a Racial Identity' at the University of Brighton. He is active in Stand Up To Racism and was editor of the Unite Against Fascism/Stand Up To Racism magazine, *Unity*.

Glyn Robbins has worked in, campaigned on and written about housing since 1990. He manages a council estate, was heavily involved in the campaign against the Housing and Planning Act and his book, *There's No Place: The American Housing Crisis and What It Means for the UK* (Bookmarks), was published in 2017.

Raphael Schlembach teaches criminology at the University of Brighton. His research is on the theory, politics and criminalisation of social movements.

David Scott works at The Open University and is a Visiting Professor at The University of Toronto, Canada. He has published 15 books on issues around crime, punishment and justice. David is a former coordinator of the European Group for the Study of Deviance and Social Control and is a member of the Academic Advisory Board for INQUEST.

Steve Tombs is Professor of Criminology at The Open University. He has published widely around the incidence, nature and regulation of corporate and state crime and harm. He has long worked with the Hazards movement in the UK, and is a Trustee and Board member of INQUEST.

David Whyte is Professor of Socio-Legal Studies at the University of Liverpool, where he teaches and researches corporate power and corporate crime. He is author of *How Corrupt is Britain* (2015) and *The Violence of Austerity* (with Vickie Cooper, 2017), both published by Pluto Press.

Bob Williams-Findlay is a long-standing member of the Disabled People's Movement and a co-founder of Disabled People Against Cuts and Left Unity Disabled Members Caucus. His research includes co-authoring the *Empire Strikes Back: Race and Racism in 70s Britain* and disability related topics such as media representation, history, education, culture and politics.

Index

social reproduction, 4, 8–10, 22
spatial strategies of resistance, 32, 39
Stewart, Mo, 91–2
student debt, 55
student fees, 54
subversive
concepts, 19–21
knowledge, xiii

Tahrir Square, 16
trade unions, 95–6, 119–20, 164
trans, 210
transformative justice, xvi, 208, 209,
212–14, 220, 223–6
transitional demands, 18–19
Trojan Horse scandal, 234, 236, 238,
241–2

ultra realism, 14
undercover policing, xvi, 172, 174,
176, 178–9, 185
university, xiv, 46, 48–50
'massification', 53–4

Vice Chancellor remuneration, 56

Wacquant, Loic, 6, 76–7
welfare reform, xv, 8, 91–3
resistance to welfare reform, xv,
20–1
dismantling of welfare state, 129
Windrush, 151, 154–6, 165
Wright, Olin, 21
women's social movements, 70–1
Work Capability Assessments, 92–3

The Pluto Press Newsletter

Hello friend of Pluto!

Want to stay on top of the best radical books
we publish?

Then sign up to be the first to hear about our
new books, as well as special events,
podcasts and videos.

You'll also get 50% off your first order with us
when you sign up.

Come and join us!

Go to bit.ly/PlutoNewsletter